Future Mind:

Artificial Intelligence

Future Mind:
Artificial Intelligence

Merging the Mystical and the
Technological in the 21st Century

Jerome Clayton Glenn

ACROPOLIS BOOKS LTD.
WASHINGTON, D.C.

ACROPOLIS BOOKS, LTD.
Kathleen P. Hughes, Publisher
Colortone Building, 2400 17th St., N.W.
Washington, D.C. 20009

Attention: Schools and Corporations
ACROPOLIS books are available at quantity
discounts with bulk purchase for educational,
business, or sales promotional use. For information, please write to: SPECIAL SALES
DEPARTMENT, ACROPOLIS BOOKS, LTD.,
2400 17th St., N.W., WASHINGTON, D.C. 20009.

**Are there Acropolis books you want but can-
not find in your local stores?**
You can get any Acropolis book title in print.
Simply send title and retail price. Be sure to
add postage and handling: $2.25 for orders up
to $15.00; $3.00 for orders from $15.01 to $30.00;
$3.75 for orders from $30.01 to $100.00; $4.50
for orders over $100.00. District of Columbia
residents add applicable sales tax. Enclose
check or money order only, no cash please, to:
     ACROPOLIS BOOKS LTD.
     2400 17th St., N.W.
     WASHINGTON, D.C. 20009

**Library of Congress
Cataloging-in-Publication Data**
Glenn, Jerome Clayton, 1945-
     Future mind.
     Includes index.
     1. Technology—Forecasting. 2. Technol-
ogy and civilization—Forecasting. 3. Artificial
intelligence.
I. Title.
T20.G54 1989   601'.12   89-6470
ISBN 0-87491-920-7

Table of Contents

Acknowledgments

Marcia U. Glenn, Dorothy C. Glenn, Stan Rosen, Carolyn Amundson, Even Dvorsek, Sherry Muller, Frank Post, Linda Maldonado, Timothy Leary, Frank Catanzaro, Andy Weil, Andy Oerke, Herman Kahn (the Late), Roy Mason, Charlie Boyle, Richard Berenzen, Kathi Friedman, Barbara Hubbard, Willis Harman, Michael Michalis, Stefanie Kott, Al De Salvo, William Halal, Dennis Holmes, John Thomas, Pat Gunkel, Richard Farman, Bruce Weinrod, Doris Mendosa, Gwenn Kelly, Jim Pearson, W. C. Banta, Thomas Cremins, Joe D'Founi, May Rihani, Lois and Max Gratzl, Terrance Liercke, Larry Hills, David Rothman, Chris Dede, Richard Hoagland, William Jewett, and the editor Adele Gorelick

There seems to be a subconscious consensus among the industrial populations about the future—that human beings will be as integrated with technology as technology will be integrated with consciousness.

Technology can already simulate the human characteristics of recognition, voice synthesis and intelligent computer programming. At the same time, it is being miniaturized for human bodies —both to replace organs and to amplify human capacity. So when the two trends come together—some time between 2025 and 2050—distinctions between humans and machines will blur and *Conscious Technology* will emerge. But toolmakers ("technocrats") and consciousness-sharers ("mystics") will have to overcome their prejudices against each other and merge the best of their respective views of the world.

Chapter One
Conscious Technology

One of the major tasks of futurists is to craft images of the future that are multifaceted and compelling enough to give meaning to our daily decisions. These images must be rational yet appealing enough to catch the imagination. They should also be on the tips of our subconscious minds waiting for the proper concept to bring many seemingly divergent ideas together.

There appears to be a subconscious consensus among the industrial populations about the future—that human beings will be as integrated with technology as technology will be integrated with consciousness. Distinctions between humans and machines will blur. When that actually happens in the 21st century, we will have a world renaissance that could properly be called the "Conscious Technology Civilization."

The leading indicators of this post-Information Age are already with us. The whole thrust of cyborg advances is to take the best of our external technology, miniaturize it, and then make it part of our bodies. There's the Jarvik heart, the Utah Arm, artificial kidneys, the Boston elbow, miniature pancreas-like pumps, the Triad hip, heart pacemakers, microelectronically driven limbs, intraocular eye lenses, the MIT knee, plastic skin, artificial ears, blood vessels, and bones. We also use technological skins and organs to enhance our abilities to move under water and in outer space. The miniaturization of technology for both remedial purposes and the amplification of human capacity represents a strong trend toward the "cyborginization" of humanity.

Simultaneously, the whole thrust of advances in electronics is to take the best of our consciousness, simulate it in computer programs, and make it part of our environment. This will make inanimate objects immediately responsive to our thoughts. We can already talk to computers that recognize over 20,000 words, giving us the eerie feeling that they are aware. Even buildings have sensors that make them seem alive, like HAL in the movie *2001: A Space Odyssey.*

Today there are more computers in the United States, from microprocessors in wrist watches and burglar alarms to personal computers and giant mainframes, than there are Americans.

What is more, computers are becoming mobile and self programming robots. The U.S. Census Bureau has been counting robots as well as people since 1984. There were 5,535 complete robots in 1984 with a total value of $306.7 million. By 1995 around 250,000 robots are expected to be part of American industry, but the total number could be well over a million if personal robots are included.

With advancing computer power, microminiaturization, and voice recognition, we can tell many inanimate objects what to do and they can tell us what to do. Our whole environment will seem to change from dumb matter to one of conscious partnership as we tell our telephones to phone home, our lights to turn off, and our music to turn on.

Concurrent with these developments is an explosion in human consciousness. Consciousness creates technology, which in turn expands our consciousness, which in turn improves our technology, and so forth. Technology is a mirror of consciousness. Looking into this mirror changes our consciousness.

At the same time that humans are becoming more technologylike with the internalization of technology, technology is becoming more humanlike with the advent of voice recognition, voice synthesis, and intelligent computer programming. When the two directions cross over into one, Conscious Technology will emerge. This will begin to be noticeable around the year 2000, but will not likely be a major force until 2025 to 2050, simply because of the time lags from laboratory to mass commercialization.

The greatest masterpiece of Chopin played by the greatest pianist of our age fails miserably if the piano tuner improperly adjusted the strings.

A virtuoso performance requires the proper state of consciousness by the pianist and the proper tuning of the instrument. The key is the proper relationship between consciousness and technology. Arthur Rubinstein spoke of his memorable performances as if he and the piano merged as a single expression of the composer. In a similar manner, the performance of civilization could be understood as the relationship of a people's consciousness and their technology.

Conscious Technology is a multifaceted view of the future of civilization in the same way that "Manifest Destiny" was a multifaceted view of the early American future. The early settlers did not have the term "manifest destiny" on the tips of their tongues, but they did have the subconscious consensus that the future would be characterized by westward expansion. Pioneers each had their own view of how they would go West and prosper. In the same way, people of the future will have their own view of how they will merge consciousness and technology in their personal lives. There will be many views of the mutual creation of consciousness and technology, but the core view will be determined by the future relationship of "mystics" or the masters of consciousness and the "technocrats" or the masters of technology.

These two opposing camps will inevitably collide as society evolves into the Conscious Technology Civilization. But the collision can be minimized. One of the primary premises of this book is that these two views can be merged and that the degree to which they do merge will determine the quality of our future.

It seems wise to bring to the attention of each what the other's best qualities are during the early days of the consciousness and technology merger. However, toolmakers and consciousness-sharers have tended to look down on each other throughout history.

The American philosopher William James, in "The Final Impression of Psychical Researchers," wrote in 1909,

> No part of the unclassified residuum has usually been treated with more contemptuous scientific disregard than the mass of phenomena generally called mystical . . . To no one type of mind is it given to discern the totality of truth. Something escapes the best of us—not accidentally,

but systematically, and because we have a twist. The scientific-academic mind and the feminine-mystical mind shy from each other's facts, just as they fly from each other's temper and spirit.

I define a mystic as one whose first reaction to a problem or opportunity is to share consciousness. This sharing can take many forms. It could be with an ill person to stimulate his or her feeling better. Or it could be with some sage to enrich the day. Or it could even be the sense of sharing life with a forest. The mystic sees everything as a manifestation of consciousness and divine meaning.

The technocrat is an adherent to technocracy, the belief that society should be managed by technical experts. His or her first reaction to a problem or opportunity is to make or share a tool. The technocrat sees everything in the most mechanical of relationships.

If you can imagine both views simultaneously, then you can experience the healthy Conscious Technology view. It is easy for us to see the human being as both a conscious entity and as a set of mechanical relationships at the same time, but it is more difficult for us to extend that merged view to the world as a whole.

In the past we either believed, as the mystic, that our consciousness was a node in a divine network or we believed, as the technocrat, that our consciousness was the product of our brain. Today, however, our belief systems are so assaulted by information overload and rapid social and technological change that we are unsure what to believe about human nature and our future as a species.

This is a dangerous situation. Historians tells us that civilizations have fallen when there is no general consensus around a positive and multifaceted view of the future. We need a new consensus to act as a perceptual glue that will hold us together as we make the transition to the post-Information Age. Conscious Technology is such a candidate world view. It could generate a new consensus by giving coherence to complex long-range trends and helping us resolve one of the greatest social polarities of all time.

We are all part mystic and part technocrat, but each of us tends toward one world view or the other. In the past these views have calcified into orthodoxy, but that need not be so in the future. It is possible to merge such different world views, if the merger is with the mystic's *attitude* toward the world and the technocrat's *knowledge* of the world. Scientists and technocrats can give us the *means* for getting organized, while mystics can give us the attitude to take during such organization.

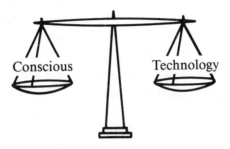

The smooth transformation from the Industrial and Information Ages to the Conscious Technology Age will require new perceptions on the part of both.

Since we each embody mystic and technocrat, accomplishing this integration of thinking will mean learning the opposite of our primary orientations. Mystics would need to study science and technology, technocrats to study consciousness. This implies that we would begin to shed our prejudice.

Prejudice is a primary inhibiting factor of many positive alternative futures for civilization—not simply racism, sexism, and so forth, but prejudice in general. As a concept, prejudice is wrong in the same way that the concept "the earth is flat" was wrong. We can know the truth about the past and present, but not the future. Therefore, prejudging the future cannot be done with certainty. Prejudice implies the illogical position that one knows the future. Just as the idea of a flat earth was wrong and prevented progress, so too prejudice is wrong and prevents progress.

The strongest prejudice throughout all cultures and times has been between the mystic and the technocrat. If these two can be brought together by a belief in the Conscious Technology future, then possibly lesser prejudices may fall by the wayside and prejudice in general may be reduced.

The last 200 years have seen a dramatic increase in social mobility and communication, putting diverse world views in direct interchange. Simultaneously, we are witnessing extraordinary advances in robots, cyborgs, computer communications, space flight, brain research, biological engineering, microminiaturization, and international commerce. These fundamental and rapid changes leave many unsure what to believe. During periods of uncertainty about big changes, it is natural for people to look over their shoulder to the past for comfort. This is the reason for the resurgence and popularization of fundamentalism in its many forms.

Eventually it will dawn on us that we are moving into the 21st century and that all this change is leading to a new *kind* of civilization. As we approach the turn of the millennium, the psychological impact of the year 2000 can act as a catalyst for us to take the best from the past as we build a new view of the future.

This book will explore the many facets of Conscious Technology and the transitions from today into the Post-Information Age. Starting with how the best from the mystic and technocrat can be merged, the book will turn to specific transitions in government and politics, defense, business and economics, Third World development, and education.

We'll conclude with three scenarios to illustrate that Conscious Technology is no panacea and that it, like any good idea, can be abused.

While reading this book, it will be helpful to keep in mind that Conscious Technology is really a network of definitions, or the interplay of six facets.

First, it is the merger of the human body and technology. With advances in bionics, we will gradually become cyborgs, who will be able to electronically link our bodies with external technology for worldwide communication of thought and action.

Second, it is the implantation of intelligent computer programming in all our external technology to make our built environment our conscious partners. Computer chips will be put in everything from houses to clothing with voice recognition and speech synthesizers. We will be able to have intelligent conversations and relationships with inanimate objects.

Third, it is the appreciation of the dynamic relationship of technological advances and consciousness growth. Advances in technology alter our consciousness, which in turn invents new technology. It includes a new cultural norm that all technology is to be designed with the added criterion that it must enhance consciousness and cut the time lag between human thought and technological response as well as between technological finding and human cognition.

Fourth, it is the merger of the mystic's attitude toward the world and the technocrat's methods of organization of the world. It is the understanding that without the best of the mystic we end up with a robotlike civilization and that without the best of the technocrat our civilization will lack the organization to absorb the pace of change and crumble into chaos.

Fifth, it is a way to view things, as much as it is a new set of things to be viewed. Just as the Industrial Age gave us a way to view resources, it also gave us a vast array of machinery to be viewed.

Sixth, it is a condition of civilization wherein the majority of people and intelligent technology are an interrelated whole. You would still be able to distinguish humanity from technology, as you can distinguish the color from the rose, but you would not be able to *separate* humanity from technology, just as you would not be able to separate the color from the rose.

This book will illustrate how each of the six facets are evolving and will become interdependent, resulting in the Conscious Technology multifaceted view of the future. It is difficult to simplify this view to fewer than these six facets while still maintaining a vision of the richness and grandeur of the next age that we seem destined to inhabit. However, it could be said that Conscious Technology can be understood as the worldview that civilization will evolve into a continuum of technology and humanity by the integration of technology with our bodies and our bodies with technology and that this integration will be improved to the degree that mystic and technocrat worldviews merge.

Because we are so polarized between those who are more mystically inclined and those who are more technocratically inclined, and because this book is intended to reduce prejudice in general, you will be asked to try to see what is valuable in the other's point of view. Admittedly, this is an exceedingly tall order, but there is benefit for the effort. The works of Thomas Jefferson, Albert Einstein, and Dag Hammerskjold, to name a few, attest to the value of this effort to blend the best of both the mystic and the technocrat.

Mystics cannot ignore the ongoing integration of technology and at the same time be a valuable influence on the future. Technocrats cannot act as if the consciousness of humanity has not evolved significantly since the days of feudal England and at the same time design products that will sell in the future. We cannot afford to be disrespectful in the process of merging technology and consciousness.

Since it will take many years to develop, popularize, and interrelate the above six facets, we have the time to engage humanity in a great conversation to prepare for the awesome prospect of the Conscious Technology Age. Futurists gave similar early warnings over 20 years ago about the potentials of the dawning Information Age. Now it is time to give a similar alert about the coming post-Information age.

Please use this book as an opportunity to consider previously rejected notions, as you explore how your views of the future tie into a rich array of possibilities for the post-Information Age. I hope this book will be equally valuable to both sides of your personality, as it will be for both orientations in our society.

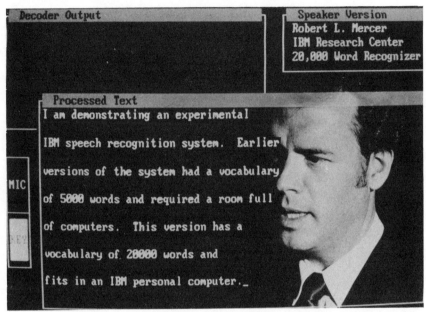

Speech-recognition research is an early but vital element of Conscious Technology. Computer recognition of human speech has moved dramatically forward with the demonstration by IBM scientists of a 20,000-word vocabulary for their experimental PC-based speech-recognition system.
Courtesy of IBM.

If we lose our mystic selves in the microminiaturized technology that will become part of our bodies and environments, we risk becoming the robotlike civilization of science fiction. But if we shun our technocratic selves by letting computers simulate our consciousness, we risk getting hopelessly lost in a civilization too complex to understand. One solution is to help our conscious mind see into our unconscious, and to adopt a spherical view of the interrelationship of people and ideas as a whole. Advances in science and technology will enable us to control our environment and destiny. Both our foreknowledge and awareness of the unknown are increasing, and as we pursue the second we expand the first (the more we know, the more we don't know).

Chapter Two

The 21st-Century Human Consciousness

Deliberately Getting It Together

The healthy mind of the 21st century will be a merger of the best attitudes of the mystic and the best awarenesses of the technocrat. We can begin to get a sense of our future consciousness by trying on some of the views of each.

See the objects around you with your best sense of reverence. Imagine each object as a reminder of something good that you had forgotten, as a stimulus to a beautiful thought, or as a divine representation. How does this feel? Relax in this feeling. This is the mystic's awareness.

Now, imagine seeing everything with a sense of detachment, objectivity, and understanding of mechanical relationships. Note each object's construction, shape, and color. How does it feel? This is the technocrat's awareness.

Now imagine these two awarenesses in your consciousness at the same time as you look around. How does it feel? This is an awareness of Conscious Technology.

It will become increasingly important to deliberately get these two parts of our minds together. If we lose our mystic selves in microminiaturized technology as we make it part of our bodies and environments, we might become the robotlike civilization of science fiction. If we shun our

11

technocratic selves as we simulate our consciousness in computer programs and place them in all kinds of inanimate objects, we could become hopelessly lost in a civilization that has become too complex to understand. As our environment becomes "Conscious Technology" and our bodies become "Conscious Technology," our minds will move in a continuum between the two with a new ease and consciousness that is uncommon today.

But how will this emerge from the world of today? Can mystics and technocrats really come together to give birth to this new civilization? Even with a generation to prepare, there is no certainty that the evolution from the Industrial and Information Ages to the Conscious Technology Age will be entirely smooth. We'll need new perceptions from mystics and technocrats both. We don't know yet if the prejudices are too calcified to keep one side from learning from the other. But one classic way of experimenting with getting our "heads right" is by coming to grips with our unconscious. And it's time to do so.

From Individual and Group to Species

We already know that our unconscious and conscious minds should get along. If an ill person's unconscious mind became known to his or her conscious mind, through self-hypnosis, free association, or other exercises, then reconciliation or wellness could follow. Most agree with this historic insight of Sigmund Freud. However, we do not live in isolation only, but in various groups as well. Individuals in a group have shared experience. Some of the shared experience may be uncomfortable. The uncomfortable experiences are also put into the unconscious minds of each individual in the group. Taken together, this could be called their "group unconscious." This can be thought of as the sum of each individual's unconscious mind that contains the uncomfortable issues of the group. If the group's unconsciousness became conscious to the group—through encounter or sensitivity sessions—then reconciliation or group wellness could follow. This is a basic assumption of holistic health.

Both individual techniques (such as hypnosis and free association) and group techniques (such as encounter, sensitivity, or T-groups) are methods that help to reveal the unconscious to the conscious mind, promoting healing. It's going to be tricky, but we must examine the mystic's subconscious thoughts about the technocrat and vice versa, to inspire a genuine healing conversation between the two.

According to Plato's *Republic,* Socrates thought the city could be understood as the individual written large. In that vein, if an individual can experience enlightenment, why not a city? a nation? or a species?

More inclusively, our species' consciousness and unconsciousness will merge through the help of global communications technology and events significant to the species as a whole. Great distances "disappear" with satellites, computers, and various miniaturization of other technologies. Part of the coming world renaissance will be the merging of our species' unconscious and conscious minds through imaginative uses of global communications. In a more distant future it seems inevitable that we will have interspecies communications with both terrestrial and extraterrestrial species. This will bring up the fascinating possibility of the merger of interspecies conscious and unconscious minds.

The following chart can be thought of as a simple overview of the evolution of human consciousness toward a more distant future.

conscious	conscious	conscious	conscious
INDIVIDUAL	GROUP	SPECIES	INTERSPECIES
unconscious	unconscious	unconscious	unconscious

Revealing the unconscious to the conscious mind as we expand our scope of life is important to create a healthy Conscious Technology Civilization. And that means we have to change the way we structure our thinking. Today, most thought is based on the view that all things are structured in levels. In the future, we will see things more structured in spheres. Until this restructuring occurs, we will never eliminate the many prejudices blocking the healthy merger of consciousness and technology.

Levels of Prejudice

Virtually all world religions and current secular views of reality are based on "Level Theory." This is a great tragedy because level theory is a major source of prejudice. Level theory holds that life stacks up like a layer cake: mental is higher than physical; spiritual is higher than mental; love and belongingness are higher than safety; metaphysics is higher than physics; the nation is higher than the city; the computer is higher than the pencil and paper; and reading is higher than cooking.

Because our cultures associate better with higher, we unconsciously associate anything on the "lower" level with inferiority. Unwittingly, prejudice is communicated every time one uses level in this fashion.

For example, people who try to understand systems tend to break everything out into levels. The less complex is categorized at a lower level than the more complex. If they were analyzing the body, they would put the cells at a lower level than the tissues and organs on a higher level than the tissues. This is called "recursive theory." When sufficient complexity is reached on one level, we move on to the next level. This approach is very helpful for mapping the functions of systems. It becomes a problem when we analyze social systems and forget that each "level" function is just as vital as the other. Presidents are not better than janitors, just as tissues are not better than cells. We seem to have a problem keeping in mind that such hierarchical mapping of different complexity of function has nothing to do with better or worse.

Most will agree that when they say something is on one level as opposed to another level, they simply mean it is different. Adding the word "level," they may feel, dignifies the statement, when it actually detracts from its meaning. Some people say "on the mathematical level," as opposed to the "psychological level." Instead they should say "mathematically" as distinct from "psychologically." Adding the word "level" brings in the possibility of transferring your prejudice to another person's unconscious mind.

"New Age" groups often lay out "levels of consciousness" with the detailed measurement of a thermometer. When pushed, such proponents of modeling the universe in levels agree that the level theory is just a way to communicate an idea.

But others still argue "levels." During the first visit of the XVI Gyalwa

Karmapa Lama of Tibetan Buddhism to Washington, D.C., in the mid-1970s, I discussed Conscious Technology with His Holiness' teacher at some length. He agreed completely with the notion of Conscious Technology. But he still held to the level theory of the universe, that is, that there are numerous levels of consciousness, higher ones being better, closer to Buddha, than lower ones. His meaning could be expressed by simply saying there are better ways to be. But Tibetan Buddhism, like most theologies and metaphysics, holds that there are higher and lower levels of consciousness.

Abraham Maslow, the American psychologist, demonstrates level theory by laying out a linear development of consciousness with his hierarchy of survival, safety, esteem, love and belongingness, self-actualization, and aesthetic needs. Claire Graves, another psychologist, does the same with his model of achieving competence, managing emotions, becoming autonomous, establishing identity, freeing interpersonal relationships, clarifying purposes, and developing integrity.

Both Maslow and Graves agree that their hierachies are not a one-way linear trip and that it is not quite as clean and neat as their one-step-at-a-time in conscious development would seem. But both base their work on level theory, making it all too easy for followers to think in terms of a "one-step-at-a-time ladder to enlightenment." Both give caveats, yet their followers give lectures that might lead you to believe that once you have satisfied the esteem need, you will not have to go back to that need, as if consciousness development were a fixed ladder to success with no backtracking.

Just as groups mold such concepts as "development" into layers, we also do so with our notion of time. Time is simply a measurement of motion. But we lay it out horizontally instead of vertically, one year after the next. Our graphic timelines point the future to the right, the past to the left. This is another common conceptualization or a consensual reality, a sense of time and history.

But the consensus can change. Some people in Williamsburg, Virginia, see themselves as living in the past; some visitors at Walt Disney's EPCOT see themselves as living in the future. People in Auroville, an experimental community of 600 people from 20 nations in southern India, see themselves as timeless. We get *Star Wars* portrayed as "a long, long time ago ... " but everyone sees it as a futuristic movie; we wait for the next "prequel" instead of sequel, since the series is not a linear chronology. Such embryonic experiments with the relativity of time instead of absolute linearity will continue.

By design alone, we can change our perception of time. Colonial Williamsburg is an environment that turns mind to slower times of the past. The experimental prototype community of tomorrow—The EPCOT Center— turns our mind to the future.

Architecturally, city-within-a-city urban planning and design can express such a nonlinear view. Many alternative styles are designed within one structure, and that structure is connected to others as one alternative within a web of such semi-self-reliant structures. The Italian futuristic architect Paolo Soleri is building a prototype of such a nonlinear city in Arizona called Arcosanti. He feels that the flat linear suburban design lowers our intelligence and that our brain's intelligence is improved by complexity and nonlinearity.

When life is mistakenly divided into levels, something or someone is always higher or better than someone else. Instead, it is possible to speak of "fuller" or "expanded consciousness.

The Spherical View

Spherical theory is a prejudice-reducing alternative to level theory. The goal of spherical theory is to be well rounded, to expand your capabilities, whereas the goal of level theory is to climb up—a climb that is often over someone else's back.

Spherical viewing is easier for astronauts and cosmonauts to understand than for earthkind, who are accustomed to seeing level streets, layered buildings, horizons of oceans, and flat lakes. In earth orbit, we find that "up" and "down" (concepts implicit in level theory) are meaningless. "In" and "out" make more universal sense and are implicit to spherical theory's models and approaches.

The origin of the term "human" has its roots in the spherical view of nature. Robert Hieronimus' report at the 1973 Washington SYNCON (a participatory conference about the future) expressed one view of our consciousness: "The term 'man' comes from "monas"—mind, to think. There is some discrepancy about the prefix 'hu' (not necessarily a prefix at all times) which meant 'Sun' in ancient Celtic languages. Therefore, human meant 'Sun mind.'" The sun is spherical and radiates in all directions. He went on the say, "Sun always symbolized spirit—you put it together: spiritual thinking." In this view our nature is more spherical than linear.

Like the sun, our brain, too, radiates a measurable spherical field. We can measure these radiations and talk about their level of intensity, but should not confuse the brain with our measurement of its radiation. The brain acts spherically; we measure linearly. We confuse the two when we speak about our consciousness as if it were a layer cake.

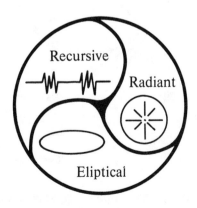

Life acts spherically, moves elliptically, and is understood recursively

A fertilized egg grows in a sphere, then differentiates, yet grows outward from its center. The sun radiates in an infinite number of directions. Ripples expand radially from the surface where a rock hits the water. Your voice emanates in all directions.

Life acts spherically, yet we seem to learn and understand in levels. We have confused our way of thinking with the nature of the objects of our thought. For example, our body radiates heat in all directions, but we use a linear thermometer to understand our temperature. Heat acts spherically, but we measure it linearly. Although we use maps to understand the territory, we must remember not to confuse the map with the nature of the territory.

In business, we know that many elements must come together. These elements are not higher or lower, more or less important. Each element must exist, or else the business will not succeed. Applying spherical theory instead of level theory to evaluation of a business, the following chart can help to show the "shape" of a business:

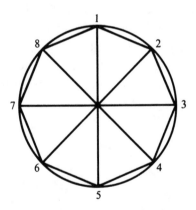

1. Entrepreneurial Spirit
2. Market Survey
3. Market Strategy
4. Supply
5. Assembly
6. Records
7. Promotion
8. General Management

If well developed, then the radiant would be longer. If less developed, then the radiant would be drawn shorter. The chart above would represent a business that has all elements fully developed. In the chart below, the business is weak in market information because of a lack of an adequate market survey, poor record keeping, and weak management. Yet, the entrepreneurial spirit has some drive that got reliable supplies, workable assembly of the product with a fairly well-developed market strategy, and promotion.

Rating each element 1-10

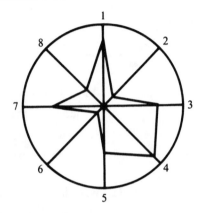

1. Entrepreneurial Spirit (8)
2. Market Survey (2)
3. Market Strategy (7)
4. Supply (8)

5. Assembly (6)
6. Records (2)
7. Promotion (7)
8. General Management (4)

The chart shows that all elements are necessary to make a well-rounded business. It helps you see your business holistically rather than in fragmented activities and helps prevent the mistake of seeing one element as more important than another.

This spherical approach can also be applied to your personal development. Imagine yourself as a sphere. Imagine that an infinite number of rays extend in all directions from your center. Each ray has a different aspect, such as mathematics, art, financial security, love, politics, and so forth, and extends as far as you have developed that aspect. Each person emanates a different shape. His or her shape is neither higher nor lower—just different in its development of the factors internal to that person. Try listing whatever factors you think are important for you and chart them:

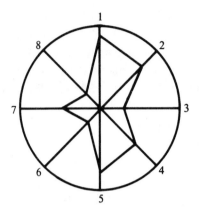

1. Relationships
2. Art
3. Science
4. Health
5. Spiritual Development
6. Financial Security
7. Career
8. Current Events

In the above chart, one would be well-developed in relationships, art, health, and spirit and less developed in science, financial security, and current events. The more developed areas could be used to develop the stunted areas. This person might draw sketches or paintings of current events in science as a new career to become more financially secure. Spherical representations allow you to see yourself as a whole rather than a fragmented identity.

If you perceive things only linearly, and if someone knows the "larger picture" of the linear system more than you do, then they can forecast your steps rather accurately. As a result, others have the potential to control you rather well or "cut you off at the pass" if they choose. You might want think more spherically to increase your unpredictability.

The major American contribution to the history of philosophy was the pragmatic position that we cannot know the ultimate truth, but we can know if an idea works or not. If it works, American pragmatism says, it is true. If it doesn't work, it is false. In this sense, much of level theory— spirit over mind, reading over cooking, and your profession over my profession—is false.

Because level theory makes it easy to stereotype people and ideas as higher and lower with the resulting prejudice, it does not work to make a civilization run smoothly for long. Spherical theory helps you see the interrelatedness of people and ideas as a whole.

In the business example, each factor is given equal importance to the whole. Each factor or radiant can be less or more developed, but not less or more significant. To repeat, the goal in spherical theory is to be well rounded, while in level theory it is to climb up, and that climb is often over someone else's back.

Philosophies of consciousness that preach the level theory see spiritual advancement as if it went up a preset ladder; hence, there is only one way. Their way is right and your way is wrong. Result? Prejudice. Philosophies of consciousness that preach the spherical theory see spiritual enhancement as if it were developing in all directions. Result? People want to learn from what they are not, by comparing notes with those who are different. This reduces prejudice.

Viewing people and ideas in this way, the mystic is neither higher nor lower than the technocrat, and consciousness is neither higher nor lower than technology.

According to Jeffrey Mishlove in his delightful history of mystics and mystical phenomena called *The Roots of Consciousness,* Ya' Kub ibn al Kindi (or Al Kindi, who died in 873 A.D.) taught spherical theory, claiming that all things radiate spherically. Unfortunately, none of his techniques have been handed down. Perhaps, some of the C-T exercises suggested later in this book designed to help bring the unconscious to the conscious mind and develop spherical awareness are like Al Kindi's.

Expanding Consciousness

Once upon at time, there was a big frog who lived in a well. He had examined every nook and cranny of the place. He knew all there was to know. He was the king of the well. One day a great bucket shattered the frog's world, lifted him up to the top of the well. Aghast at what had happened, he jumped from the bucket and hopped around the ground like Alice in Wonderland or Dorothy in Oz. The frog's consciousness had been expanded enough so that a quantitative increase in his awareness made a qualitative change in how he viewed the world.

This painting, courtesy of Champion, gives you the perception of walking through time. "Walking" through such artwork expands one's view of evolution.

In the spiritual model of personal development, as awareness of anything increases, the volume of one's sphere increases. Neurologically, it means more complex cerebral activity. Your consciousness does not go up any ladder; it simply becomes more and more complex. It can also shrink and become simpler. Standing on your head, drinking alcohol, meditating, smoking marijuana, jumping into snow after a sauna bath are some ways to alter your consciousness.

If the altered consciousness does not erase the previous awareness but gives more depth of perception, then consciousness has expanded. If altering consciousness erases other awarenesses, overall awareness may not have increased. If you alter your consciousness to achieve a state of bliss and step on a cobra's tail as you walk through the forest, you are not enlightened—you are dead. Expanded consciousness doesn't mean you become blind to what is right in front of you.

With expanded consciousness, it is easier to see the next step toward becoming more enlightened and contribute to the First World Renaissance. With a stagnant or shrinking consciousness, you resist, resent, and shut off the very ideas and people who bring the next age.

According to Sri Aurobindo one of the leading Yogis of India, as recorded by Satprem in *Sri Aurobindo, or The Adventure of Consciousness:* "In yoga experience the consciousness widens in every direction, around, below, above, in each direction stretching to infinity."

WARNING: Just increasing your awareness of things can quickly lead to an overload condition, leaving you confused and indecisive. As you expand your consciousness, seek a sense of improvement, goodness, perfection, wholeness, and balance. All growth requires quality control. We want to move toward enlightenment and not develop a needlessly busy brain.

The C-T exercises presented later will provide a variety of specific techniques to expand consciousness.

Are We Ants on a Log Floating Down the Evolutionary River?

After extensive travels around the world and in my own country, I have come to the conclusion that the dominant world view is fatalism—the kind of fatalism that pessimistically and aggressively asserts that you can't really make a difference that matters. This is a poison in the human spirit that must be countered.

There are many sophisticated points of view offered to dissuade deliberate efforts to create better civilization. Here's a sample:

From the point of view of DNA, bodies are merely vehicles to stay immortal. Our brain simply keeps the body from dying prior to passing on the genes to a new body. From the point of view of the known universe, life on earth is barely a blip on the cosmic screen. There is no guarantee that earth will have any significance, and a fast-moving comet or asteroid could wipe us out at any time. From the point of view of Freud, we are controlled by unknown forces in our unconscious mind. Drives we don't understand have more to do with our behavior than what we do understand. From the point of view of macroeconomics, we are net loss or gain, grist for the mill, and at the mercy of the forces of supply and demand.

So, they argue, who are we kidding when we think we can deliberately become more enlightened while creating the first world renaissance? Aren't we like so many ants on a log floating down a river? How foolish such ants would look taking readings of wind speed, temperature, and depth to determine how to steer their log down the predetermined course. The ants think they are controlling their lives, but they are not. The river determines their course, not the ant's judgment.

Aren't we like these ants? No. Not any more. We have begun to make genes and new species as only the forces of evolution did before. We have begun to make spaceships to put us where we want to be as only the forces of matter and energy did before. We have begun to understand the physics and chemistry of the brain, changing our moods and making the unconscious conscious as only random chance did before. And we have begun to build a communications and transportation system that means that anyone can buy or sell directly to or from the world market, letting people create there own economy, as only natural resources and physical force did before.

To quote the futurist Herman Kahn: "200 years ago almost everywhere human beings were comparatively few, poor, and at the mercy of the forces of Nature, and 200 years from now, we expect, almost everywhere they will be numerous, rich, and in control of the forces of Nature." Our consciousness is a product of the past, but increasingly it will be our deliberate construction in the future.

Determinists will still argue that these new capabilities to shape the future are merely determined by the river of evolution. They say free will implies an "uncaused cause." Each event, they argue, is caused by some cause or set of causes, and each event causes new events. To have an event that is not so determined by the past implies something happened that was not linked by causality to the past.

But such philosophers forget that the Scottish philosopher David

Hume wiped out causality. His unrelenting logic in *On Human Nature* demonstrated that we can talk about correlation, but not about causality. Hume showed that we really cannot know what causes events with enough certainty, but we certainly can talk about observed correlations. As a result, the basic assumptions of the determinists are unfounded.

From the pragmatists' view, we can demonstrate that those who believe that a better future is possible, and who are free to help bring it about, are more likely to leave a better trail than the one they found. Those who are pessimistic, fatalistic, and believe it is all predetermined tend to leave little improvement. It is easy to list the great optimists of history, more difficult to list great pessimists who added much to civilization.

While designing the educational approach called "Futuristic Curriculum Development" in 1971, I visited schools and discovered a correlation in students between constructive behavior as seen by the teacher and what I saw as a positive view of the future. In one school for the near criminal or mentally ill, I found that all of the 15 students I interviewed saw the future in terms of their personal death, coupled with the end of civilization, such as thermonuclear war, environmental collapse, or the disintegration of civilization in general. They didn't believe they could do anything to change the disastrous course their log was following down the evolutionary river. As a result, they believed it was pointless to cooperate with anything that meant change. Today, they believed, was bad, but tomorrow would be worse. Change brought tomorrow faster; therefore, they fought any form of change.

I asked the group if it was 100 percent necessary that we were all going down hill. "No," came a hesitant voice. "Then what was the possibility of making it better?" Silence. "Come on now," I fought back. "If it is only 99 percent, then what about the 1 percent?" One hesitant voice admitted that if we had enough energy (this was two years before the 1973 oil cutoff), then we might be all right. Building on that sliver of hope, I asked: "How do you think we could make enough energy?" Eyes moved around the room. They were beginning to think, rather then acting like robots. One brave soul broke the silence: "How do we make energy anyway?" Aha! I had them! And I began teaching how energy is made.

The students' positive thinking and learning behavior did not begin until the negative and deterministic view was altered. And it cannot be altered by the naive, positive thinking of teachers who simply say all will be better in the future or who espouse the fatalistic belief that all will get better by predetermination. Those who believe everything will necessarily get better because it is predetermined are at the mercy of those who disagree. Even our delightfully blissed-out friend dies after stepping on the cobra's tail. Following the flow in India can lead some to starvation. The faithful have been eaten by lions.

Positive thought must be plausible or else the students will see the teachers as "air heads," hopelessly naive or not serious about the real problems in the world. If education does not break negative deterministic thought, it cannot hope to get students to learn how tomorrow can be improved.

Foreknowledge and the Unknown

Those who agree that we can exercise free choice to create our future disagree quite broadly about what that really means. For example, one of the fathers of future studies, Bertrand de Jouvenal, in *The Art of Conjecture,* argued that freedom is the act of choosing with foreknowledge of the consequences. If you don't know the consequences of your choice before choosing, then you are guessing and your freedom is illusion.

Arnold Lesti, in *The Existential Computer,* argues that we cannot know enough of the consequences in the short term, and know even less in the long term. "The more we choose," Lesti argues, "the more unknown consequences occur." As we are attracted to the unanticipated consequences, more choices occur, yielding even more unanticipated consequences. His way out is Zen instead of foreknowledge. Zen is the Japanese version of Buddhism that says we should choose in such a way as to make diversity become a unity.

We are curious by nature, and we act as if learning comes from exploring the unanticipated. This implies that we are choosing from abstract foreknowledge of consequences; that is, we will learn more if we explore the unknown. This abstract foreknowledge does not give us any indication of the concrete consequences of our choice.

Interestingly, both de Jouvenal and Lesti would agree with the German philosopher Hegel (1770-1831) that "the history of the world is none other than the progress of the consciousness of freedom"—de Jouvenal because of increasing foreknowledge and Lesti because of the increasing unknown. Both foreknowledge and our awareness of the unknown are increasing at the same time. The more we know, the more we don't know. Each is describing his half of a yin/yang:

Both are right, but not complete. Each tells the truth of a different side of the same coin. The resolution and balance can be illustrated as

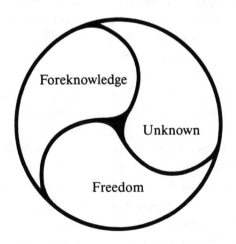

The more foreknowledge we have from forecasting, the more freedom we have to follow our curiosity to the unknown, the unanticipated. The more unknown we pursue, the more we learn to improve our foreknowledge.

We can also see patterns in change. Change is not pure chance and random consequences. The greater and faster the pace of change, the easier it is to see the patterns. However, patterns are not necessarily the concrete foreknowledge of consequences that would make our freedom of choice escape the charge of being an illusion.

Nevertheless, both conclude that the proper attitude is that tomorrow can be better and we can make a difference, but there are no guarantees.

It has become popular among some writers of subatomic physics to say that the unpredictable actions of subatomic particles show that there is free will in nature. Unfortunately, this may say more about our instrumentation and ability to predict than it says about the nature of reality. Just because we cannot predict a thing does not necessarily mean the thing has free will.

Ronald S. Valle, in a chapter in *Relativistic Quantum Psychology,* takes a principle of physics and applies it to the human issue of free will versus determinism. An element of the "Principle of Uncertainty" states that we can either know the location of a subatomic particle or its speed, but we cannot know both at the same time. Valle applies this principle to psychology by saying that we can either know our condition as the result of free will at a given moment or we can know it as the result of determinism, but we cannot be aware of both at the same time. Again, our ignorance of a thing or our inability to comprehend a condition is not a reason to claim knowledge of its possession of free will.

Although modern philosophy has agreed that free will necessarily implies an uncaused cause, contemporary pragmatism does not try to resolve it as such. Instead, it simply says "I act as if or with the belief that I have free will. I cannot act as if I am determined. Belief in determinism does not add to my life. Belief in free will works; belief in determinism does not."

To say that the particle or human is not predictable with certainty does not necessarily imply free will or uncaused cause. It may well imply that no system of control (requiring human predictability) will take away our "freedom" and that unpredictability is necessarily a statement about the predictor, but not necessarily about the predicted.

In summary, we are becoming less and less like the ants on a log floating down the river beyond their control. The forces that have determined our fate are becoming influenced by our action. As a result, we are more and more becoming the masters of our own future. In the museum of errors, the idea that people are not free to improve their lives should be placed next to the idea that the earth is flat.

It is important to refute fatalistic belief because it nurtures acceptance of dictatorships and saps our will to try for a better tomorrow. It is imperative to fight such negative thought. People who espouse such thought poison our youth's spirit and their willingness to try and implement dreams of a better life.

New Factors Affecting Your Consciousness

Let's go back to the beginning of this chapter: we put things in our unconscious mind that we are unwilling or unable to integrate into our day-to-day thinking. These impressions fester among themselves, invisible to our conscious mind, but are expressed later in ways we do not understand. If it's true that human consciousness will transform, as we pass from the Information Age to the Conscious Technology Age, then we can anticipate some elements of our 21st-century consciousness. To do that, we must become more aware of some of those new impressions that we have pushed into our unconscious.

Some of these factors include the integration of biology and technology; space exploration; the search for extraterrestrial intelligence; television; women's growing economic power; intercultural synthesis; changes in family structure; fears of nuclear destruction; communications connecting people into a common view of reality; general interest in things mystical; and the reanalysis of human nature, which is accelerated by the popularization of computers, robots, and bionics.

Dr. Steve Paddock of the National Aeronautics and Space Administration (NASA) has identified the trend of making structures, repairing structures, structures making themselves, and eventually structures merging with humans in outer space. This merger of structures and humans to create outer space-adapted organisms is what Paddock calls "cyber symbiosis."

Each year, computers and robots become more complex, more mobile, more like us. Each year we become more bionic, more cyborglike, as more of us acquire contact lenses, steel joints, artificial skin, computer chip implants and become more mentally dependent on computers. Each year it appears that distinctions between humans and technology blur. If these trends continue long enough, we must eventually become Conscious Technology.

Space technology has given us the chance to see the planet as a unified whole, and seeing it as such has altered our consciousness like our frog in the well. Astronauts and cosmonauts speak of their orbital or lunar experiences as if their view of life had improved. They come away with strong loving feelings for the whole earth and all of its inhabitants, with broadened or expanded spiritual or mystical awareness, and are more caring about humanity in general.

The greatest potential enemies in history shake hands in space.

The Apollo-Soyuz encounter in earth orbit involved numerous exchanges of information and an increase of mutual trust between the US and USSR, something never seen before between potential enemies. Such sharing of consciousness and technology will increase as more humans lift off to orbital dwellings. In 1984 the US President put forward an international space community as a 10-year goal. Others are lobbying for a joint Soviet-America human landing on Mars. Soviets have always had space migration as a national goal. As a result, some humans will become space-kind in our lifetime.

As we go into outer space, our nervous system—the physiological basis of our view of reality—will necessarily alter, and with good reason: (1) there is no atmospheric distortion of the electromagnetic spectrum, giving us a new sense of the intensity of color; (2) all objects will be seen as moving in straight lines rather than along curved lines because of a difference in gravitational forces; (3) the fluid in our inner ears will float in a weightless condition, altering our sense of balance; (4) the spinal column will tend to straighten out; and (5) mental organization will change from "up and down" to "in and out."

All these differences add up to an altered perception of reality, similar to (but stronger than) the way it changes when we plunge under water and look around while scuba diving.

Another factor growing in our collective unconscious was brought to us by writers and moviemakers. It is becoming a fashionable idea that extraterrestrials are walking among us in our daily lives. The creators of such movies as *2001: A Space Odyssey, The Man Who Fell to Earth, Star Wars, Close Encounters of the Third Kind,* and *E.T.* tend to present these beings as fairly mammalianlike. But extraterrestrials could also be imagined like wheat or virus or as transceivers in inanimate objects like the Empire State Building. As transceivers, extraterrestrials could observe, decide whether to transmit, and see if or how people respond.

From the extraterrestrial point of view, this could be a way to screen the public for intelligent contact. Using such a sensing "bug" is safer than showing up as a cytoplasmic being in a farmer's cornfield. After all, America sent such robot transceivers to Mars and out of the solar system before sending people. Why expect extraterrestrials to be less cautious?

In any case, the notion of an extraterrestrial presence is a novel thought influencing some people's view of reality. A more likely reality is that extraterrestrials may form part of our future.

We look back over history and can imagine our distant ancestors as more primitive than ourselves. Yet we have a difficult time imagining our distant progeny as far more advanced than ourselves. Could you believe that your grandchildren might be born in orbital space and be quite different from you? Could their children become space-adapted creatures, as in the "cyber symbiosis" described by Paddock? Could their offspring marry an extraterrestrial? If you saw no possibility of your great-great-grandchildren marrying an extraterrestrial, would you perceive your life differently than if you did? How would you feel about casting your genetic votes toward an intergalactic future? Identifying and wrestling with these futuristic questions alters your present consciousness. One hundred years ago, these questions would have seemed implausible.

But today, we are growing a global consciousness through the medium of television. In the United States, half of all leisure time is spent in front of the electronic fireplace. By the age of 15, children have watched 18,000 hours of TV compared with 11,000 hours in school. The major factors influencing how we are to act as human beings are programmed by television producers instead of teachers, preachers, and neighbors. Children grow up with television actors as their role models for behavior. As a result, an increasing number of people act in "real life" as actors do on camera. This tends to create artificial personalities.

On top of that, TV rarely shows people working hard, which programs an entire generation with lazy work habits. And TV actors usually exhibit average, rather than exceptional or excellent, behavior, perhaps reflecting the influence of media polls, which identify the tastes of the majority of average intelligence. As a result, and I believe unwittingly, our television networks are programming society to become average, rather than advanced.

But the hero of excellence is slowly returning to popularity, and the potential to bring out our best via TV is the next programming frontier. Computer games are becoming educational. If TV does not respond, then the personal computer will replace the personal TV for those who want a better future.

Intercultural encounter via TV and other media, along with intercontinental air transportation, is weaving the fabric of a global culture leading to a world renaissance. The Beatles' integration of American rock 'n' roll with Hindu music is a bellwether of what is in store as different myth systems come to expose each other's speculative foundations. People around the globe increasingly realize that no one has a monopoly on metaphysical truth. The new view of reality that can accommodate the great interplay of cultural myth systems does not yet exist: the future myth system is up for grabs.

One million women per year move into the so-called man's working world in the United States. By 1983 over 55 percent of the work force were women and over two-thirds of all American married women will be employed by 1990. Over half of all the 26 million investors in the stock market are women and 702,000 businesses are owned by women.

The divorce rate is high, the singles phenomenon grows, and one-fifth of all leisure time is spent being lonely. Single women own one-half of all condominiums and one-tenth of the houses in America. One-quarter of US households consist of people living alone or with an unrelated person. There is an explosion of computer networks that help people find those with whom they want to communicate regardless of geographic distances. This new form of extended family, explained by Murray Turoff, the inventor of computer conferencing, in his *Network Nation,* may grow entirely new forms of human linkages, loyalties, and lineages.

The nuclear family will not die, but its members will have increasingly complex relationships beyond the biological family. Children will have many father and mother figures for the many facets of adult roles. The adults will have many relationships ranging in intimacy. The singles phenomenon will evolve new patterns formed by interest via communications technology, with other singles as well as with members of other nuclear families.

This will transform our cultural boundaries. It will give us a greater sense of psychological independence, beyond the more simple focus on family and original culture. Through new telecommunications linkages worldwide, we will experience a far richer and more intense set of human affairs. And as the computer communications lead to the 24-hour work day and 7-day work week, we will pick our working times rather than adapt to a cultural norm of 9 to 5. Both space and time cultural constraints will fade.

These forces acting in our unconscious mind will increasingly put us in a conscious search for a new myth to pull us together.

A reformation may be occurring in the mystical world. Just as Martin Luther felt one could be one's own priest interpreting the Bible and experiencing divinity directly, so too the mystic temples' secrets seem to be becoming public with much of the "New Age Movement." Most national surveys show that half of all Americans and 36 percent of Britains claim to have had mystical experiences. According to a Gallup poll, 64 percent of Canadians who attended college believe in ESP, whereas only 26 percent of those with a primary education accepted ESP as a fact of life. The Netherlands government has a hotline for those having a psychic crisis. Mystic faith in the limitless consciousness is becoming accepted.

The nuclear weapons technology also influences the way we think about reality. For the first time a war could mean the end of all wars and life itself. This radically alters the nature of force in politics, brings the world together in a shared interest, and has begun the first substantive arms control and reduction in the history of warfare.

The interdependent crises of energy, inflation, debt, and population have forced the world to be aware of itself as a single system. Satellite television, voice, and data flows around the world are giving birth to what the American politician Adlai Stevenson called the "global village." The human race is breaking through its parochial blinders and prejudices. We have begun thinking as a species.

Our species is beginning to communicate more deliberately with other animals and will eventually communicate with plants. The pioneering work of the American medical doctor John Lilly with dolphins and the British animal sociologist Jane Goodall with the great apes are examples. Such contributions expand our interspecies consciousness of what is possible for human communications with our fellow DNA-based beings. We have had simple communications with animals for as long as dogs participated in the hunt and protected our homes and horses gave us the upper hand in war and pulled our plows.

But these communications in support of the human economy are nothing like the inventive communications reported by Lilly and Goodall. John Lilly has claimed we are all suffering from "interspecies deprivation." We will continue to make progress to get to know our earthly neighbors, but when electronic attachments to the human brain and animal brain are developed for direct communications, this process will truly be revolutionized. The mystical attitudes toward life will complement our capability to find the proper measurements and analysis to make this process truly enlightening. When we increase and improve such interspecies communications, we will be a healthier species.

A note of interest: as we develop a better appreciation for our fellow earthlings, the National Academy of Sciences documents a 40 percent drop in the destructive use of lab animals over the past 10 years.

All these factors simmering in our unconscious minds are preparing us for a 21st-century consciousness characterized by extraordinary intensity and complexity. We will consider it normal to experience near simultaneity between thought and response, regardless of time and national boundaries. Why not in a global system that forms a continuous web of thought and technology? By 20th-century standards, we will appear enlightened masters of technology and personal discipline.

As we weave our new consciousness from the cloth of ancient wisdom and futuristic technology, we will bump our way through some bizarre and startling transitions on the way to Conscious Technology.

How can mystics and technocrats, so long at odds in their vision of the universe, find a common path to the future? The healthy mind of the 21st century will be a merger of the best attitudes of the mystic and the best awarenesses of the technocrat.

Mystics must give up their insistence on the empirical truth of their metaphysics, and technocrats must stop denying the truth of anything that cannot be proven empirically, for both the mystical experience and technology transcend religious and cultural differences. And it is the transcendant quality of each that will allow them to merge in the Conscious Technology of the future.

Chapter Three

Building Our Minds from Views of the Past

"Off the Wall" Becomes Establishment

With all this change we will experience many bizarre behaviors that just several years ago would have been unthinkable. Teenagers are telling computer executives and Congressional hearings how to program more efficiently and protect their security. Women gather to share bread and wine in Holy Communion without an ordained priest. Former "revolutionaries" have become quite establishment. Jerry Rubin holds business salons in New York City. Abbie Hoffman was hired as a professional protestor by Mount Pleasant, Bucks County, Pennsylvania, to help protest the diversion of river water for a nuclear power plant. Eldridge Cleaver joined Charles Colson of the Nixon White House in evangelical Christian revivals. And Timothy Leary debates G. Gordon Liddy on human values.

In the political arena, Star Trek fans worked through the White House to overrule NASA and had the first space shuttle named the "Enterprise" instead of the "Constitution." There is an effort to get the U.S. Congress and government bureaucracy to recognize enlightenment and consciousness growth as a political issue, according to the events chronicled in *The Aquarian Conspiracy,* by Marilyn Ferguson.

Naming the first space shuttle the "Enterprise," the first political act of science fiction fans.

Experiments over 50 years ago at the University of Pennsylvania that showed that reaching out with feelings toward plants affects growth are generally accepted today. In the 1970s, Fordham University held a once-a-week scream session to release tensions. Homosexual couples sue for alimony. Dr. Barney Clark was kept alive by a plastic heart. And America's tendency toward overweight gave way to joggers of every stripe from California to the halls of Congress.

There's a drive-in funeral parlor in Georgia and a drive-in church in California. Rich people can pay $500 to be matched with a poor family by the Class Exchange in Massachusetts to see how the other half lives. Witch doctors and African government medical officers cooperate in rural health programs.

We will see more rapid changes in world opinion. In the past it took generations to get new ideas and events known worldwide. Today satellites get news to nearly everyone "all-at-once," allowing for quick changes of mind.

In the late 1970s questionable research indicated that aerosol spray cans might knock out the ozone protective layer around the earth, letting in cancer-causing ultraviolet light. Within several months sales of these cans fell off by 25 percent. Later it was established that the effect on ozone was negligible and that the ozone layer was three times tougher than had been expected. Nevertheless, as this example shows, quick world response to both good and faulty information will become more common. We are likely to see some wild fluctuations in what the world sees as "in" and what is "out."

In the 1950s and 1960s Americans worried that one day in the not too distant future the Chinese pepulation would grow to such proportions that millions would eventually invade America. What happened instead was an invasion of another sort. Oriental philosophies invaded the minds of Americans in the form of gurus teaching transcendental meditation, Karma, Yoga, Zen, reincarnation, acupuncture, and other ways of thought "off the wall" to the Western mind. "New Age" businesses, universities, and communities were set up, complete with newsletters, magazines, books, and conventions. Unfortunately, a good deal of this activity is full of superstitious mumbo jumbo and enthusiastic frauds.

The combination of computers, robots, and rapid communications will bring more power to more people in less time than most expect. Because increased power without increased widsom can increase the abuse of power, people in general will have to become wiser if we are to avoid massive abuse of power. In order to have the technocrat effectively participate in the merger with the mystic, we have to help identify what is worthy in all this "off the wall" mystic phenomena and what is not.

How to Judge Between Genuine Mystics and Fakes

The primary value of the mystic's contribution is an attitude toward life, not a particular set of metaphysical beliefs or card tricks. Genuine mystics increase freedom to experience life, whereas fakes try to take over their followers' lives. To repeat what the English philosopher Bertrand Russell said: " . . . mysticism is to be commended as an attitude towards life, not as a creed about the world."

It is the mystic's attitude toward the world that this book seeks to merge with the technocrat's, not a particular metaphysical vision of how the universe works. Mystics tend to stress "direct knowing" or intuition, while technocrats stress reason. When genuine, both acknowledge the other's way of knowing.

The mystic tends to turn fraudulent when claiming knowledge of how the universe works. Les Ericson, in *Omni,* July, 1982, points out that "more than 5,000 studies have been published in parapsychology journals since 1930, yet even parapsychologists admit that evidence of psychic phenomena or psi, is flimsy at best." William James, in 1909 in his "Final Impressions of a Psychical Researcher," cautioned, "Tactically it is far better to believe much too little, then a little too much . . . better a little belief tied fast, better a small investment salted down, than a mass of comparative insecurity."

Philosophers and scientists throughout the ages have said that intuition was key to their knowledge, but how to know when one intuition is right and another is wrong? Since Galileo, the answer should be empirical experimentation. Any mystic that does not accept that should be held with some suspicion.

On the other hand, any intuition not yet scientifically verified or proven cannot be dismissed as false either. An intuition should be enjoyed and held without claiming certainty that its contents are a true description of how the universe works. The mystical intuition of the divinity and beautiful wholeness of life need not be proved; it simply can be experienced and possibly shared with others.

Mystical literature can be enjoyed for the aesthetic response it gives, just like we enjoy great music, good wine, lovely perfumes, and excellent body exercises. It does not have to be taken seriously as if it were describing how the universe works. Mystical literature and systems describe visions of one's experiences, but many visions differ and appear contradictory. We tend to say one is better than an other as a matter of taste, just as we do when we choose music, wine, perfume, and exercise. We don't claim universal truth for these, and neither should we should claim such truth for mystical literature and systems.

Utopians are originally stimulated by a vision or intuition of a better world, but they should not be confused with mystics. The utopian believes in the perfection of humanity; the mystic merely finds that an interesting idea. The utopian will kill for perfection; the mystic will joke about a perfect world.

The old saying "There is no worse lie than a truth misunderstood" applies to many of the mystical teachings and teachers who are taken too seriously. It is true that people can be taught to meditate and improve their awareness by concentrating on parts of their bodies. Classical mystical teachings of the Orient point out seven "Chakras" (a Sanskrit term meaning wheel) to teach people aspects of life. Many teachers have come to take these points as physical locations in the human body with specific size, shape, and color. But Dr. Rammurti S. Mishra, psychiatrist, endocrinologist, Sanskrit scholar, and yogi, points out in his *Yoga Sutras of Patanjali* that "the seven Chakras are purely psychological classifications which have been adopted as focuses of concentration in yoga."

Techniques like automatic writing, crystal ball gazing, and tarot card reading are ways to bring the unconscious to conscious awareness. For example, tarot cards have pictures of universals such as love, death, chance, birth, and wealth. Placing these cards in various combinations gives rise to questions that might not have been asked, such as "What death is blocking your love?" "What does birth have to do with your wealth?". The questions tend to bring to the conscious mind perceptions that are suppressed or have not been questioned. The reader can see your reactions and get an insight into your life not normally revealed to others. Where the reader may go astray is in demanding that we believe there is some mystical force guiding the cards. Both the mystic and the technocrat can agree that it is at least a good way to bring up and out some issues that may need some airing.

Mystical experience, like technology, transcends religious and cultural differences. The experience of the universe as divinely alive and interconnected is essentially the same for both Catholic mystics and Buddhist mystics. Such transcultural commonality has the potential of being a uniting factor, rather than a divisive one. Unfortunately, the desirable attitudes generated by the experience tend to get lost when followers calcify the experience into orthodoxy.

Arthur M. Young, the American engineer who developed the first Bell helicopter and has worked to integrate experimental science and consciousness research for some years, comes to an interesting conclusion. He believes that if you increase sensitivity of each sense organ and all of them at once, then you experience mystic intuition or Extra Sensory Perception (ESP). But he says there is no ESP as such. "It's all sensory; it's just extended sensory perception. The way to get ESP is to train and develop your normal senses. Then you pass through some threshold." Beyond this threshold, one could say, is expanded awareness, psychic power, mystical awareness, or ESP, but there is nothing extraphysical about it.

An interesting test of Young's hypothesis would be to try it on a robot. Imagine a robot equipped with sensors for hearing, vision, touch, smell, and taste wired to its computer. Have the robot give a general report on its environment, then increase the sensitivity of each sensor to see if a unique kind of report is generated, just as the "ESP" human report seems unique compared with the average human report on its environment.

In his popular book series about Yaqui Indian sorcery, Carlos Castaneda made the observation that one acts *as if* there is power in the object, but only a fool believes that there *really is* power in the object. The object is a tool to focus consciousness. It helps bring to mind the appropriate thoughts, feelings, attitudes, and knowledge necessary to help right action. Patriots use national flags to conjure up courage; Christians use the cross to focus love. If one does not already possess the experiences, then the object is useless. Hence, masters of consciousness may do things with objects that work for them, but to copy their manipulation of objects without their wisdom is folly.

It is popularly believed that alchemists tried to turn lead into gold. These were the fakes. The genuine alchemists' perception was a recognition of lead and gold as metaphors. They sought to transform earthly experience (lead) into wisdom (gold). The pursuit of this transformation is the basis of alchemy.

Genuine martial arts teaches wisdom as it teaches power to prevent the abuse of power. If one abuses power, then one's teacher is obliged to correct the student's abuse. It is said that the Kung Fu master Bruce Lee was killed at the order of his master after two warnings. No one objected to his making movies, but wisdom was not taught in proportion to the power to kill that was shown on film. If he was a martial arts lightweight, it would not have mattered, but he was actually quite advanced. Little children imitating Bruce Lee after seeing one of his movies actually killed other little children by mistake imitating the actor's moves. Those mistakes are Bruce Lee's responsibilities.

David Carradine, who popularized Kung Fu through a television series by the same name, was dramatically different. Although he is an actor, and not a Kung Fu master, Carradine adhered to the ethical standards of the martial arts far better than did Bruce Lee, by illustrating ancient teaching of wisdom more than the power to kill.

On January 19, 1983, The People's Republic of China announced in the West that it decided to promote Kung Fu and would even make a movie on it. The announcement said it would separate Kung Fu from its Buddhist origins and teachings. This is a mistake. Separating the killing power from its spiritual heritage is likely to increase murder. The purpose of martial arts is to protect the sacred from the profane. And it is that perception that is the key to force. While some say that "might makes right," others in the martial arts say, "it is right that makes might." If you are fighting the right cause against evil, your might will rise to the occasion. The awareness of the situation is a source of precision and strength, something like the mother who exhibits more than expected strength to lift a heavy object pinning her baby.

Historically, having more power than one needs tends to go to one's head. "Absolute power corrupts absolutely." In Hindu philosophy one is not to seek power or what is called the Siddhas. It is believed that the powers will be given as the occasion warrants. Again, right makes might.

It is indeed unfortunate that one who has taught so many the basics of simple meditation seems to have broken this rule. Maharishi Mahesh Yogi of Transcendental Meditation (TM) fame sells power or Siddhas training at a high price to the consumer. He even advertised in *Time* magazine (December 13, 1982): "The world Government of the Age of Enlightenment [one of his organizations] offers to every government the invincible strategy of defense," the ad declares, "which uses the infinite power . . . " He teaches that enlightenment is reached as the brain patterns measured by the electroencephalogram (EEG) move toward coherence. His organizations want to get as many people with the same brain coherence as possible, which might be very useful for anyone wanting to take over people by mass hypnotic suggestion. Possibly a good insurance to prevent such control might be to have many other people of differing EEGs. The more diverse the forest, the better it survives a variety of problems.

Similar distinctions are made in African witchcraft. To oversimplify, good witch doctors use power to solve problems; bad witch doctors use power for personal gain. If one has been wronged, according to the rules of the culture, then one can go to a witch doctor for medicine or power to solve the injustice. Once the problem is solved, then and only then is payment for services made. If one simply wishes power or revenge or is motivated by jealousy, then payment is given to a malpracticing witch doctor to entice the sought action.

Author with African witchdoctor 1968.

It is the job of the good witch doctor to kill the bad witch doctor. The ethics are strikingly similar to martial arts, with an extra twist: If a "good" witch doctor sees such malpractice and does not act, and both are seen by another good witch doctor, then the third is to kill the first two. It's quite a stern quality control system.

It is also the job of the witch doctor to protect the village from the unknown. He or she has to know the difference between what is dangerous and what is irrelevant. He or she must be first to act on the real danger and spend no time with the irrelevant. They have to always separate the noise from the signal.

I had the pleasure to study with witch doctors for two years while a Peace Corps Volunteer in Malawi, working with leprosy and tuberculosis control programs. Thirteen years later I returned to double check what I had learned. I observed that it is not the roots and spells that made good witch doctors stand out. It is their ability to command without dominating. They say everything that is necessary and leave silence for the rest. This is done while being continuously gentle, uplifting, and mannered so as to strengthen others. They tend to know that we do not know the truth of the universe. Yet they also know that if villagers are to be motivated to do their part to make the village right, then these villagers need to believe that good conquers evil.

There is some logic to the belief. The good witch doctor is supposed to know both good and evil practice. The bad witch doctor knows evil practice and not enough of the good practice to be good. So, the good is supposed to win 2 to 1.

Reading too much into coincidences so that they seem to prove some preconceived notion is another sign of fraudulent activity. Sometimes people give up their own better judgment to a fake who unveils amazing parallels, coincidences, and omens; they become mesmerized by the apparent awesome understanding of frauds who try to demonstrate how the universe works. One classic example of an amazing set of coincidences was published in *Quote* magazine:

> Both Abraham Lincoln and John F. Kennedy were concerned with civil rights. Lincoln was elected President in 1860; Kennedy in 1960. Both were slain on Friday and in the presence of their wives. Both were shot from behind in the head. Their successors, both named Johnson, were Southern Democrats, and both were in the Senate. Andrew Johnson was born in 1808, and Lyndon Johnson was born in 1908. John Wilkes Booth was born in 1839, Lee Harvey Oswald was born in 1939. Booth and Oswald were Southerners favoring unpopular ideas. Both Presidents' wives lost children through death while in the

White House. Lincoln's secretary, whose name was Kennedy, advised him not to go to the theater. Kennedy's secretary, whose name was Lincoln, advised him not to go to Dallas. John Wilkes Booth shot Lincoln in a theater and ran to a warehouse. Lee Harvey Oswald shot Kennedy from a warehouse and ran to a theater. The names of Lincoln and Kennedy each contain seven letters. Names of Andrew Johnson and Lyndon Johnson each contain 13 letters. The names of John Wilkes Booth and Lee Harvey Oswald each contain 15 letters. Both assassins were killed before being brought to trial. Both Johnsons were opposed for reelection by men whose names start with G.

Things may actually be laid out in some elaborate play by the masters of the universe. But we don't know that. To claim to know is another sign of fakery.

The same year the first robot, Voyager, left our solar system (depending on your definition of the edge), we discovered the first evidence of another solar system. In 1983 we found objects orbiting Vega —the first magnitude star, by which all other stars are judged in brightness. It is tempting to read all kinds of meaning into this coincidence: that the first time we leave our solar system, we discover the first solar system beyond our own, which turns out to be of the first magnitude star. One might want to read into this that it is the first signal for extraterrestrial contact, but there is no basis in fact. Such coincidences should be seen as entertainment, but not as science. We should draw lessons and pleasure from such parallels, coincidences, and omens, but not metaphysical certainty of how the universe is rigged as a system by which we predict the future or upon which we make life's critical decisions.

It seems odd that some religions and gurus tend to ask people to rely on faith rather than reason and logic. If God gave us a brain, then why would God want us to throw it out? There is nothing wrong with faith and beliefs that a little reason and logic can't improve. The popular revival of mystical pursuits has also brought a prejudice against intellect as somehow anti-intuition or anti-ESP. This shows a lack of understanding of things intellectual. The history of great philosophers is replete with their reverence toward intuition, even though they are seen as the most intellectual among intellectuals. Most philosophers would agree that faith and belief begin where reason and logic leave off, and intuition is the bridge.

Mystical groups, like other groups, try to prevent their own overthrow. Reason and logic seem to such groups as the primary forces that could overthrow them. Hence, they preach the irrational position to trust the spirit and distrust the mind. But what is the spirit but the mind minus idea?

Again, we have to remember that not all mystics or mystical groups are irrational. It was a mystic from Egypt who loved logic and reason, Hamid Bey, who taught me the definition of spirit as mind minus idea.

Real magic, also called spontaneous or natural magic, is a bit controversial and difficult to define. But for the purposes here, I would define it as those acts done while in an expanded state of awareness that perceives multidimensional realms of reality *and* is not shocked by those perceptions but plays with them joyfully. Such magicians see more than about them than the average person. This allows them to take something from the areas others do not see and "materialize" it into the areas others do see; they do the opposite for disappearance.

Stage magic is the use of some technology that gives the magician the edge over the audience's ability to figure out what is going on. A new material with properties unknown to the general public will do the trick. Stage magicians share their wonder and delight with a twinkle in the eye. They do not exploit their technological edge to gain power over others.

Be wary of those who seriously claim some superior psychic power, such as bending forks and talking to extraterrestrials. Uri Geller, one such stage magician from Israel, seems to abuse power. His agent called the Committee for the Future to appear at one of their SYNCON conferences. When the agent was asked why Geller wanted to appear, he answered, "To become famous." Why did he want that? "To give the people 'The Word,'" said the agent. What if people don't believe him? "Then he will still their tongues with his power," was the response. That clearly identified him as one who might abuse power.

Encouraging hero worship of the guru and the duplication of his personality in his followers is another indicator of potential abuse of the mystic's way. Allowing followers to run around like little clones of the guru can deny the followers' individuality, self-discovery, and development. Since the wisdom of a guru comes from many sages in the past, focusing worship on the one teacher denies the reality of history. It tends to foster naivete and lays a foundation for mass insanity like Nazism in Germany or the Jonestown mass suicide in Guyana.

"Civilization is doomed . . . the world is coming to an end . . . nuclear war is inevitable . . . any effort to work with the current world systems will corrupt you and will end in failure," and other such feelings of impending doom switch people's loyalty from the here and now to the fantasy world of the guru's paranoia. Such false prophets encourage people to leave everything and follow them in preparation for some future that will be theirs, if they are willing to become sheep in the guru's flock.

Negative extrapolations and romantic deliverances teach hatred for humanity as if humans were carriers of the disease "progress." Prejudice against humans, technology, progress, civilization is in marked contrast with the genuine mystical attitudes and experience of humanity and the universe as divinely interconnected, alive, and evolving toward increased enlightenment. Granted, we should not close our eyes to problems of hunger and crime, but neither should we give up, turn tail, and run. These fake mystics encourage planetary irresponsibility.

Exaggeration of scientific research that appears to confirm mystical experience is another form of abuse. Genuine mystics feel no need to be justified by scientific research. The majority of the claims in "New Age" literature that I have cross-referenced with the researchers in question proved to be misleading. New Age cheerleaders in their exuberance to "give the word" to the masses, tend to grasp at any scientific straw to make their claims acceptable.

For example, several publications indicated that mystic psychic power was measured at the Stanford Research Institute (SRI). When I checked with Lawrance R. Pinnero, the man who was alleged to have performed this scientific breakthrough, he responded in a letter: "I assume it was about work at SRI we carried out from 1972-74, trying to find out if thought words (i.e., silent) could be detected by pattern analysis of the scalp Electroencephalogram. Only moderately successful, the project ended in 1974 and in 1975 I retired and have done no further work on it.

Since the results were inconclusive it was never published . . . " This is a typical example of how we can be misled.

Again, it is the mystic's attitude toward the world that this book seeks to merge with the technocrat's, not a particular metaphysical vision of how the universe works.

Mystical experience, like any other phenomenon, is a perfectly proper subject for scientific study. But the neurotic quest for laboratory justification cheapens the genuine mystic. On the other hand, there is no doubt that science will learn more about these phenomena in time.

Researchers like Ralph W. Hood at the University of Tennessee at Chattanooga are trying to build a foundation for such future research, by measuring mystic states of consciousness relative to people's reported belief systems. Unfortunately, one cannot be exact in such psychological measurements as quality, depth, and intensity. Subjective ratings on scales of 1 to 10 are misleading, since one person's measurement of 5 may be a 7 to another or to the same judge on a different day. Nevertheless, putting together scales is necessary, as was the thermometer to thermal dynamics. Yet a 2-degree Celsius reading is universally verifiable, but a 2-degree mystical experience is not. Nevertheless, the work of Hood and others like him is to be applauded, for they are trying to build a foundation of understanding, rather than using science to justify claims of wisdom.

Another area of potential abuse can be found in guided meditation. It is a popular and usually honorable method to expand consciousness and assist in self-healing. In this method, a guide suggests that meditators increase their internal imagery, awareness of their body, or other forms of attention. In good guided meditation, a guide might suggest that meditators feel the area on the scalp from which the hair grows begin to relax and that this sense of relaxation slowly moves down their body until they feel their whole body as a single relaxed unit. Another variation is to suggest that meditators needing healing focus attention on the edge between the healthy tissue and the damaged tissue and then imagine healing happening. In these two examples, the form of the fantasy is given but the meditator fills in the content of the image.

Proper guided meditation increases the individual's mental command over his or her own imagining process. As long as the form and not the content of the meditator's internal imagination is suggested, there is less likelihood of abuse. The possibilities for abuse are similar to those in hypnosis or subliminal suggestion. Abuse can occur when the guide suggests the content of his or her views on those of another. People are more easily influenced or vulnerable in the hypnogogic state and become dependent on the guide, who may suggest images that are not within the meditator's norm.

The abuse of psychic power is more difficult to detect than that of technological power. When someone holds a gun to your head, you know what is going on, but when someone seeks power over you by mystical means, it is far more difficult to detect. The following chart is offered as a simple checklist to help distinguish mystics from fakes:

Indicators of Abuse	Indicators of Genuine Use
Claims certainty about knowledge of how the universe works	Shares attitudes of delight about experiencing the universe as divinely interconnected
Believes truth can be found in objects	Believes objects can help thought
Teaches power for money without teaching sufficient wisdom	Teaches wisdom before power and according to need
Belittles need to counter evil	Actively counters evil
Forces meaning into coincidence	Enjoys or is entertained by coincidence
Puts down intellect, reason, and logic	Uses and enjoys intellect, reason, and logic
Allows or encourages worship of guru or teacher	Discourages worship of guru or teacher but encourages worship of life
Encourages negative view of the human future	Encourages positive view of the human future
Humor at expense of nonbeliever	Humor at the delight of life

Witch doctor receives payment prior to solving problem	Witch doctor receives payment after solving problem
Exaggerates scientific research to support ideology	Has little inclination to be justified by science
Seriously claims psychic power and authority over others	Shares a sense of humor about magical abilities and empowers others
Gives form and content to guided meditation	Gives form but not content to a guided meditation
Certainty	Humility
Grave	Humorous

Please keep these distinctions in mind throughout this book. When the term "mystic" or the "mystic's attitude" is used, it is meant as described in the second column and not the first.

Sample of Mystic Metaphysics

The experience of the universe as a divinely conscious whole leaves you feeling love for all. "What can't be said, can't be said, and it can't be whistled either." Just like the experience of love, the mystic experience leaves you with an inability to adequately explain what happened. Our attempts at expansions and interpretations of such experience can foster beneficial or harmful attitudes.

If you were to recall your most spiritual thoughts and wisest insights while looking at a glorious evening sun casting beautiful colors across the sky, some new insight might trigger within you. This new insight might answer a series of paradoxes. Could this be an experience of enlightenment? Can brain activity alone account for mystic experience?

The technocrat has shied away from meditation or other deliberate attempts to experience the mystical, because the technocrat is not convinced of the mystic's metaphysics. If the experience can be explained in more conventional or physical terms, then the technocrat might be more willing to try mystic techniques. Once having experienced the mystical awareness, the technocrat might tend to be more open to exotic views and less prejudiced against the mystical, and be part of the merger of mystic and technocrat. And if the technocrat refers to the chart above, he or she is less likely to be sidetracked into avenues that might lead to abuse.

Philosophy is the mind core of civilization and has always accepted the "Platonic flash" or intuition as a key source of all knowledge. Philosophers may argue about what such illuminating experiences are, but that will not be resolved here. Instead, the following section will share a sample of mystic intuition and metaphysics to show how the attitudes derived from these views can be helpful.

MIND CAN CONTROL THE BODY. We can worry ourselves sick and laugh ourselves well. Thinking that good thoughts can improve the body improves your body awareness and helps you to have a healthier outlook on life. An electric current in a wire produces a magnetic field, and a magnetic field induces a current in a wire. It may be similar with our nervous system. Neural activity produces ideas and ideas induce neural activity. Neural activity affects the endocrine system, which affects the immune system. Hence, the mystics teach that right thought makes you healthy and wrong thought makes you ill.

The new scientific term for the study of the relationship of the mind, brain, and the immune system is psychoneuroimmunology or PNI. The mystic would say, "Fine. Do your study. When you are finished, you will conclude that right thought keeps you well."

However, this can get carried to extremes by people who are less competent in the control of thought, leading to some some pretty bad errors. One very ill person with cancer swore off doctors, thinking that she could think herself well and died in the process. Right thought, meditation, internal visualizations, and chanting have been shown to help, but unless you are a master of consciousness like Jesus or Buddha, see your doctor, too. Doctors are well aware of the role of the patient's mental attitude in the healing process. Let the doctor do his or her part and you can do your part with your mind.

TRANSCENDENTAL OR FOURTH-DIMENSIONAL CONNECTION TO EVERYDAY LIFE. This view can help us have a loving attitude toward all beings, keep us from being lonely, eliminate prejudice, and encourage us to work together for a world renaissance. All beings are different in shape, size, and so on, but one in the spirit. We can all equally participate consciously in the "transcendental reality." We can share "mind space" or experience the same awareness simultaneously, as distinct from "reading" another's mind. Some say this is the source of "psychic powers."

What is referred to as the "transcendental reality" may be the fourth dimension. We can see length (first dimension), length and width (second dimension), and length, width, and depth (third dimension). The simultaneous movement of length, width, and depth from the center point to the outer surface and outer surface to the center point is fourth-dimensional motion.

As direction is a characteristic of the first dimension, area the characteristic of the second dimension, and volume the characteristic of the third dimension, consciousness and time may be the characteristics of the fourth dimension. This dimension's simultaneous movements from center to outside and outside to center could explain one classic transcendental view. How can it be that "the Kingdom of Heaven is within you?" Imagine fourth-dimensional motion with you and the universe. Your awareness radiates spherically out as you perceive the universe and you receive perceptions of the universe into your awareness. This is a simple secular view of fourth-dimensional motions between you and the rest of the universe you perceive. But now consider the universe as divinely interconnected. With fourth-dimensional motion, the divine interconnections are received by you and radiated by you. In this way the Kingdom of Heaven is within you and more than you at the same time. This fourth-dimensional interpretation is consistent with our consciousness of the continuous flow of inner and outer awareness. As the third dimension does not transcend the second but is inclusive of it, so, too, the fourth dimension does not transcend the third but is inclusive of it.

Awareness of "inner" self and "outer" reality is one way to define consciousness or, as the American Philosopher Will Durant put it in his delightful *The Story of Philosophy,* "a point at which the sequence and the relationship of thoughts coincide illuminatingly with the sequence of events and the relationship of things."

The transcendental view has often led people away from the concern with terrestrial matters. Many neglect their basic survival needs and hold an outright prejudice against civilization and progress. " Why," they say, "be concerned with earthly human affairs that are always in flux, when the transcendental is the only true unchanging reality?"

The fourth-dimensional view, like the spherical theory view, holds that one dimension is no more or less real or important than the other. Volume is no more or less real or important than area. Again, the truth or falsity of mystic vision is not verifiable, but the attitudes associated with beliefs about such experience can be constructive or destructive. We know that the transcendental view tends to be associated with prejudice of hierarchies, while the fourth-dimensional or spherical view does not.

The fourth-dimensional interpretation of mystic experience, relative to the transcendental interpretation, does not in any way detract from the significance of such vision, but gives the added benefits of prejudice reduction, is more internally consistent with other mystical insights, and may help solve the mind-body problem as one dimension is continuous with the other.

CONSCIOUSNESS OF SUBATOMIC PHYSICS. Gary Zukov's delightful book called *The Dancing Wu Li Masters* gives a variation on continuity of the mind and body. Zukov relates subatomic physics to mystical experience, as did *The Tao of Physics* by Fritjof Capra. Zukov points out that a three-particle event of an anti-neutron, anti-pion, and a proton can jump together out of "nothing" and return to "nothing" called a "zero point vacuum fluxation." He further says that noted scientists, Brian Josephson, Jack Sarfatti, and Nick Herbert "independently have speculated that human sensory systems might detect the zero-point vacuum fluxation of the dance of virtual particles in empty space predicted by the uncertainty principle. If this is so, such detections might be part of the mechanism of mystic knowing."

We are just beginning the systematic study of the brain and subatomic physics. It should be a law in science that whenever we study something, we always find more than we expect. Possibly Zukov's speculation will bear fruit and reassure those who, when having mystical experience, wonder if they are going insane. William James wrote:

I firmly disbelieve, myself, that our human experience is the highest form of experience existent in the universe. I believe rather that we stand in much the same relation to the whole of the universe as our canine and feline pets do to the whole of human life. They inhabit our drawing rooms and libraries. They take part in scenes of whole significance they have no inkling.

Throughout the history of philosophy, it has always been held that metaphysical statements cannot be proven true or false because of their sweeping generalities. But this may begin to be chipped away by science. Granted, mystic experience needs no scientific justification, but, as stated earlier, it is still a legitimate subject for scientific study.

Mystics experience the universe as one interconnected whole. Einstein's work and later scientific experiments proved that this is so in terms of the relations of matter, energy, and speed. Maybe there will be another Einstein who will prove the relations of consciousness, brains, and distance. Until then, we should keep an open mind to the notion that our body, consciousness, and cosmos are a continuum.

AKASHIC RECORDS AND KARMA. The Akashic Record is like having your phone bugged by God. The *Akash* is a very ancient term used in many mystical traditions meaning "the consciousness of the universe." The Akashic Record is the memory of this consciousness. Some mystics like Edgar Cayce claimed that it was possible to mentally "tune into" this record to know things of which they had no previous experience. Cayce gained his reputation by "reading" the Akashic Record and passing on such readings to help his patients find proper medical cures.

Karma, a term recently familiar and popularized in the Western world, is the spiritual law of cause and effect. In Christian terms it is "As ye sow so shall ye reap." In popular terms it is "The 'vibes' that you put out are the 'vibes' that you will get back," or the universal credit card for the celestial old-age home.

Jurisprudence holds that people are less likely to commit a crime if they believe they will be caught and punished. Unfortunately, our legal system is not perfect and criminals believe they can beat the odds of conviction and punishment. The belief in Karma and the experience of the Akashic Record would be a powerful deterrent to crime. The attitude derived from such belief is honesty, the hallmark of civil behavior. Maybe that is a reason Karma-believing Japan only has 25,000 lawyers in the whole country.

History shows that masses of people are held together by myth. Although it would be nice to have civilization work without the resort to myth, so far it seems hopelessly romantic to believe it is possible. In the meantime, it is less romantic and more practical to point toward such mystical experience as Karma and the Akashic Record as underpinnings of civilization.

THE LIFE FORCE. Mystics speak about feelings and acting with an energy that the Buddhists call the *Chi;* alchemists call *Azoth*, the invisible fire; and the movie *Star Wars* popularized as "The Force." The coordination of mind and body, as if movement and thought were one, gives rise to this feeling of Chi. When this feeling seems to take on its own momentum through motions of the body, then the force behind that momentum is the Chi. Joining with this momentum would be acting with "The Force."

Whether the experience is illusion or not, it reduces fatigue by helping you concentrate on your task and helps separate the "noise" from the "signal" to help accomplish that task. This is acted out all over China in public parks when people practice T'ai Chi Chuan before going to work. Japanese productivity is partly attributed to the fact that factory workers hold group meditative calisthenics before beginning the day.

Constant attention to balance is required not to abuse this "energy." Or as Obi Wan Kanobi reminds us in *Star Wars*, there is a dark side of "The Force." Some prefer to believe that evil is merely ignorance or lack of wisdom, but this view is easily countered by remembering that although newborn babies are ignorant, they certainly are not evil, even if they do need their diapers changed at all hours. Maybe evil can be wished away, but so far the abuse of force has been more predictably countered by more force or counterforce.

Mystics have to give up their insistence on the truth of their metaphysics in the coming dialogue with technocrats. They need to concentrate instead on the values and attitudes that result from their metaphysics.

*This Kirlian photo shows residual pattern of a leaf,
after a portion has been cut and removed. Does the
leaf prove a life force?*
Photo courtesy of Thelma Moss.

Technocrats will have to give up their insistence on calling anything not yet
proven in empirical science false. They need to concentrate on how such
values and attitudes may derive from mystic metaphysics and how they
improve the organization of civilization.

As this dialogue is carried out over the next generation, we will see a
new interest in the role of philosophy as the mediator. Philosophy need
not be a ponderously difficult pursuit, as it becomes more public in the
21st century. But its value to help pose the questions of what is real and
how do we know that will be increasingly called upon as the mystic and
technocrat merge.

Always be suspicious of opinions that cannot be verified. Mystics see the universe as divinely alive and conscious, while technocrats see it as mechanically interdependent. In the future, both will see the universe as one. Expanding your abilities to their limits is implicit in the spherical theory of personality, and more and more people will join astronauts and "psychonauts" in doing this. "Both/and" thinking allows us to support others in actions different from our own.

*"But the greatest men who have been philosphers
have felt the need both of science and of
mysticism: the attempt to harmonize the two was
what makes their life, and what always must, for
all its arduous uncertainty, make philosophy, to
some minds, a greater thing than either science
or religion."*

Bertrand Russell
Mysticism and Logic

Chapter Four
Philosophy to Mediate the Transition

As life increases in complexity, moving from a physical to more mental and aesthetic focus, the popularization of philosophy (which Rousseau thought would be a disaster) may be inevitable. Philosophy is to the mind what push-ups are to the body, a kind of cerebral exercise that helps us penetrate complexities to get to essential matters. It toughens our judgment so that we are less likely to be brainwashed or hoodwinked by the increasingly complex information world and ideological mind games. It gives us an appreciation of logic, the mathematics of ideas. Logic is slowly becoming more popular as more and more people buy home computers and begin to logically arrange their mental activity.

It is commonly held that philosophers and mystics are incapable of living in the conventional world and so they retreat to their "Ivory Towers" instead. This is a myth that should be debunked. When I used to introduce the speakers on international affairs while an undergraduate at The American University, I got to read many biographies of ambassadors and other players in the world of conventional politics. The plurality of undergraduate degrees of these speakers was philosophy.

According to Michlove's *Roots of Consciousness,* Emanuel Swedenborg (1688-1772) was one of the integrators of academic philosophy and mystic practice who

> participated in the engineering of the world's largest drydock. He developed an ear trumpet, fire extinguisher, and a steel rolling mill. He learned bookbinding, watchmaking, engraving, marble inlay . . . engineered a military project for the King of Sweden which transported small battleships fourteen miles over mountains and through valleys.

Even more recent figures like Bertrand Russell and Albert Einstein were in trouble with the authorities in England and Germany for their social involvement in contemporary affairs. Maybe the Ivory Tower myth gets passed from one generation to the next because philosophers can so push the tolerance of the average person that they'd like to send them off into ivory towers.

But there is a less ponderous way to use philosophy to help us through future complexities. The British philosopher Alfred North Whitehead argued that all explicit metaphysical statements were implicit epistemological statements and all explicit epistemological statements were implicit metaphysical statements. For example, "God created the universe" is an explicit metaphysical statement. For us to believe that this statement is true, we must be given a way to know (epistemology) that it is so. Divine revelation, personal appearance, or laboratory research would be epistemological evidence supporting how one came to know that metaphysical statement. These epistemological statements in turn imply metaphysical statements, that is, there is such a thing as divine revelation, God did show up, or there is a laboratory with such research conclusions. What does this mean? And how does it help?

First, metaphysics is the study of being. What is being in and of itself? What do all beings have in common that distinguishes being from nothing? Epistemology is the study of how you know that. So, if someone says that something exists without a way to know that, then we should hold his or her opinion in abeyance. And if someone says there is a way of knowing but there are no objects identifiable from that knowing, then again we should object. This little trick can help us separate noise from signal in the pursuit of truth. In the preceding section, metaphysical issues were discussed; later epistemological issues will be discussed. You might compare the two for consistency.

Philosophers who countered Edmund Husserl's (1859-1938) views of phenomenology argued that it was impossible to know consciousness, since it was a conscious pursuit itself. It is like defining a word with the same word. You could never see consciousness as-a-whole. You could not be objective. We could not understand our consciousness because it would be like trying to turn around to see the back of your head. Ironically, one can indeed turn around and see the back of one's head, if two mirrors are used. Technology can mirror consciousness. Scientists infer consciousness through interviews, EEGs, blood tests, and other physiological indicators. Mystics infer it through the meaning of acts. If you can do things with your body that others cannot, like sleeping on nails, walking on coals, being buried underground and survive, and the like, then you have developed a consciousness that others have not.

In the Western view, to know a thing you had to be separated from it in order to know how it was different from you. It is the reverse in Oriental epistemology. The degree to which you become the thing is the degree to which you know the thing. Today, we make technology like robots and computers that help us know ourselves. In the future we will merge with these to be adaptable to "outer space." Hence, we are likely to use both ways of knowing ourselves and become more enlightened.

Mystics often teach that the ultimate journey ends with the discovery of your self. We learn about our brain as we make computers; we learn about our earth as we study Mars. And we learn about our consciousness as we build our technology. We will duplicate life through technology, and during this duplication we will discover ourselves. We make the mirror and see ourselves.

East and West do agree that our basic nature is curiosity, which creates changes, and we are making tools to increase these changes. Mystics have seen the universe as divinely alive and conscious. Technocrats have seen the universe as mechanically interdependent. Merged, they see both as one. *Star Trek: The Movie* (better know as "Star Trek I") ends with the "conscious machine" and the human merging to create a new life form. Whatever consciousness that merger or new life form represents may be the consciousness we are moving toward, if current trends continue. Granted, some extraterrestrial culture might intervene to create an entirely new situation, but that cannot be predicted.

The German philosopher Hegel held that God devolved into us and we will evolve back to God. The continuity in this process is consciousness. Could it be that we will develop technologically and evolve into conscious technology, with consciousness still being the continuity in the process?

Some say consciousness is simply a set of chemical reactions in the brain. Brain produces thought and thought produces brain activity, which can affect the rest of the body. The cerebrum alone seems to have all the enzymatic processes to support the major metabolic pathways, which are found in the rest of the organs of the body. The brain is like its own little chemical unit that can affect all the others.

Will Durant, the American philosopher, said consciousness is "a point at which the sequence and relationship of thoughts coincide illuminatingly with the sequence of events and the relationship of things." Neither the anatomical view nor this particular philosophical definition contradicts the other, and both are assumed as "consciousness" as used here.

Hamid Bey, a mystic philosopher from Egypt, defines it as mind minus idea. You might think of consciousness as attention minus the object of attention. The most conventional definition is the awareness of being aware. Take your choice. They are all valid for the purposes of this book.

In the earlier discusion of factors to consider that affect the consciousness, one was left out that seemed more appropriate here. All significant earthly migrations ended in America. The great Asian migration that established the "Indians" from Alaska to the tip of South America was followed by the European migration that brought the Africans, culminating the three main racial migrations in America. Cultural diversity and complexity greatly increased in America because of these migrations. As the complexity and intensity of interaction increased, we began to see the relativity of views of life. One view seemed correct relative to one situation, and another view seemed correct relative to another situation.

Now culture-at-large is evolving a relativity of consciousness. One indicator was the popular view "You do your thing, and I'll do mine." Each person was the center of his or her value system. In the relativity of Einstein, each point in the universe is the center of the universe. One result of the blending of cultural relativity and contemporary physics will be the relativity of consciousness. This will eventually replace absolutist views and their inherent prejudice to want to keep things the way they are. Relativity implies the futility of trying to keep all things the way they are.

Another impact of Conscious Technology is the ease with which you can identify your unique "next steps," be they in general or in particular to the next moment. If you are more aware of how consciousness is affecting you than you are of technology, then technology is your next focus. We live in a world of both mind and machine. Balancing both influences will make us more fully alive in this world.

As an example, you might be very aware of all those in a room, know your mind's ideas, and yet be unaware of your physical surroundings. You might be sitting in an uncomfortable way that makes you look silly and leads to your knocking a glass of water off the table. The practice of C-T would make you simultaneously aware of your physical and conscious relations with your environment. As you straighten yourself in the chair, to feel a sense of balance between your relationship with your consciousness and technology (chair), note what new perceptions come to mind. Do these new perceptions lead to better action? And maybe the glass of water stays on the table.

Implicit in the spherical theory of personality is the notion of expanding all your abilities to their limits. Tom Wolf traces the story of test pilots and astronauts who pushed the "outer envelop" of their skills in his book *The Right Stuff.* The "right stuff" is that which pushes the outer limits beyond previous performance. It challenges Satan for sport, loves the impossible, and laughs with the unknown. Pushing the limits of perception by psychonauts was portrayed in the movies *Altered States* and *Brain Storm.*

Astronauts and psychonauts comprise a small section of humanity, but their ability to push beyond previous performance will become more commonplace. Research is going on to make us all super beings. According to *Sputnik,* a Soviet export magazine, Professor Vladimir Kuznetsov, the director of the Laboratory of Reserve Human Potential, All-Union Research Institute of Physical Culture in Moscow, claims that "Everything is vital here: pulse, breathing, the movement of an arm, even the angles of the turn of the head . . . " What is the appropriate speed for each activity like surgery, sewing, etc.? He goes on to say "As soon as man no longer needed to adapt himself to nature, [this may be a premature conclusion] his evolution stopped. But the disappearance of natural selection dooms biological species to degeneration. It follows that man should take control of his own evolution." Kuznetsov is pioneering this study of the maximum human performance for the USSR and calls it "anthropromaximology." This recognition that we can re-create humanity is here to stay.

The German Philosopher Leibnitz (1646-1716) felt that the universe and all its elements were wound up like a clock by God. Each element ticks out its motions regardless of whether or not others malfunction. A crab digs just before high tide, whether at its home on the beach or after transporting it 20 miles inland in a marine biologist's metal pail. NASA is now seeing if plants, like crabs, will go through their cycles in orbit as if on earth. But it seems that all of this is moot since we have already overruled the genetic determinism with genetic engineering and bionics. We will wind up our own little Leibnitzian clocks and make our own little universes.

But there is a limit to this. The universe is likely to contract or implode. It's a hot topic in astronomers' circles. Some think we won't contract but continue to expand out to a cold death. Either case portends a dismal long-range future. Granted, we have billions of years to figure out how to rig the universe so that it neither contracts nor expands to the danger point, but it may take us billions of years to figure it out, and we might as will get our astronauts and psychonauts on the job.

Meanwhile, back on earth, more philosophies are running into each other in less time. People will accommodate the different views by applying pragmatic relativity. A view that is true (or works) for one person, relative to his or her situation, may contradict another's view of what is true.

You need not blindly accept specific views of others in this relativistic philosophy because there are at least four tests: (1) does it indeed work; (2) are the metaphysical and epistemological statements mutually consistent;

(3) does it increase or decrease the balance of consciousness and technology; and (4) is there consistency between one's inner feelings and outer expressions or actions?

Another set of ideological fallouts deal with the role of belief in the absence of certain knowledge. For example, if we believe in multi-realities rather than in one absolute reality, then one philosophy need not argue to the death with another. Instead, they might acknowledge the relative validity of each to their unique situations and find the common links. The technocrat may not buy the Akashic Record and Karma as the mystic does but might concede that such a belief can act as a force keeping people more honest, since everything "counts." Both agree that the belief influences behavior. Again, the technocrat might not believe the universe is a "divinely conscious entity" but would concede that such a belief can act as a force to make people treat their environment more responsibly. The beliefs in mind over body and self-hypnosis have produced extraordinary feats documented by medicine.

Gertrude Schineidler's research into ESP demonstrated that those who believed in ESP scored above chance in tests to "psychically" guess cards without seeing them, whereas those who did not believe in ESP scored below chance. A French author, Emile Coure, and the consciousness training group Silva Mind Control encourage people to use a self-hypnotic suggestion for healing themselves by repeating "Everyday, in every way, I am getting better and better." No one doubts the role of belief and morale in Olympic games or military victory. We don't have to know the ultimate explanation of these activities in order to try them out and share experiences. The trick is to do it without claiming certain knowledge of the mechanism involved. Sure, we would like to know the ultimate truth of things, but in the meantime, we can look at the consequences of belief.

Many warrior cultures believe they can alter their consciousness by drugs, chants, rituals, or pain to bring forth superhuman ability. Don Juan's stories, told in the popular books by Carlos Castaneda, speak about getting into animal states of alertness. *The Wizard of the Amazon* recounts the stories of jungle hunters who imitate bird calls, quick head movements, or balancing on tree limbs like birds to bring out capabilities not considered normal for human beings.

If we were to dismiss all this as primitive nonsense, then we would cut ourselves off from the discovery of some potentials of consciousness. Ontogeny recapitulates phylogeny; that is, during the embryo's development, the evolutionary summary of the individual species is repeated. You were like a fish, a reptile, a primitive mammal while growing up in your mother's womb. Since the structure of DNA is the evolutionary summary of the individual, maybe we can tap some of our previous potential, as the jungle warriors claim. We don't need to know the relationship of the brain to DNA, to consciousness, or to behavior to give it a try. If some feats are experienced and we are surprised, perhaps we are surprised only because our world view was so poor or limited.

Under hypnosis, people can recall details of birth such as their mother's hair style and behavior of people around them, according to David Chamberlain, a psychologist in San Diego. His study of 10 mother-child pairs corroborates earlier research of David Cheek, a San Francisco obstetrician-gynecologist, which seems to indicate the possibility of memory without language. What other capabilities may be humanly possible that mystics allude to that are yet to become part of our futures? And how do we know when we are fooling ourselves?

Epistemology and How Do You Know What to Do?

As we move toward the first world renaissnace, the merger of mystic and technocratic ways of knowing is the key to discovering what we can do to create a more enlightened world. The technocrats believe that we know by logic—deduction and induction based on sense impressions augmented by tools. Mystics believe we know by intuition, direct knowing, ESP, or listening to our feelings.

All deduction (all men are mortal, Socrates is a man; therefore, Socrates will die) is based on induction. The major premise "All men are mortal" is a conclusion from inductive reasoning. We see a series of individual cases with the same result, then generalize that all future such cases will therefore have the same result. But how many individual cases must be observed in order to make such a universal generalization? 5? 5,000? 5,000,000? There is no universal, absolute rule for such certainty. It is judgment, intuition, feelings, or the research money ran out. Objectivity is based on subjectivity. Our knowledge is based on deduction, which is based on induction. Induction is based on feelings as to what is a sufficient number of cases to make the generalization. There is no certainty about the correctness of these feelings. Hence, all our Western logic is not as solid as we would like to believe.

The American philosopher Nelson Goodman, in *Fact, Fiction, and Forecast,* flatly states "Although Hume's dictum that there are no necessary connections of matters of fact [i.e., causality] has been challenged at times, it has withstood all attacks." Goodman goes on to say of Hume's analysis of causality that

> When an event of one kind frequently follows upon an event of another kind of experience, a habit is formed that leads the mind, when confronted with a new event of the first kind, to pass to the idea of an event of the second kind. The idea of necessary connection arises from the felt impulse of the mind in making this transition.

Hence, "felt impulse" is the key to such perceived certainty. Again, Goodman goes on to note the role of feeling in the history of epistemology: "A rule is amended if it yields an inference we are unwilling to accept; an inference is rejected if it violates a rule we are unwilling to amend." If our feelings are strong enough, we change logic.

Using logic alone can get you into some pretty twisted situations. For example, there is no truth or falsity about the future. You can say, true or false, that it is raining. You can say, true or false, that it rained yesterday. But you cannot say, true or false, it will rain tomorrow. Truth and falsity is required for logical inferences to be sound. Therefore, logic cannot judge current statements about the future. But this conclusion is self-referentially inconsistent. Logic judged logic to be unsound when making statements about the future. But that statement is a statement about the soundness of logic in the future. And so it goes.

This is not to say that we should throw out our logical analysis, as the anti-intellectuals would have us do. It is simply to say that analysis alone is not enough. Technocratic analysis has helped us systematically build our knowledge to make more humans successful. Scientific method has accelerated this process. Unfortunately, we create more hypotheses in scientific analysis than experiments to test them out. This results in a daily backlog of hypotheses, beyond our ability to cope using science alone. Instead, we make judgments about which hypotheses to pursue. These judgments are based on feelings cross-referenced by analysis.

As analysis is reason about reason "feelysis" is feelings about feeling. Just as there are many forms of analysis, there are many forms of feelysis. The following is a partial list of some forms of feelysis:

1.   How do you feel about a certain proposition or course of action? Then, how do you feel about your reaction to that course of action? For example, I feel excited about feelysis as an addition and cross-reference to analysis as improving my epistemology. How do I feel about that reaction? I feel some concern about excitement because that has sometimes in the past been premature. How do I feel about that? I will rededicate myself to ascertaining where and how the prematurities might have occurred. Our conscious ideas do not account for the sum total of experiences. The unconsciousness can be brought into play to add to our consciousness, what we may have experienced about a proposition that we have temporarily forgotten. Meditation can be such a method to allow for the feelings or the sequence of feelings to come to mind. The belief that one can discover the essence of divinity and the universe by simply looking within is the essence of egocentrism. But if you balanced such subjective feelysis with objective analysis, ego involvement can be reduced.

2.   What are your bodily feelings as you analyze a course of action? Is there tension in your legs, fingers, or a straightening of your back? As you note the tension, relax the area and note what comes to mind. Does this add improvement to your original awareness? For example, I felt some discomfort in my feet while considering this idea just now. Then I straightened my feet making them more comfortable. Next I noted a sense of calm and centeredness in my mind and went on writing to give this example I was looking for. The brain is connected to the muscles. Changing one affects the other. Mental blocks can be affected by changing physical blocks and tensions.

3.   Drawing or doodling about some issue that is troubling you can allow the unconsciousness to fill in the blanks. What doodles in your drawing make you feel better about the troublesome issue? Does it feel better to

make it more symmetrical, balanced, and in proportion? Go with your feelings as you doodle, but don't force a symmetry or pattern that does not feel right. Nature often has that little bit of irregularity. This form of feelysis externalizes some of your feelings about your feeling. Drawing is a technique to help you bring forth from your unconsciousness that which may complete your feelings about that troublesome issue.

4. Feelysis can be used to check intuition or direct knowing or ESP by noting the feelings associated with these experiences. Is there a consistent pattern of feelings associated with intuitions that were correct? Is there a different pattern of feelings associated with intuitions that have turned out to be wrong? This requires you to feel the least noticeable difference, which is quite demanding. This particular form of feelysis is developed with much time and attention.

5. If your feelysis gets stalled, then center your attention, seek a sense of balance, note any new feelings that arise and continue again.

6. When we hit a conscious brick wall, we reach for a smoke, coffee, psychoactive drugs, physical exercise, clean up our environment, go to the bathroom, or make some other form of change. This gives us time for the unconscious to come up with a clue to solve the problem. Psychoactive drugs are one of the most dramatic tools to change your consciousness and possibly to experience different feelings. The philosopher William James used nitrous oxide and peyote; the author Aldous Huxley used mescaline pills; the psychiatrist Sigmund Freud used cocaine; the medical doctor John Lilly and futurist Herman Kahn used LSD; and the authors Ernest Hemingway and Edgar Allan Poe used alcohol. Such substances bring the unconscious to the conscious mind as a cross-reference to previous feelings, analysis, and perceptions. These may not add to our knowledge per se, but do loosen the inhibitions of feelings to expand the scope of feelysis. Other nonchemical techniques for altering our consciousness like chanting or extremes in physical activity can produce similar additions to feelysis. Granted, one can overuse and may oversynthesize the awareness and relationship of feelings and ideas. It can lead to foolishness, like too much of anything.

Think of these altered states as cross-references to normal states. If your expanded feelysis by altered states comes to the same conclusion as you do when in a normal state of consciousness during analytic reasoning, then you can be more certain that you are correct. If there is contradiction, then it seems you have to do more work to complete either your feelysis or your analysis.

7. A more subtle form of feelysis uses your body as an epistemological tool. In this technique you hold an idea or issue in your awareness, while doing some physically difficult act like balancing on a rope or juggling. As the internal feelysis progresses, note any alterations in your balance or juggling. At what feeling did that alteration occur? What feelings arise as a result of that alteration? This technique can help you to note more subtle feelings that might not have been noticed by still meditation. If there is not a good correspondence of body coordination and feeling at this point during your feelysis, then it may be that there is a tension between the conscious and unconscious. This tension could cause the physical glitch. The standard lie detector that registers body alterations in breathing, pulse, and blood pressure is based on the same principle as this technique.

8. As doodling can help the sequence of feelysis, so can rhyming. Doodling helps visual-feeling associations to be made. Rhyming helps verbal-feeling associations to be made. Making rhymes about a proposition forces the mind to both find words that rhyme and words that mean something about the proposition. As the mind searches for words, unexpected words and their associated feelings arise. Note the unexpected and how that adds to your feelings.

These eight forms of feelysis have many variations and more focused applications. Some are listed in the C-T exercises section. But the best techniques may be those that you develop yourself, since feelysis is by definition a more subjective activity than analysis with its more objective forms of verification and replication.

We do not use feelysis to know the truth about how many chairs there are in the room. We count them. We don't use mathematics to know the truth about what kinds of chairs we like. We use feelysis. But we must use both feelysis and analysis to buy the chairs we like. The interplay of analysis and feelysis informs our beliefs and judgments about right action. To come up with a better tax policy or indeed a better civilization we should use both feelysis and analysis.

Another variation of knowing what to do involves a confusion of "or" thinking and "both/and" thinking. People waste inordinate time debating whether one course of action is right as opposed to another course of action. We say a thing can be true or false. In logic this is called "two-valued logic" because there are only two values for any proposition. This way of thinking incorrectly spills over into "if this course of action is right, then that course of action is wrong." This confusion can be straightened out by saying *both* this course of action *and* that course of action is right. The correctness of one does not necessarily negate the correctness of the other.

So often our minds seem to think that a course is right or wrong and if we believe this, then the other course must be wrong. Notice how much time is taken up in this confusion at your next meeting. There are so many things to do to bring about a better future. We need to figure out how to do the many, rather than pit one against the other. We need to think strategically. First, we should say "How can we do both?" Then, if we are sure we cannot, then and only then should we prioritize. "Both and" thinking allows us to support other people in their different courses of actions than our own.

We need to know when to use two-valued logic and when to use strategic thinking, that is, how things fit together for successful action. Two-valued logic is good for figuring out why the sky is blue. Strategic thinking is good for figuring out how to keep it blue. The stereotypical view of the industrialist and environmentalist holds that each believes he or she is correct and the other is wrong. Two-valued logic reinforces this polarization. Strategic thinking puts the two views in a relationship such that together they can know how to act. The environmentalist can point out energy-efficient ways to create products, and the industrialist can point out production techniques as to cost/effect. The two could work together to plan better approaches, if each accepts the validity of the other's basic principles—the value of environmental health and the value of economic health. The two could see themselves in a yin/yang relationship:

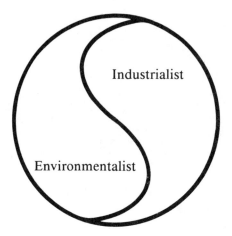

rather than one versus the other. This could be expanded to the Tamoyan:

Expanding this same approach to the world one could imagine

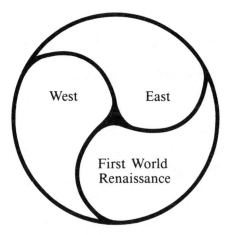

Traditionally, Oriental thought sees the world as a whole with relationships. For example, man in proper relation with woman:

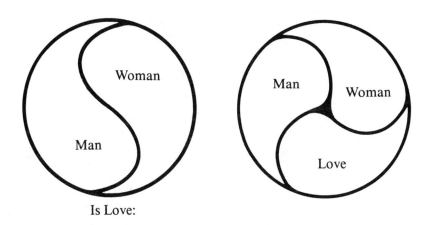

Is Love:

Hence, the strategy that resolves the contradiction between man and woman is love.

This is all to suggest an addition of ◐ and ◑ to logical notation. These additions may be helpful to resolve adversarial thought and confusion. There is no simple logical notation that indicates two propositions standing in a relationship of mutual improvement or creating. There is also no simple notation that indicates a strategy to resolve contradiction. There is

X v Y   X or Y

X & Y   X and Y

U [X & Y]   Both X and Y

but there is no X ⊘ Y, meaning X mutually creating Y, nor is there (X ⊘ Y) ⊘ Y, meaning X and Y resolved by Z.

Mystics like to talk about things being and not being at the same time — loudness in silence or fullness of emptiness. In logical notation that would be A & ~A, which is impossible. With the new notation it could be represented as A ⊘ ~A.

In the Hilbert-Ackerman system of logic, silence implies loudness and loudness implies silence would mean that silence and loudness are the exact same thing:

$$[(S \supset L) \ \& \ (L \supset S)] \ = \ [S \equiv L]$$

So, that won't do it either, but S ⊘ L will. The example of love resolving conflict between man and woman would be written as

$$(M \ ⊘ \ W) \ ⊘ \ L$$

This may seem a bit extreme, but remember that the original observation that two-valued logic has been confused by public sentiment to say (incorrectly) that either you are wrong and I am right or I am wrong and you are right. It may be helpful to begin to get logical notation to include the mystic's notation of ⊘ and ⊘ in order to influence our epistemological thinking.

As we move from the duality of "or" to the strategy of "both," we will become more aware of how other conflicts can be resolved. We will notice more coincidences, as our scope of vision includes more elements to be seen as coinciding. As our strategic thinking becomes more holistic, we will see how more things fit together. This is compatible with a mystical epistemology: if the rate of synchronicity or "divine coincidence" increases, then you are acting more advantageously; and conversely, if the rate of synchronicity decreases, then you are acting in a less balanced fashion.

Please note throughout this discussion that we are talking about how we can be more certain, rather than how we can know the truth. The positive correlation of feelysis and analysis increases certainty, but does not guarantee truth. In a similar manner, the more fully the principles of the industrialist and the environmentalist are engaged in a mutual strategy, the more certain we can be that their action will be beneficial. Hence, we can know that we are not as "correct" when there are opponents to our action. The burden of proof is upon us to fit their self-interest and principles into ours and ours into theirs. Or, as Einstein was said to have believed: "Two sides disagree because they are both wrong!"

We can think of a world view as what constitutes reality, how we know that, what is valuable, and what are meaningful events. A witch doctor's world view may appear quite different from a New York stockbroker's. These may be quite different from a Soviet ideology instructor's. Yet, there may be points or areas of their world views that overlap. All three prefer to express love in a safe environment rather than be hated in a dangerous one. It may be an impossible task to delineate all the world views and find all the cross-over points or areas of overlap. But the attitude that pursues such philosophical cross-referencing is the one we need to discover the foundations for the first world renaissance.

This can begin less grandly, on an individual scale. Cross-reference your own world view with others and identify patterns of overlap. In time, these patterns can become your world view. This allows you to be more at ease with more of the world—if your action is in concert with your newly evolved world view. Our seeing should be cross-referenced with our being. The American poet Andrew Oerke calls this "trueing." You must act as you speak and believe in order to find out if what you speak and believe is true. This creates a self-correcting feedback loop of being and perception. You "true" your world view by action and you true your action by your world view.

The popularization of the computer may also help us to behave more honestly. First, humans can be fooled. It is harder to fool a computer. You make a mistake with a human, and it is possible to talk your way around it. But a computer? It simply and patiently comes back with various ways of saying that you goofed. Second, humans tend to hear with a well-developed sense of self-interest. Computers hear just what you tell them.

Hence, the computer is imposing a bit of rigor to our honesty. This will help us become more precise, clear, and more efficient. These attitudes of the mind will help us through the increasing complexity and shocks of the future more smoothly.

The cross-referencing of feelysis with analysis, your world view with others, and trueing of belief and action has an interesting implication. It becomes prudent and pragmatic to drop your prejudices. This in turn reduces your fear of the unknown — a major block to increasing knowledge.

So, listen to all, but cross-reference everything until action follows. And see everything, but notice consequences until action follows.

Form your own meditative techniques, trust your own creativity, think positively, and eat light amounts of fresh non-animal food. Be aware of potential dangers to our minds and nervous systems. The built environment can enhance consciousness (Arcosant, Williamsburg, EPCOT). Our bodies are our most immediate environments; and improved health and quality of life are the goal of meditation, dance, fasting, aerobics, biofeedback, encounter groups, hypnosis, sensory deprivation, surrealist art, and dreams (but their misuse can be dangerous). Conscious Technology exercises include eye balancing, seeing the unconscious, balancing with your center, walking in time, sensory pushups, peripheral seeing, good morning, wisdom in a chair, solace, relational meanings of objects, boomerang, visualization, four ball sequences, spherical perception, doodling.

Chapter Five
Beginning Today

Policy Recommendation and Implications

Begin with yourself. Is your view more weighted toward the mystic or the technocrat? Are you more mystically inclined at the expense of your awareness of technology? Or the reverse? Perceive the consciousness of those who are different. Find the overlaps.

Create your own meditative techniques so that others will not consciously or otherwise control your consciousness. You should trust yourself. Believe that you can bring forth your own creativity in making yourself more spherically whole, as explained in the "Levels of Prejudice" section. Think of your personality as a many-faceted diamond. Polish the diamond on all sides, rather than playing level's advocate.

Your brain interacts with the endocrine and immune systems through the nervous system. Thoughts of health and illness have physiological effects, like ulcers and stuttering. Thought influences action, or as the Buddhists teach: "Right thought; right action." Can you play your role to think the world right? Can you imagine transforming or unraveling evil? Heal what you can.

Since you are what you eat, become more aware of the relationship of food to your mind. Eating fresh, locally grown food in season, in light amounts that are lower down the food chain should help. "Enter your kitchen with a calm mind, cleared of distractions," says Lima Ohsawa in *The Art of Just Cooking,* "and concentrate as you would for any other act of meditation. Develop a sense of dedication to the art, for from this dedication not only you and your family, but all of mankind will benefit. Make your kitchen the center of your home, radiate creativity and joy." The process of cooking and serving feeds more senses than just taste.

On a more ominous note, the recent rapid proliferation of electromagnetic devices in all aspects of life may affect our minds, compared to the environment when our species roamed in the wild. Magnetic fields induce electric currents. As you put a wire in and out of a magnetic field, electric current is induced and measurable. As we move through different fields created by electronic activity of different frequencies, at different intensities, from various distances and lengths of time, what induction may result in our nervous systems?

For ten years I have asked the relevant engineers, physicists, biologists, and medical doctors about the biological effects of electromagnetic waves. No one has the overview. The research has been too fragmented to draw conclusions, beyond the conclusion that there is some effect.

Let us assume the worst for a moment: slowly but surely the species is being driven irritable and maybe mad by artificial inducement of cerebral activity from electronic devices in space and on earth. Let us further assume that the situation is far too subtle and complex for intelligent and rapid government or international response.

What's our reaction? Smashing transmitters in a neo-Luddite or anti-technology binge is not the answer and could cause more damage to evolution than the original problem.

Assuming again that this is a real and not an imagined problem, we might as well use our own consciousness to try to influence our nervous system for the better. Until governments and corporations correct the situation, there doesn't seem to be much else to do. We could center our consciousness on any new sense of self-awareness that we feel might be due to the increased electromagnetic activity. And then meditate on this sense of change while imagining improvement. We could visualize a drama inside our bodies that defends our nervous system from the external influences.

The recent science of psychoneuroimmunology has documented a variety of positive results from such visualization techniques in cancer cases. The idea is that thought has a biochemical corollary in the nervous system. If this is so, then this might be one approach to defend ourselves from electromagnetic pollution.

As we move into the Conscious Technology Age, we should become more aware of the potential dangers to our minds. For example, a September 1975 U.S. Defense Intelligence Agency document, DST-1810S-387-75, asked: Is there any evidence of a connection between the Soviet science of Opinionology and psychotronic research?" The Public Information Office of the U.S. Department of Defense says that no further study was done on this question, or any of the other points within the document. Well, was there or is there any connection? If so, and the Soviets are experimenting with that connection, then would they be trying to affect U.S. opinion? How would it surface? Would U.S. opinion reflexes begin to shift from self-respect to self-destruct?

Remember *V*, the movie and series for television? The hero's boy changed his opinion reflex from liking baseball to not liking baseball. Notice your value shift, over time, recognize the trends, understand why, and imagine it better next time you try. Easier said than done, true, but this is the kind of self-care that will become increasingly important.

If indeed the Soviet Politburo were able to apply opinionology and psychotronic research to change your world view and affect your values, how would you defend yourself? The Canadian Society for Clean Energy claims it detects extremely low frequency transmissions from the Soviet Union entering North America and that it is in the frequency range to affect our alertness. Although the EPA says the energy in the field is too small to cause biological damage, no one knows the long-term effects. So how do you prepare your psychic self-defense? Short of Canadian or American governmental response, we are left with visualization techniques mentioned earlier and C-T exercises at the end of this section.

A Standford Research Institute report paraphrases "Assessment of Psychotechnology" by G. A. Miller in *Psychotechnology: Electric Control of Mind and Behavior*:

> What is the best protection against misuse of consciousness-altering techniques by authoritarian governments, mad zealots, and fast buck artists? Probably wide-spread knowledge and understanding. If a potentially destructive technology is controlled by the few, the many are endangered by that power; but if the ability to use the technology is distributed, the danger is lessened.

This is strange advice. Should everyone get the bomb? the psychoplasmic blaster? the button to blow up the world? hand guns?

Maybe what is to be distributed is the knowledge of Conscious Technology so that people could master their mind/body's reaction to technologically induced effects.

We should arrange our environments to improve our perceptions. Messy rooms, random storage, and furniture that doesn't fit your functions forces your mind to do unnecessary work. Clutter in; clutter out. A poorly used mind gets poorer, while an effectively used mind gets more so. The evolution seems fair on this point.

Taking the environment to include large numbers of people, we can have cities or cities-within-cities that enhance or inhibit enlightenment. A city is like the autonomic nervous system or subconscious support system of society. We create city technology to do those things we don't want to do and hence, our consciousness can be freed and secure to do those things we want to do. As the unconscious needs to be brought to the awareness of the conscious for an individual's mental health, so too, the city must be brought to the awareness of society for social well-being.

The architect Frank Lloyd Wright addressed this perception in his concept of "form follows function." His student Paolo Soleri coined the term "arcology" or the merger of architecture and ecology. They believed that the built environment could enhance consciousness. If we wanted to experience such enhancement to speed-up our enlightenment, then why not build so that these experiences can occur?

Holy shrines, zoos, Disneyland, and other cultural expressions are examples of built environments that architecturally express alternative realities. As mentioned in Chapter 2, Paolo Soleri is building a sample alternative as a small community in the Arizona desert called Arcosanti. It is being built by people who live there, who believe that flat suburbia, like fewer folds in the brain, will not increase human intelligence. Granted, satellite communications can make the most isolated or suburban place quite sophisticated. Nevertheless, Soleri makes an excellent point that a city must be perceivable as a whole to be lovable as a whole object. His arcologies are intended to be one sculpted machine for people to experience and be sustained by.

Arcosanti is an experimental mini-city being constructed in the southwestern desert of the United States to see if it can improve human consciousness.

Begun around 1970, Arcosanti was under construction long before sufficient funding was achieved. Only bits and pieces of the idea have taken shape in the dry southwest of America. The suburb was the developer's grand-scale work. A new challenge for future developers will be to make microcities like Paolo Soleri's Arcosanti in a city.

Williamsburg, Virginia, is another current attempt to express through architecture an alternative reality. Houses have been restored to the pre-American Revolutionary period. People dress in period costumes, use tools of that time, and some even imagine that they are really living in a different time zone. Tourists are perceived by some as visitors from the future.

Walt Disney's dream of building an "Experimental Prototype Community of Tomorrow" was partly materialized in Florida and is called EPCOT. Exhibits of how we will live under the sea or in orbit around the earth show the tourist that reality might be quite different in the future.

Such examples merely point out that alternatives can be conceived and built. In the history of ideas, it has never been recorded that vast portions of civilization ever believed that they could invent tomorrow.

But exactly that belief "future shocked" the world in the mid-twentieth century.

Our present action can be thought of as the interplay of the past we believe and the future we expect. Therefore, social change is achieved by either changing our view of history or the future.

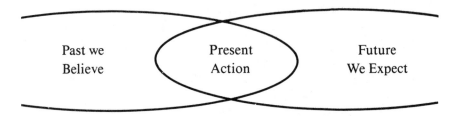

Past we Believe | Present Action | Future We Expect

Imagine changing your expectation of the future of human habitats. Instead of dividing our built environment into rural, suburban, and cities, imagine them instead as one continuous structure connected in a variety of ways. Like Paolo Soleri, architect Winslow Elliott Wedin believes that the goal is a "symbiotic relationship between the built world and the natural world." But there he parts company with Soleri and claims a continuously connected, horizontal, habitat that follows the natural forms of rock, sand, water, and soil is a new approach to our future.

All of humanity could be housed as one. He writes: "If the fine gray line of demarcation between that which we intelligently conceive and that which has existed in nature becomes nearly invisible, then the goal has been achieved. The design process requires a metamorphosis of subtle changes of color, scale, form and proportion as rock becomes the dwelling or the mountain becomes the city."

This Zen approach to architecture, where the inside and the outside are characterized by continuous flow rather than demarcation by cement walls, is more difficult to implement than Arcosanti. It does illustrate an alternative future and an opportunity to reduce prejudice. Wedin offers six observations:

1. The horizontal is commonplace; the vertical is unique.
2. Small changes in height are very noticeable; small changes in the horizontal are hardly perceived.
3. We do not know the "neighbors" above or below.

4. We, as social animals, relate more easily to each other on the horizontal plane than above or below.

5. Grade separation eliminates circulation conflicts.

6. Our field of vision (physical perception) is greater in the horizontal [seeing left and right] than the vertical [seeing up and down].

Environments should offer different views of reality so that we may be able to see others' views more easily. This allows us to know the points of overlap, the keys to unlock prejudice.

David Spangler, in the *Vision of Findhorn Anthology,* calls for environments that could "create a magnetic center that has physical, emotional, mental, spiritual aspects, calling for being, knowing, feeling and doing, in a harmonious synthesis." The Findhorn experimental community of 300 people in Scotland and another called Auroville with 600 people in India are such centers that are "synergetic in their nature and therefore require for success both individual transformation and group endeavor."

There seems to be a value in small clusters within bigger urban structures. Jack Calhoun in rat research at the U.S. National Institutes of Health has demonstrated that "as a group size increases the average social velocity decreases." If we have this in common with rats, and if we want to increase our social interaction with those of different views, then it is beneficial to have small clusters of diverse people, rather than megalopolises. It is physically easier for us to find points in common with people in smaller diverse clusters than within larger ones. Even physiological common bonding will occur, according to Mary McCarthy in her book *The Group.* She writes that Harvard psychologist Martha McLintock proved that women in small communities tend to menstruate on the same cycle.

Our bodies are our most immediate environments and they too should make us more awake. Martial arts exercises are done to open our awareness to cosmic consciousness. Prana Yoga is the discipline of breathing to awaken the mind. Jazzercize and aerobic dancing classes act like human consciousness filling stations to make you more lively. Fasting alters your consciousness and saves you time—no cooking, washing dishes, buying food, or opening the refrigerator door. Creating exercises that can be integrated into your life style to become as normalized as possible will keep your body environment tuned up and enliven your consciousness.

So, our policy of consciousness is to create technologies that improve our consciousness. Our body is the technology of our mind. Our city is the technology of our society. And we must become aware of how our thoughts are the technology of our future.

We can think in terms of "both/and" or in terms of the yin/yang. For example, it is pointless to argue against the reductionist who feels that continuously subdividing something is the way to know. Put the discussion in a yin/yang relationship. It is pointless for one necessary part to argue against another necessary part. Both holistic and reductionistic thought is necessary.

Conscious Technology Exercises
Introduction

Our hands are tools. Unlike hammers and nails, our hands have sensors to alter our awareness. Our awareness alters our hands. Our hands give information to and receive information from our brain. Our hands are conscious technology. As there are exercises to improve our body technology, there are exercises to improve our conscious technology, or more precisely, our internal conscious technology.

Humans, more than any other animal, have externalized technology. Microscopes and telescopes are external technology for our eyes; submarines and space ships are external technology for our hands and feet; telephones for our voice box; and computers for the brain. We need exercises to improve our conscious relationship with our external technology relationship as well.

Health is the proper relationship between consciousness and internal technology; "qualitivity" (quality and productivity) is the proper relationship between consciousness and external technology. Hence, the purpose of conscious technology exercises is improved health and qualitivity.

Many C-T exercises practiced by mystics are well documented in other books and training programs and have been passed on through the oral tradition. The proof of their effectiveness is demonstrated by amazing feats. One documented by Dr. L. K. Kothari in 1973 at Ravindranath Medical Center College, in Udaipur, India, was Satyamurti's eight-day meditation in a sealed underground pit. This was reported on in *Omni* magazine March, 1982, by Roy Walford, Jr. Houdini and other quality magicians develop a special relationship between their consciousness and both internal and external technology, although they tend not to share these C-T exercises with the public.

C-T exercises can also be thought of as perceptual toys or think tricks. One version, called the Futures Wheel, I developed in 1971 to move the mind from concepts to multi-concepts formation. The name of a concept is written in the middle of a piece of paper. Short lines are drawn spokelike from the word in the middle of the paper. Words are written at the end of each spoke that connote a necessary correlation with the concept. Next, correlations are added to each of the primary correlations to form the multi-concept. This exercise is used by futurists to uncover and display consequences of trends and by school teachers in futuristic curricula.

Another example of the perceptual toy or think trick version of C-T exercises is the work of M. C. Escher. His paintings showed the dualistic interplay of forces to alter consciousness from one-dimensional thought.

C-T exercises make us more aware of intuition because they take the mind beyond conventional awareness. Intuition has always been the bridge between the known and the unknown. But how to know when to trust it and when not to? Charles Whitman had an intuition that his brain needed to be checked out. No one paid attention to his intuition. Later he killed his wife and mother. He then shot over 40 people from the University of Texas tower. It turned out that he had a brain tumor the size of a walnut pressing on the aggressive area of his brain. On the other hand, people have been getting intuitions that the world is coming to an end for years. C-T exercises may help you develop your own "logic of intuition" or feelysis, as described earlier.

Techniques such as automatic writing, crystal ball gazing, and tarot card reading may be ways to bring to consciousness our unconscious knowledge. As described in Chapter 3, tarot cards have pictures of universal symbols of love, death, wealth, and so on. By laying them out in various patterns, we may find questions that we might not have thought to ask. Such traditional techniques are designed to affect our consciousness.

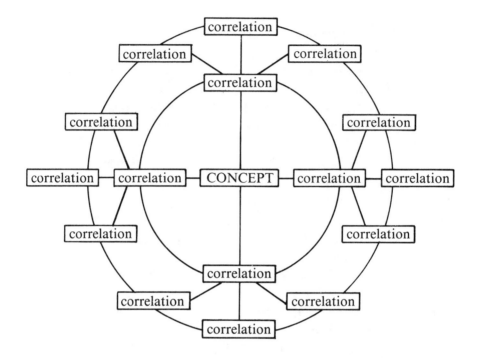

Basic Futures Wheel.

Conscious Technology is the perception of something that we use to focus our awareness. I might look at some family heirloom to increase my awareness of wisdom and strength or stare at a mountain to increase my awareness of the power in life. When I forget to see objects in this fashion, I perceive a less exciting environment, and one that is not increasing my brain functioning. By looking at a meaningful object, I associate memories of similar meaning. This can give me some sense of change over time and direction of a trend in my learning or awareness. From such comparisons of past and present perceptions, one can be helped to see ahead.

C-T exercises are intended to make new cerebral activity that leads to better-balanced perception. Exercises like balancing on a rope or juggling should stimulate cerebral activity for balance and a sense of centeredness. Both hemispheres of the brain are equally engaged in these exercises. In addition, sitting still, we can fool ourselves about how balanced or centered we are, but there is no way to fool yourself when juggling or balancing on a rope. If you are off center or unbalanced, you fall off the rope or drop what you are juggling.

Some of the better-known categories of C-T exercises are meditation, dance, fasting, biofeedback, chemical ingestion, encounter groups, rite of passage ceremonies including physical pain, hypnosis, sensory deprivation, art (most noticeably, surrealism), and dreams. These ways of consciously using your body as a tool have their dangers. For example, the Stanford Research Institute's Center for the Study of Social Policy under contract to the U. S. National Science Foundation identified the following areas of the misuse of technologies to affect consciousness:

1. Danger to mental health
2. Conflict between social responsibility and ecstasy seeking
3. Who should control
4. Religious freedom
5. Power-seeking cults
6. Missing the benefits/opportunities through failure to pursue consciousness research primarily in health education

This same report points out the value of such exercises:

1. Unconscious processes comprise a majority of significant human experience (intuition, etc.).
2. World-and-self perception are strongly influenced by unconscious processes.
3. Access to unconscious processes is facilitated by attention to feelings and emotions.
4. Access to unconsciousness processes is facilitated by imaginal thought (visual imagery in contrast to verbal associative thought).

Considering how influential our unconscious processes are, it is amazing how little we know about them. This report points out this fact by boldly stating that "We have no adequate theoretical framework to explain hypnosis." Yet hypnosis is now so well established that a man was filmed using self-hypnosis prior to surgery thereby controlling his blood flow during the operation.

Dreaming is less understood than building muscles by lifting weights. C. G. Jung called dreams "the spokesman of the unconsciousness." This spokesman speaks through our nervous system. This inner technology must be a transceiver, since I can *receive* signals that my left eye is twitching and *transmit* awareness of stillness and healing until my eye twitching ends. If the nervous system has such communications wiring, can it create a field when consciousness and unconsciousness communicate? An electrified wire creates a magnetic field. In a similar fashion our neurons, like these wires, may create a "biomagnetic field." If so, then as the magnetic field induced by the electric wire has different densities, so too our biomagnetic field could have different densities.

A C-T exercise called cosmic push-ups is intended to increase this density, while balancing our feeling of centeredness. Imagine expanding your awareness to outer space, passing the planets, galaxies, and your imagination. Then return to yourself. This "in and out" sense of consciousness expansion and contraction as distinct from "up and down" is difficult to experience, since level theory is so ingrained in our veins.

The density of consciousness might be thought of as a warping of our attention in the same way that the denser the mass, the more energy that passes by the dense object is warped. A healthy person with a more balanced and denser consciousness warps you into feeling good. An out-of-balance and consciously dense person warps you into feeling negatively. You can also warp yourself by thinking too much of yourself or that you are better than others. You can be seduced by your own density or power. So be careful that your increased density or sense of density does not warp your attention or you might get seduced by the "dark side of The Force," as in the movie *Star Wars*. If you begin to feel this, then imagine seeing divinity on your other shoulder.

Alvin Toffler suggested that the "noble savage" always seems to lurk around the corner of each new image of the future of our species. Genetically speaking, we are our past, which includes savage capabilities. Hunters and warriors depicted in books like *Wizard of the Upper Amazon* and Carlos Castaneda's tales of the Yaki teacher's experiences in the night jungles and deserts bring forth this former savage alertness and body awareness. As noted in Chapter 4, these hunters and warriors put blood of the kill on their faces, imitate the calls of birds, and lie still like the crocodile to heighten their awareness. Possibly, we can have both the alertness of the savage with the wisdom of civilization. Spend the night alone in a forest and see how alert and how aware of your inner technology you become.

Much has been written about both the use and the abuse of psychoactive chemicals. There is no need to explain or expand on that here except to say that the more stable individual can use them as an exercise to prepare for more difficult times. Alan Watts said in the *California Law Review* that the psychedelic experience "can very easily be an experience in which you have to test your soul against all the devils in hell." Better to do it on a trial run to improve your reflexes, so that if you do run into some bad parts of life you have some experience and reserve to handle it. This would be like getting some dead polio virus to activate the body's defenses to ward off the actual disease. But since these substances are illegal in most areas, you may have to visit temples in the Orient where this is practiced under experienced supervision.

It is not necessary to try all or any of the C-T exercises. The following are only illustrative to give you a sense of what such exercises are like so that you can develop your own. The most effective techniques are more likely to be the ones you create for your own health and qualitivity, rather than ones you merely copy.

Sample C-T Exercises
1. EYE BALANCING   Look at your right eye in a mirror for 5 to 10 seconds. Then look at your left eye for the same time. Next, look back and forth from right eye to left eye until you notice any asymmetry between them, such as one iris more contracted than the other, one eyelid drooping more than the other, or whatever differences strike you. Now look at the mirror image of your face and focus somewhere between your eyes so that the asymmetry begins to disappear in your peripheral vision. You can tilt your head, blink your eyes, raise your eyebrows, or whatever

helps you to focus on your image that gives you a sense of symmetry and balance between your two eyes.

Once you have found a comfortable place to focus your gaze on your face in the mirror, keep that focus while reducing your awareness of the point of focus. Now increase your awareness of your two eyes simultaneously. You should be looking at some point between your eyes but seeing your two eyes directly in your increased peripheral vision. Try to hold this for 10 to 20 seconds to get the sense that your focus in "peripheral" and your previous peripheral vision of your two eyes now becomes your main or direct seeing.

A variation on this is to focus on your forehead while increasing your peripheral awareness of your two eyes. Move the point of focus around on your forehead until your two eyes seem symmetrical.

2.   BALANCING WITH YOUR CENTER   Focus your attention so as to be aware of your center. When you feel you have found it, imagine becoming more balanced. Feel the symmetry of your body and adjust your body and perception to balance with that symmetry. Now feel centered. Practice this several times remembering the key words "center," "balance," then "symmetry."

A variation on this is to imagine your body as lines of force as you read this. Note what is symmetrical and what is asymmetrical. Adjust your body to increase symmetry. Note what is the next body relationship that feels asymmetrical. Move again making yourself more symmetrical.

3.   SEEING THE UNCONSCIOUS   Hold your hands about four or five inches in front of your face as if you were holding a pair of binoculars. Look at the skin on your hands for a couple of seconds. Then look through your hands as if you were looking through the binoculars. See whatever is in the distance. Now try to see the space between the distant scene and your hands. Whatever comes to mind, or you imagine seeing in that empty space, has come from your unconscious.

A variation on this is to see what arises in the space among three objects. Focus on an object in your room while noting what object first comes to your peripheral attention and then what comes up next. Fix your gaze somewhere in the middle of these three objects so that you can equally see

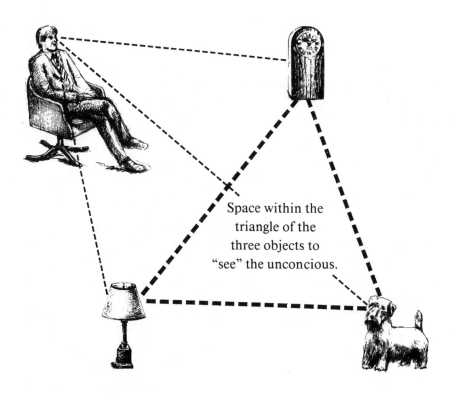

Space within the
triangle of the
three objects to
"see" the unconcious.

them. Now notice what the unconscious mind fills the space with within the triangle of the three objects.

You can get ambitious and use the two-hands version to look at the triangular space and note the space between your hands and the triangle.

4. WALKING IN TIME   If you toss a glowing coal in the night, you can see it leave a "trail of light." Of course there is no trail as such, but the sharp contrast of the night and the light of the coal leaves an effect in the eye for a brief moment, long enough to make you "see" a trail of light in the darkness.

In a similar way, one can imagine holding the image of oneself walking along behind oneself. "Seeing your trail" and seeing your legs moving in the present can give you the sense of time depth perception. Now imagine seeing your foot's movement a split second before it occurs. In this exercise you can get a sense of seeing yourself with a trail of yourself and a head of yourself with your normal self in the center.

5. SENSORY PUSH-UPS   Sit quietly with your eyes closed. Withdraw consciousness from your senses. Become less aware of noise, pressure on your bottom while sitting, and other bodily sensations. Then slowly increase you awareness of bodily sensation, noise, and smell, open your eyes, and intensify your awareness of your environment. Then repeat withdrawing awareness of your senses and refilling your sensory awareness several times. Try to get the sensation in your feelings of doing push-ups similar to the sensation in your muscles when doing physical push-ups.

6. PERIPHERAL SEEING   In Carlos Castaneda's *The Eagle's Gift* an excellent exercise is explained: "He used to make me walk for miles with my eyes held fixed and out of focus at a level just above the horizon so as to emphasize the peripheral view. His method was effective on two counts. It allowed me to stop my internal dialogue after two years of trying, and it trained my attention." You might not want to start by walking miles, but try this walking in your local environment, first for short periods of time.

7. GOOD MORNING   Wake up lying still. Consider each sound, sight, smell, and taste in your mouth. Be aware of your body in the environment. Then lean your head over the edge of your bed and slowly move into a head stand while breathing deeply and evenly for 15 to 30 seconds. Feel the body, inner technology getting ready for the day. Then roll over and begin your day with a smile.

8. WISDOM IN A CHAIR   Look at an empty chair in your room. Then imagine the presence of a very wise person in that chair. Ask a question to that wise one and note what response comes to your mind. The first time I did this exercise, I imagined Socrates and asked how does one do philosophy? This is a question that I had pondered for years. The response that came immediately to mind was: "Be it." That is a response that I had never considered before, which I have found useful ever since.

A variation on this is to sit in one chair pretending to be a mystic talking to a second chair with an imaginary technocrat. What would you, the mystic, say to the technocrat? Then get up from your first chair and sit in the second chair imagining that you are now the technocrat speaking back to the mystic. What will you say to the mystic? Go back and forth and see what consensus is achieved.

9. SOLACE   After my father's death, my mother ran across a line from the Roman Lucullus: "Wouldst cheer thine heart? Then think upon the good qualities of thy friends." So she made a list of her friends, and beside each name she wrote the main quality that endeared them to her— traits like humor, sincerity, dependability, whimsy, talent, youthfulness, kindness, drama, imagination, honesty, common sense, eagerness, etc. Next she imagined these same friends surrounding her in a tight circle, each holding in front of them, like a shield, a placard bearing the one magnetic, descriptive word that she had used to characterize them. "As I read one after another," she wrote to me, "magic happened: I was safe, comforted, infinitely strengthened within that invisible human fortress of protective caring. From that moment, I knew I was not alone. Further, I realized that love I had concentrated for so many years upon just one could now be diffused, spread not only among my friends, but among all those with some kind of need."

10. RELATIONAL MEANINGS OF OBJECTS   Some engineers and physicists who want to make sure their calculations are correct, keep the terms or abbreviations with the numbers while solving equations. For example:

$$1 \text{ ft} \ \times \ 2.5 \text{ ft/sec} \ \times \ 2 \text{ sec/lb} \ = \ 5 \text{ft}^2/\text{lb}$$

If they expected to get an answer in terms of lbs/ft^2, they would know that they made an error. But if they set up the calculation as $1 \times 2.5 \times 2 = 5$, they might not catch the error. In the same way we can keep meanings attached to objects as we or others move them around. For example, an old chair could have the meaning of a stately grandmother, a drawing table the meaning of drafting precision, a book the meaning of perseverance to finish projects, and a knife the meaning of courage. Arranging these objects could help us to remember to be stately in our precision while having the courage to persevere until we complete our projects. If another set of values needs to be remembered, then we might put together another arrangement of different objects. I am told that Zen masters who spend their time arranging their garden die when each object is in relation to all others, yielding a pattern of meaning that is their unique learning from life.

11. BOOMERANG   The boomerang is one of the most unsung tools of consciousness ever invented. If you are feeling angry or depressed this Australian tool can bring you back. Imagine holding a boomerang in your hand, pretending that all the rage or depression you feel pours from you into your boomerang. Then raise you eyes to the sky and fire it from your hand with a whip of your body and a roar like Obi Wan Kanobi of *Star Wars* sending the Sand People away. Watch your boomerang and emotions fly out toward the sun, then turn and fly on its own. Imagine your emotions turned into graceful circles in the sky.

The principle of transference is practiced by everyone to some degree. We flip a coin to transfer decision to the chance turn of a coin. We hire an accountant to transfer our financial anxieties to a professional. We pray to transfer our guilt to God. And you can imagine unloading your personal angers and depressions into your boomerang, then throwing it to the sky. At the moment that it changes direction, imagine the anger or depression being jettisoned. Then see it come back like a clean slate as your hands and boomerang become one again.

12. VISUALIZATION   This is a fairly well-known technique, and has even found its way into executive management training programs. Essentially, one visualizes some condition in the future, imagines each step from the future back to the present, and then acts out the steps like an actor following a script in a play. Another variation is to go from the present out to the future. For example, one might try self-healing by imagining the edge between the healthy area and the damaged area. Then one visualizes the healing area expanding toward or into the damaged area. This is done a number of times each day until the healing process is accelerated.

This can be a dangerous technique for two reasons. First, we can fool ourselves about self-healing and die as a consequence. And second, we can forget that other people exist in the future whose lives count too. Hitler used projections of Eastern Europe on a screen in his planning room at his Eagle's Nest and superimposed projections of his troops invading. He is said to have practiced this visualization technique until he then acted out the invasion.

More Subtle, Sophisticated, or Abstract C-T Exercises

13.   FOUR BALL SEQUENCES   The key graphic for R. Buckminster Fuller's *Synergetics* was

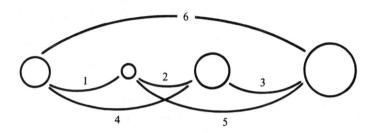

This can be used as a think trick. Imagine yourself as the first ball talking to one of less political power than yourself about some solution to a political problem. This person, symbolized by the smaller second ball, then runs your idea by someone of more political power than you. This person, symbolized by the third ball, in turn runs it by one of greater political power than the rest of those in the diagram. Imagine the relationships using this diagram. What is the first relationship and what would be said? In the same way, imagine what would be said in the other relationships. This may bring forth better thinking for political strategy.

Another variation on the Four Ball Sequences is the use of abstract symbols such as:

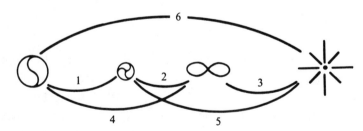

The first relationship would be dualism with the resolution of dualism or some triadic view. The second would be triadic with magic (some use the infinity sign as the magician's logo). The third relationship in this example would be magic and the unknown, consciousness, or divinity. This think trick can help to raise some pretty interesting questions. As these questions arise, so too may your curiosity, intuition, and unconscious processes.

Try the Four Ball Sequences at a party. Walk into the party. Who or what do you notice first? Then in turn, what is that object or person noticing? And so forth carrying out the sequences. This may bring you together with a person at the party that you would have preferred to be with but would not have met had you not used this C-T exercise.

14. SPHERICAL PERCEPTION   Imagine yourself in the center of a sphere with a radius of maybe 5 feet. Then be aware of the outer surface or "skin" of that imaginary sphere. Now return your awareness to your physical center.

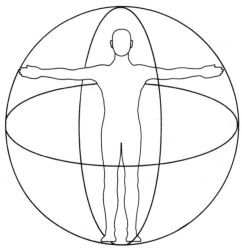

Continue moving your awareness from your center to the outer surface of the sphere and back again. If this seems difficult, begin moving your awareness between your physical center and physical skin.

The main idea is to sense the expansion and contraction of the scope of your awareness. Once you achieve this awareness, then begin to make the radius of the boundary of your perception increase. Be aware of sounds from a distance and then return to the sound of your breathing.

15. DOODLING   Aimless drawing helps many to concentrate and others to understand their thoughts. Since the doodler is not sure how the drawing will end, unconscious thought may finish the sketch. The un-

conscious addition may bring clarity or wholeness or completeness of thought.

Make doodles of your ideas, problems, questions. Play with your pen or pencil "aimlessly," and see what comes to mind. The technology of pen and paper may have done more to alter consciousness than all the other tools of humanity put together.

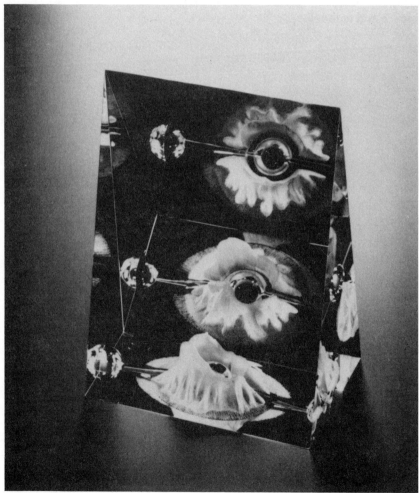

Photo of Stueben Glass's "Mountains of the Inner Eye"

These 15 C-T exercises are offered simply to stimulate you to come up with your own exercises to improve the relationship between your inner technology and your consciousness, as well as your external technology and your consciousness. A result of the improved relationship is to first balance your mystic self with your technocratic self and then to merge them.

Now that many facets of the Conscious Technology view of consciousness have been covered, we will turn to the Conscious Technology view of science and technology.

A Cyborg is a human who is dependent on technology for some vital function. We are miniaturizing that technology and making it part of our bodies. While early work in this field focuses on *maintaining* the human body, future implants will seek to *enhance* it until eventually we have learned to regrow our bodies. Already being developed . . .

- implanted "nerve chips" which are electronic interfaces for individual nerve cells to communicate with a computer;

- TOK, the interactive worldwide computer/audio/video individual communication and retrieval system and its applications;

- voice-actuated microphones and memory chips instead of keyboards;

- "biochips" from organic compounds no bigger than large molecules.

Chapter Six
The 21st-Century Human Body and Technology

Scientists and technocrats give us methods for *how* to get organized. Mystics give us the attitude to take during such organization. This relationship will become increasingly important as consciousness and technology merge.

Once we discovered how to make fire and give our fellow beings compassion, we took on our own evolution quite uniquely on this womb planet.

Will We Become Cyborgs?

Before you knew it, we started wearing eye glasses. Then we put on contact lenses. And now we are surgically implanting all kinds of technological advances to see better. We also throw out old bone in our bodies and replace it with stainless steel. Plastic is becoming a substitute for destroyed skin. Slowly but surely we are adding more technology to our bodies. We are becoming cyborgs.

Although the early technological additions to our body have been for remedial purposes, we will also add technology to enhance our capabilities. We have created temporary cyborgs for working under water and in outer space with artificial skin, lungs, lighting, and robotic attachments. Contact lenses with zoom vision, miniature shotgun hearing aids to hear selected sounds at greater distances, or miniature transceivers to "reach out and touch someone" are just some of the ways future cyborgs will go beyond our inherited biology.

The day will come when the first human being will have over 50 percent of the volume of his or her body composed of technological implants. We need not worry about becoming like a robot if our future civilizations grow up with some of the perceptions of reality and ways of knowing discussed previously.

Cyborg technology is the internalization of technology, and will become a key factor in the merger of consciousness and technology. In the past, humans have externalized a significant portion of technology, while other creatures have internalized theirs. For example, some frogs emit chemical warfare to ward off the enemy lizard. These frogs carry their weapons technology with them in their body, whereas our guns are external. Monarch butterflies have iron in their wings that helps them act as a conscious compass. The lung fish of East Africa can go into quick suspended animation when their ponds dry up, bears hibernate during winter, and we have seen frozen fish dropped in water swim away. So life seems to be able to use its technology to keep alive under varying conditions that we humans only approximate with mystic meditation or the use of external technology.

The whole thrust of cyborg advances is to take the best of our external technology, miniaturize it, and then make it part of our bodies. As we have noted, there's the Jarvik heart, the Utah Arm, artificial kidneys, the Boston elbow, miniature pancreaslike pumps, the Triad hip, heart pacemakers, various microelectronically driven limbs, intraocular eye lenses, the MIT knee, and artificial blood vessels. We even use ceramic retinal tacks to flatten and reattach retinas. Australians have developed an implantable hearing prosthesis that inserts 22 electrodes into the inner ear which is connected to a pocket speech processor that allows the deaf to hear on a multichannel device. Next we will make a microminiaturized computer hearing aid with a thin microphone, which will be voice activated and could be programmed to "hear" certain sounds and not others.

A grid of microcircuits attached to nerve cells will replace rods and cones in eyes of people with certain forms of blindness. These might also be programmed to allow sighted persons to see different slices of the electromagnetic spectrum other than light.

Again, the early work in cybornetics will focus on maintaining the human body; more futuristic work will focus on enhancing the human body. And as we learn more about how to simulate biological growth, we will prefer to regrow our own bodies rather than have bionic implants. As a result, the longer range future of cybornetics will be to make superhuman beings.

As mystics may talk about shared mind space, we will have technology simulate the experience. If you had the ability to plug your brain into the same electronic device as another person at the same time, then the two of you could experience the same awareness at the same time. If the two were aware that they were equally plugged in, then they would begin to experience shared mind space. This would be an example of how technology could become a training wheel for consciousness.

In 1974 I laid out a research scheme showing how we could experience another's cerebral activity in *The Future of Vision,* a television documentary for the American Optometric Association. With enough subjects, one after the other looking at the same visual screen, we could correlate the brain's activity and the seeing of colors and shapes giving us the ability to "decode" the brain. With such a code programmed into a computer, we could let people see what others are seeing by having them connected via electrodes on their scalp to the computer. This could be thought of as a training wheel for mental telepathy. Ten years later this concept was was portrayed in Natalie Wood's last movie called *Brain Storm.*

Robert Prehoda in his book *Your Next Fifty Years* suggests replacing the skull bone with a computer of the same size and shape to assist the brain. More likely would be the insertion of a transceiver to communicate via radio or micro waves with other computers or brains simulating "mind reading."

We have already used fluorochemicals to replace 80 percent of the blood of mice, rats, and dogs with no ill effects. In April 1979 a Japanese man was the first to use artificial blood that accounted for 25 percent of the fluid in his veins. We will make motors one molecule thick of ACTIN (a muscle-contracting protein) and myosin (a muscle molecule) and insert them in our capillary walls to pump medicine in our bodies.

According to Dr. Williams Dobelle of the Institute for Artificial Organs in New York City, "by the turn of the century, every major organ except the brain and central nervous system will have artificial replacements." By 1983 the annual installations of manufactured parts cleared 3 million and by the most recent data in 1985 it had jumped to 3.6 million. So, the trend of cyborganization of humanity has begun and it will continue to build the 21st-century human body.

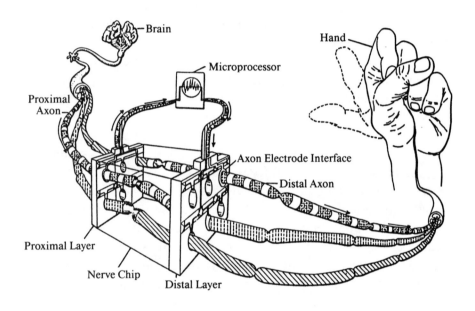

Artist's concept of how the brain, nerve chip, microprocessor, and hand will be connected.
Courtesy of Stanford University

One strategic element of our future conscious technology, called a "nerve chip," is being developed by scientists at the Stanford University Medical Center with support from the Veterans Administration. It is an electronic interface for individual nerve cells to communicate with a computer. This human-machine linkage will be used to program and control artificial hands, regenerate damaged nerves, and enhance human capability in ways not yet imagined.

As with any significant change in life, many humans will call such a cyborg future unnatural. Some will say it is not within biological evolutionary dynamics, and it is not part of God's plan. After all, isn't our future to become like Buddha, Mohammed, and Jesus? Yes, in terms of attitudes toward life, but in terms of what we do and what we physically become? Buddha is portrayed as physically obese, Mohammed was involved in war, and Jesus said that people would go beyond his example in the future. Take, for example, the Christian Bible, John 14:12, which says "Truly, truly, I say to you, he who believes in me will also do the works that I do; and greater works than these will he do . . . "

Is the Dali Lama less spiritual because he wears a wristwatch and a pair of glasses? Are you less of a human being because you lost your hand and now have a mechanical one? Paralyzed people dependent on specialized wheelchairs that have robot arms and voice systems report feeling like test pilots for the next generation by having these devices. Others that are partially paralyzed and use electrodes to simulate their muscles know they are on the cutting edge of human evolution.

Our cyborganization is a straight trend forecast. It should seem as natural to us as the evolution of the spider's ability to spin webs or the beaver's construction of dams.

A more far-reaching possibility (and more strategically important) is the notion that robots one day might wrest control from humans over the course of years of subtle events. The British science fiction writer Arthur C. Clarke has said that humans will create technology that will replace us, as we replaced dinosaurs as the dominant force on earth. Science fiction has portrayed this possibility of humans being deselected in the evolutionary process in favor of the more capable robot civilization. We might avoid the possibility of being dumped in the dustbin of evolution by merging with future technology.

Dinosaurs did not anticipate that mammals would take over the earth and none tried to mate with mammals to keep them in the evolutionary race. But humans, like Clarke, have anticipated that we are making the seeds of our takeover as we microminiaturize computers. This may not happen, but we could make sure that it does not by mating with advancing technology and becoming cyborgs. If it turns out that we can't beat them, than why not join them and evolve together? We could all become like the

Many of us are temporary cyborgs. The Plantronics earphone augments the efficiency of the busy executive.

"Six Million Dollar Man" after the price comes down. After all, computer prices fell at an annual rate of 23 percent during the 1980s.

We humans like to talk about dinosaurs as if they were a great failure. But consider that we have been a species for 3 million years, give or take a million. Now remember that the dinosaurs roamed the earth for 181 million years, give or take several million. So, for us to be as big a failure as we think the dinosaurs were, we will have to hang around for another 178 million years, again give or take some millions.

If you relate the species life of the dinosaur to the life span of an individual human, then by comparison our species is still in the womb. And maybe we are. We could think of the earth as our womb and ourselves as intergalactic life growing on the womb planet until we are ready to be born into the solar system. The solar system could be thought of as our local shelter from which we venture forth to our neighborhood, the Milky Way. We then mature into adolescence visiting new neighborhoods or other galaxies. On February 20, 1980, NASA announced the existence of amino acids—the building blocks of life—in a meteorite found in the Antarctic that had "right-handed" molecules not found on earth. So, we may not be alone.

When we finish trying on roles or experiencing galactic cultures, we will mature with a sense of responsibility to try and prevent the implosion of the universe that creates the big bang all over again. Our consciousness would permeate the entire universe as gravity does today and would act as a kind of conscious glue preventing both the implosion or the endless expansion of the universe for our "cold" entropic death.

These bench marks into the universe constitute quite a long-range task. Consider the astrophysics. We are 8,500 parsecs from the center of our Milky Way galaxy (3.26 light years to a parsec). We are orbiting around that center at 230 kilometers per second. It takes about 225 millions years to make one orbit. There are about 100 billion stars in our galaxy, all moving 50 to 80 kilometers per second away from the "center" of the known universe. The particles of which we are composed have been traveling away from the "center" for about 15 billion years. There are at least another 100 billion galaxies besides our own Milky Way. So stopping the implosion of the universe is a big job, but somebody's got to do it.

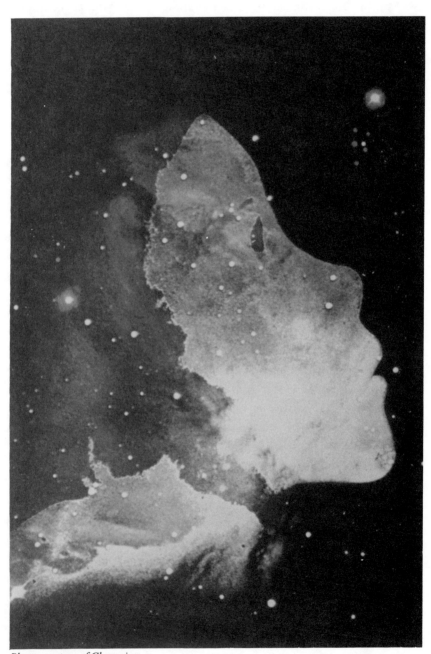

Photo courtesy of Champion.

THE 21ST-CENTURY HUMAN BODY AND TECHNOLOGY

Our Machines Become Conscious

Meanwhile, here in the present, computers are becoming mobile and self-programming robots with perception and controlled responses. (The term "robot" comes from Czech meaning forced labor and was coined in 1921 in the film/play called *R.U.R.*). Increasingly we see robot farms, robot mining, robot manufacturing, robot fishing, robot toys and house aids. As mentioned in Chapter 1, the U.S. Census Bureau has been counting robots as well as people since 1984. Then there were 5,535 complete robots, and by 1995 we expect 250,000 in American industry. There could be well over a million in the United States alone if personal robots are included.

With advancing computer power, microminiaturization, voice synthesis, and voice recognition, we can talk with inanimate objects. What was dumb matter to our parents will become Conscious Technology to our children.

If you add up the imbedded computers in our wristwatches, pencils, and so on, plus the more conventional computers, the total is more than the total of the U.S. human population. All the vital elements of our buildings will be connected to computers and robots making us feel that our shelters are alive.

According to futuristic architect and President of the Home Automation Association Roy Mason, nearly 1,000 American homes by 1988 had an electronic interface between their personal computer and systems such as the burglar alarm, heating, lighting, and air conditioning. There are even more in Europe and Japan. Keith Phillips, Vice President of Smart Homes, a joint venture of utility companies and home manufacturers, estimates they will have completed 4.4 million such intelligent homes by 1997, of which 76,000 will be retrofitted existing homes.

Alan P. Hald in the August 1981 *Futurist* gives us a nice scenario:

> Imagine a house called Fred, who, while performing routine roof maintenance, discovers a leak. Fred first seeks help. Not from you, but from Slim, a ranch-style home down the block. Slim has recently undergone roof repair and can provide Fred with needed advice. Fred then calls you at the office to present his plan of action. You've

learned to trust Fred's judgment, so you approve the repairs. The rest is rather straight forward. Fred calls the roofer and directs her to the leak. After it is repaired to Fred's satisfaction, funds are electronically transferred from your account to the roofer's account. Fred promises to give her a good reference and stores the entire experience in his memory banks for future use, to share with other homes and humans.

If we project the trend of humans becoming more technologylike and project the trend of technology becoming more humanlike, then can we imagine the two trends crossing over and becoming one trend, the trend of Conscious Technology? This seems to be the direction of science and technology today. Robots will get biochips and humans will become cyborgs. Dr. Philip Handler, former President of the National Academy of Science, said of solid state physics "So profound is its impact that one may wonder whether in so doing, man has guided his own evolution—in the sense that a human being combined with a computer represents a new species."

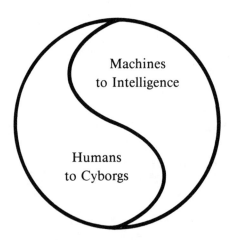

Machines
to Intelligence

Humans
to Cyborgs

From Copernicus to Einstein

Originally, science was a method to test the empirical hypothesis in epistemology. Would we know more, if we relied on our sense impressions of controlled experiments? The answer was yes. The knowledge, technological, population, and wealth explosions all began around the same time—the time of the empirical age.

Today science and its technological spinoffs are destined to give us what would have been thought by our ancestors to be godlike powers. The philosopher Hegel taught that God created humanity, which in turn creates God. Maybe that's what's going on. The purpose of science and technology today is to reinvent life in our own image and our images come from the mystic insight.

Unfortunately, the general public does not live with what is known today. Children are taught "sunrise and sunset" rather than morning and evening "earth turning"; we don't "see" ourselves revolving around the sun 93 million miles away, speeding toward a star called Omicron Hercules at 19 km/second. We don't understand that our bodies are a successful summary of the history of the universe. We don't feel the relative interdependence connectedness of a dynamic body, consciousness, earth, and universe. But help is on the way.

From Einstein to Everyone with the Tree of Knowledge

With the trends of microminiaturization, technological systems integration, portability, communications, and biological sensors, it is not difficult to imagine an attache case that connects you to the world for nearly everything for which you would want to be connected. Let's call this attache case the "Tree of Knowledge" or TOK for short. It would be a world-wide computer/audio/video localized communication and retrieval system via high-powered satellites, such as ACTS (Advanced Communications Technology Satellite), with low-powered, inexpensive, portable ground transceivers adaptable to telephone, radio, and TV. This Tree of Knowledge would be your real passport to the global systems of the future.

The TOK would have the following as standard equipment:

1. Computer
2. Microphone
3. Speaker
4. Video screen
5. Biological sensors
6. Recording disks
7. Modem
8. Satellite transceiver
9. Roll out solar panel/AC/DC plugs
10. Printer
11. Camera
12. Weather-proof case
13. Radio (AM,FM,short wave,ham) and Television

The TOK will move the general public's perception closer to the mystic's view of the universe as being consciously interconnected. Einstein demonstrated that the universe was interdependent through a heroic effort of physics and mathematics. With the Tree of Knowledge, anyone will have more rapid information and communications access than Einstein did. Time between thought, question, and answer will shrink. Curiosity will increase.

If you were in the middle of Africa 500 years ago and heard about a great body of water to the east, your curiosity would be frustrated, because the effort to get there would probably have been too great. Put in Skinnerian terms, this situation would have "negatively reinforced" your curiosity. But the TOK's rapid feedback will positively reinforce your curiosity, allowing you to follow your curiosity through the countless inquiry paths, and with such speed that your unconscious mind will become consciously engaged in your pursuit of wisdom. The TOK is the appropriate technology to enhance curiosity and it was curiosity that was the source of Einstein's great gift.

Imagine setting the TOK on the ground. Roll out the solar panel, fold out the umbrellalike satellite receiver and transmitter, and flip on the switch that runs the solar-generated electricity through TOK's electronics and exposes the video screen with the main menu:

1. AUDIO   [Granted, TOK's menus would be image
2. VIDEO   maps with hypermedia links rather
3. COMPUTER   than hierarchical menus: these are
4. BIOLOGICALS   shown merely to show capacity.]

If you selected 1, your screen might show
   1. Past audio recordings
   2. Connect live
   3. Record
   4. Voice attunement

If you selected 2, your screen might show
   1. Input number
   2. Search by:
          a) Name b) zip code c) association d) dates
   3. List sequence of those trying to reach you
   4. Match priorities and display numbers

If you selected 3, your screen might show
          1:20 am 1/4/98 Sally Gibbs (audio cuts in to give 15-second
                              message)
          9:18 am 1/3/98 John Talbert (audio 15-second message and title)
          4:20 pm 1/3/98 Ho Dzie (audio 15-second message and title)

Let's say that you were looking for the John Talbert call. So you say "Break" to your Tree of Knowledge microphone, and then say "Dial 9:18 am 1/3/98." But the line is either busy or John is not taking calls at this time. Instead of just leaving a 15-second message and title for him, you chose to end the "telephone tag" by leaving a full message. But there is some information that you want to get 100 percent clear, so you respond via the computer print telecommunications option instead of the audio option.

The TOK is a key example of how we can consciously design technology to enlighten our consciousness, which in turn will enhance our technological design. For example it will be very nice for inventors. The day's notes can be recorded and electronically signed for later patent defense if necessary. Scientific research abstracts can be searched to make sure mistakes are not duplicated. Research teams can be organized around specific experiments, regardless of geographic distribution of the team. Advanced market research teams can monitor progress so that inventors receive bids from investors, as was the case with much of the early work in bioengineering. And the same TOK will connect the inventor to data bases for patent search and application. Since the inventor's notes are electronically signed, legally protecting theft, the average person could be allowed access to this information to keep abreast of new developments without the usual worry of theft.

The TOK will also be nice for the student, who could, for example, search for the course in Algebra designed by the three leading mathematicians, several logicians and a learning theory analyst. Since the course could be taken by say 1 billion students, the curriculum team could afford to get the best the world had to offer, take as long as necessary, and produce a classic that might cost less than 1 cent per user.

Based on 1989 statistics that show that international data communications time charges averaged around $0.20 per minute, communications costs would be larger than the cost for the entire Algebra course. Yet it would still be cheap enough for anyone in the world to access it via their nearest school's or library's TOK.

In this scenario, the producers of the Algebra course would make enough net profit that they could turn around and produce the best course on laser mechanics over a several-year period. With this use of the TOK, all students could get access to the very best minds the world has to offer.

You could choose the BIOLOGICALS option on the main menu if you didn't feel well. First, you would respond to questions from the

Man under umbrella-like solar cell sprayed transceiver using TOK at the beach: all alone while participating in a world-wide community

built-in expert computer program. This program would be periodically updated by international data communications into your TOK. If the program needed more information, you might be instructed to open the TOK's storage compartment and use a sterilized blade to get a blood sample and put it in a special slot with sensors for local and then on-line international medical analysis. More sophisticated internationally accessible medical diagnosis programs could then pin down the problem through asking a sequence of questions. If it turns out to be simple, a prescription would be printed out simultaneously on both your TOK and at the several nearest pharmacies or medical stores.

More sophisticated diagnosis would get transferred to a computer-matched doctor who had "on-line duty." You would switch to the AUDIO option on your TOK and then add the VIDEO option to see the problem.

A doctor could run a speech analysis program to determine if or what type of emotional distress you might be experiencing. With your permission, the on-line doctor could access your TOK's memory to help analyze the synergy of other elements such as diet, personality, genetics, and healthy and unhealthy habits. Added tests could be requested of you by the on-line doctor, such as inserting feces, or phlegm, or whatever the doctor requested to be placed into the sensors of your TOK. This would continue until the diagnosis was confirmed and you were on your way to becoming well again.

This procedure has the advantage that doctors could monitor a specialty on a worldwide and daily basis. Patients will get doctors who have an easier time remaining at the state of the diagnostic arts through telemedicine, and doctors in turn will be able to see many more patients a day, perhaps reducing per-"visit" charges. People have been known to give personal information more freely to a computer than to a doctor in person, even though the computer is connected to a person. This should also make for better analysis.

The BIOLOGICALS options could also be used to plot a personal index of the probabilities of what diseases and lead times match your condition. Recommendations could be given such as diet changes and exercises so that you could act in time to prevent the potential illness.

The TOK can also help with time management. You could leave a question for a specific person that would be played prior to the TOK's notifying you of the call. Let's say you know a Mr. Jones will eventually call to find out if you are ready to buy something. When he tries to contact you, he will hear the prerecorded message "Have you completed your cost/benefit analysis of your product compared with Mrs. Smith's?" If he answers no or not yet, then your prerecorded message "Well, please let me know when you have. Until then, take care of yourself. Bye for now" would respond to him and end the communication. If Mr. Jones answered "yes," then you would be notified and your TOK would alert you that Mr. Jones is ready to communicate.

If the conversation was stressful, then when you hung up you could switch on one of the computer programs for biofeedback, stress reduction, or other consciousness-enhancing programs that you have tailored to your preferences to calm down again.

These applications of the Tree of Knowledge give us even more time to expand our mind than advances in the Agricultural Age and Industrial Age did. It is widely believed that philosophy came from the leisurely priestly caste in Egypt. Who knows what could come from a leisurely global caste that grows up in the future?

In the past, oral tradition was passed on by traveling masters. This is still going on today, but most public information is now passed on by television "talents" who may know little of the content and quality of the information they transmit. Television quality control follows public ratings. But because the TOK is an interactive system that enables cross-referencing of information, anyone can handle his or her own quality control.

The telephone allowed us to greatly expand human contact, giving rise to a variety of relationships of varying degrees of intimacy, and increased the complexity of human affairs. The TOK will expand this complexity and intensity of human interactive experience. It also fits Schumacher's three criteria for methods and equipment: it is cheap enough that it is accessible to virtually everyone, suitable for small-scale applications, and compatible with our need for creativity.

One of the strongest technological trends is the integration of many technologies into a single tool, like the TOK. When Isaac Newton was 42 he merged earthly physics and celestial physics with the theory of gravity. René Descartes merged algebra and geometry with coordinate graphing. And the TOK will merge a vast array of storage and communications capabilities.

Quality and honesty should be increased because you will be electronically with the people at the time that those people are in your mind.

We can already see the elements of the TOK in operation: (1) telemedicine; (2) integrated financial services (credit cards that can handle transactions among brokers, banks, and supply companies); and (3) international television, telephone, and computer conferencing.

Eventually, the TOK will be further miniaturized to be sewn into clothing or added to jewelry. In a more distant future it may even become an implant in your body, so that we would be a conscious technology Tree of Life. What the printing press was to the written word and memory the TOK will be to the spoken word and action.

Although the TOK is a significant technology in our future, it is only one of many emerging tools that will influence our consciousness. As you look over the following list of technologies that we are likely to experience over the next several decades, reflect on how each might change your view of reality and how the combination of these technologies will further grow our human consciousness.

Future Technologies That Will Grow Your Consciousness

1. Typewriters and computer keyboards will be replaced by microphones and memory chips that can accept dictation. As a result, you could give dictation, drop your disk or cassette into a computer, and go off to do something else while the computer carries out your instructions.

IBM is currently working with an experimental personal computer that can understand 20,000 words. Depending on how sophisticated their PC marketing requirements become, it may be commercially available in the early 1990s. Recognition of continuous speech without pauses and the ability to recognize different accents without adjusting the program are tough problems to solve.

Since the public domain is several years behind the military, we can assume that a good deal more than 20,000 words can be understood by military computers. Japan expects to have a commercially available "talkwriter," a computer that has a 10,000-word recognition, by 1991. Hence, it is not too far off that these talkwriters will replace the keyboard in the same way that the hand calculator replaced the slide rule.

Speech recognition of your voiceprint is more precise than fingerprints or signatures for personal identification. Your voice will be your computer sign-on code, password in security checks, and authorization for electronic funds transfer.

2. Maps stored in computers will be built into cars so that you can tell your computer where you are or where you want to go, and it will tell you where you are or where you have to go. These dashboard map displays could be telecommuted to remote computers that display demographic information, people of similar interests, or other functions of interest along your way.

3.   Video conferencing with 56K digital service is already available through public telephones for your camera, computer, and home use via modem. Coupled to video disks that can store images of 100,000 of the world's greatest art treasures, people could interactively produce new art forms integrating computer graphics, film, photos, slides, sound, and live video.

Along with data packet switching that allows worldwide print communication at pennies per minute, Koji Kobayashi, head of NEC, expects to offer in the year 2000 voice packet switching with automatic translation. You will speak English to a friend in Japan, and he will hear it in Japanese. He will respond in Japanese, and you will hear his words on your telephone in English.

Integrated Services Digital Network (ISDN) will offer voice, data, and video via fiber optic telephone lines making your personal computer a multimedia machine for two-way communications. An individual fiber optic wire is 3/1000 inch thick and covered in plastic making it as thick as horse hair. These fibers are bundled together making a telephone line about as thick as a human finger and can transmit 200 books a second or carry 240,000 conversations at the same time. Normal communications around the beginning of the 21st century will make nearly everything in all media available to anyone. We will even see holographic broadcast television via digital transmission by then.

4.   Airplane weapons have already been aimed by pilots' eye movements. Next we may use brain waves and the plane's radar for throttle and wing control. These technologies will spin out to applications for spacekind's industrialization in earth orbit, not to mention replacing the steering wheel on terrestrial cars.

5.   Biochips or computer chips that will be formed from organic compounds no bigger than large molecules will permit direct, surgical, brain-to-computer links.

6.   Recombinant DNA or gene splicing of bacteria has so far induced the growth of human insulin, Interferon to kill cancer cells, and growth hormones (for bigger fish, cattle, etc., so that we can get more milk, eggs, and meat per animal). Gene splicing has also made possible a biodegrad-

able plastic called "Biopol" that can be inserted into damaged bone; the needed bone tissue then grows in where the biodegradable plastic is absorbed by the body, eliminating the need to reopen the patient to take out the implanted plastic.

Areas for future impact include energy (alcohol produced by enzymes rather than fermentation), industrial chemistry, agriculture (salt and frost resistant crops, as well as animal-plant hybrids for better nutrition), forest products, mining, public health, medicine, even genetically engineered drain cleaner to digest hair that clogs your pipes.

As of 1989 the U.S. Patent Office has approved over 4,000 biotechnology patents.

7.   Techniques for physical excellence used by Olympics athletes will be available to the general public. You will be able to use computer simulations of bone/muscle combinations to find the optimal sports for you to enter as well as the optimal movements for you within those sports.

Nan Davis was paralyzed from the ribs down, but walked again in 1982 with computer-sequenced electrical stimulation of her legs simulating the normal walking sequence. The same technology will make it possible to electrically stimulate your muscles from computer programs simulating top athletes' movements. Such systems can be packaged in expert computer programs available to the general public through the Tree of Knowledge.

8.   Machines will reproduce themselves in space. Gerald O'Neill, physicist at Princeton University, has calculated that if we put 100 tons of equipment on the moon and another 100 tons of equipment at L-5 (a point that forms an equilateral triangle with the earth and the moon), this equipment could replicate most of itself from lunar materials and thus create the foundation for future space industrial civilization.

One big-ticket item for this industrial capability in orbit will be giant solar satellites that receive solar energy 24 hours a day with no atmospheric interference and beam down energy via radio waves to all points on the earth. O'Neill estimates that $8 billion over 5 years would produce the orbital capacity to manufacture one solar power satellite per year. Each solar satellite could be sold for $10 billion and produce the equivalent of 10 nuclear power plants on earth. Giant orbital food farms will also be

In the future, a new science called gene splicing could produce miracles—like the regeneration of limbs, a cure for cancer, even the flowering of a "better" human being. But who is going to decide what makes a "better" human being?

constructed to feed the new spacekind as well as serve as a back-up for earthkind's supply. We will come to realize that industrialization is better suited to space, leaving the earth as a Garden of Eden.

9.   "Biological awareness rooms" will have four walls, and ceiling and floor that are all video screens. There will be no normal visual references in the room. The screens will display your biofeedback in exciting color and sound combinations that will become an art form and an aid to meditation. Your body and the room would be connected to a computer programmed to display biofeedback. These rooms will allow you to "see" and "hear" your heartbeat, EEG, EKG, breathing, blood pressure, and temperature. Along with improving the balance between mind and body, it is likely to be used to intensify sexual experiences was well.

10.   As our bodies break down, we will replace the effected parts with spares from a variety of sources. Along with the bionics already mentioned, we will be able to clone our own cells to grow our own organs. If we decide to improve on our DNA inheritance, then we could clone specially engineered DNA to produce custom-made "designer body parts." A more macabre option will be to keep cadavers functioning and harvest their parts as needed or to grow "neomorts" as a biological parts factory.

11.   The Nobel Prize for the invention of the laser was shared by Charles Townes of America along with Nickolai Basov and Alexander Prokhorov of the U.S.S.R. based on a 1905 paper on coherent light by Albert Einstein. Lasers will alter our awareness of precision. They can already see the recoil of an atom when it emits a photon. The size of an atom relative to a golf ball is about the same as the golf ball to the whole earth. Laser cameras can take a picture in less than 1 millionth of a second. With IBM's Light Compressor 12 quadrillion exposures are possible in one second. Laser pulses can now send a datum in 1 ten trillionth of a second. A NASA invention allows lasers to be pulsed 10 billion to 200 billion times a second, which gives the same number of cooling times a second to cut things like human tissue with little heating.

Our sense of precision is also being altered by the breakthroughs in subatomic physics. Consider this quote by Steven Weinberg of Harvard University in *Scientific American*: "When a charged particle moves through a transparent medium faster than the speed of light in that medium, it emits a cone of blue light called Cerenkov radiation. The radiation is an optical boom analogous to the sonic boom generated by an airplane moving through the air faster than the speed of sound in air." Just as increased awareness of outer space expands our consciousness, so too increased awareness of inner space sharpens the precision of our consciousness. It is exciting to realize that we are evolving a consciousness that can expand while simultaneously becoming more precise.

12.   We will pay more attention to our sense of smell than we have in the past. Traditionally we have limited ourselves largely to perfumes and after-shave lotions. In the future we could put scents in air conditioning systems and motors or fans in our computers. Smell could be added to old forms of media. For example, fragrances will be emitted by a record's groove as it is scratched by a needle to enhance our experience of the recorded event.

13.   Holographic technology was invented in 1947 by Dennis Gabor. In the future, this technology will improve robotic memory and vision so that it will miss nothing, make it possible to send a hologram of an ancient relic for distant examination, create conferences among humans geographically dispersed giving each a sense that they are all meeting in their own location, store images in crystals for later recall, replace glass lenses, continue to improve encryption, give us the ability to measure changes of force on an object as slight as that which shows as little as one-half wave length difference between the original hologram and the one after applied force, and will give interior design a completely new feeling of light and depth not achieved today with solid hues.

14.   We will improve our auditory environment with "noise neutralization devices" that "hear" sounds and then transmit sound of equal amplitude but opposite intensity. You could program it to neutralize just the specific sounds you want to avoid like airplanes and fire sirens. The principle has been proven by the Technology Integrations and Development Group in Billerica, Massachusetts, by placing countersound transmitters on a diesel truck.

15.   Hibernation is a state between death and sleep that can be chemically induced, according to Peter Oeltgen of the Veterans Administration Hospital and the University of Kentucky. He is isolating the amino acid that induces hibernation. He and his colleagues took plasma from hibernating animals and injected other animals who normally do not hibernate. Result? Hibernation.

It seems that humans could indeed become Rip Van Winkles. This ability will extend life, help insomniacs, reduce weight by sleeping it off, improve surgery, help the storage of organs for transplants, improve recovery from illness (hibernate for a week or so to get over the illness), and serve as an aid to space travel. On a more grim note, we might hibernate to avoid the secondary effects of a nuclear disaster, since there seems to be less damage from radiation during hibernation.

16.   Total gene screening may be here before the year 2000. This could be the greatest single innovation in disease prevention since the vaccination. Prevention of 4,000 known inherited diseases could be accomplished from isolating the problem gene and performing "gene therapy" by inserting a healthy gene for the diseased one.

17.   Cancer cures are on the horizon. Monoclonal antibodies, Interferon, and Interleukin-2 and 3 presage the end of cancer.

18.   Robots will become cheap enough for us to have robot police and armies as well as toys and maids. Robots are already making robots in the Fanuc factory in Japan, driving down the price per unit. Anything that is repetitive can and will be broken down into sequential steps, digitalized, programmed, and automated.

An important addition to conventional computer programming to make robots more effective will be artificial neural systems or neural networks. This use of a computer is patterned more closely to cerebral functioning. Instead of relying on data stored in specific locations and the execution of programs, neural networks in computers have processing elements that receive weighted input signals and can distinguish the various angles of reception of these signals. This allows each processing element to respond uniquely and the status of the entire neural network to be different after each response. Information is distributed over the whole, rather than in specific locations.

Neural networks working in partnership with conventional computer programs will allow robots to more easily recognize and learn patterns of speech, vision, and other forms of generalizations about patterns that the very precision of programming makes difficult.

19.   Nearly 40 percent of all engineering research in the 1980s was in materials science. New materials are being developed, such as metal that dissolves in water, alloys of metal and plastic, and materials that seem invisible (clear like glass but will not reflect light from the surface like glass). Other new materials will include those that form with light, such as methyl methacrylate. When this plastic powder is sprayed in an area that has lasers shot through, it will form small plastic filaments to make a three-dimensional object. The object will dissolve by altering the light wave pattern and form a new shape.

Improved materials will be forged by containerless melting, called "acoustic levitation," which is created by 160-decibel sound waves. The waves suspend materials in furnaces for cleaner melting to produce improved fiber optics and lenses. Engines will be made from one ceramic mold or glass that cools at 1 million degrees Fahrenheit per second. We will see ceramics that are harder than diamonds and stronger than steel.

Water-jet saws can cut 6-inch stainless steel and optical glass with no heat to affect their properties.

20.   Artificial gills for scuba divers and submarines have been tested. Sea water was forced through artificial gills made from a foamlike polymer and hemoglobin. The hemoglobin takes out the oxygen and electricity releases the oxygen from the hemoglobin to be breathed by the diver or people in the submarine. This technology could be used in the construction of undersea walls for marine cities.

21.   As we transfer genetic traits between species, we will begin to blur the distinction between species and develop new views of life. Pigs fitted with human growth hormone genes grow faster; humans fitted with other species' genes will avoid disease; and we may create new capabilities for ourselves only dreamed of in the pages of science fiction.

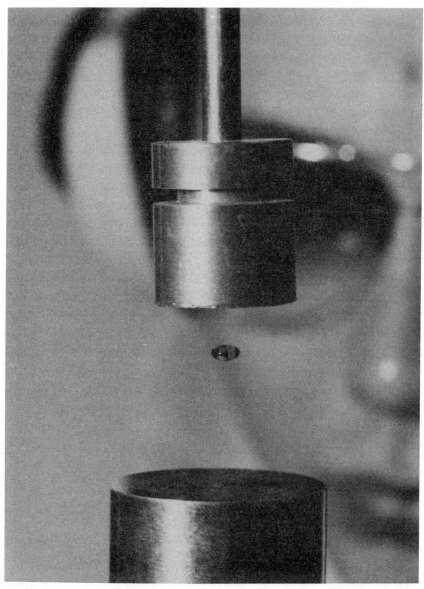

The above droplet of water is levitated in air by sound waves. Such magnetic levitation can be used to contain molten materials in low gravity furnaces in space.
Courtesy of NASA.

22.   Fibrin sealant or "organic glue" will replace stitches. It uses fi-brinogen; hence, it acts like clotting of normal cuts but sets faster and the result is tougher than the natural clot. Fibrin has no red blood cells and gets absorbed by the body.

23.   As gene splicing gets simpler, less costly, and fun, a new genera-tion of "gene hackers" may popularize inventing life forms. The first "manufactured DNA" was duplicated in 1967 and by the summer of 1983 Harvard had created the first artificial chromosome.

24.   Oil spills will be burned off by lasers shot from helicopters or eaten away by bacteria sprayed on their surface. Laser beams shot from satellites and from the earth will focus on areas where the ozone has been depleted to patch the "hole."

25.   Current computer systems that work linearly with yes/no gates for memory will give way to holographic memory through "neural net-works," which are closer to our brain's functioning. In the meantime, we expect microprocessors will compress 10 million transistors onto a single chip in the old yes/no mode by 1990. We already have the HSP-2 super-computer at NASA that can handle 1 billion computations per second.

Just as the silicon chip is giving away to the much faster gallium arsenide chip, so too will it give way to the diamond chip. Vladimir Deryagin of Moscow has already demonstrated that microwaves can ex-cite a mixture of methane and hydrogen to deposit a thin film of diamonds suitable for computer chip technology. Future "optical" computers will have laser-driven transistors that will be 200 times faster than those of the mid-1980s. Erasable optical disks will use heat from lasers to change mag-netic orientation, which in turn changes how light is reflected. Such re-movable 3 1/2 inch disks will hold 160 megabytes of information for both print and video.

26.   One way we will clean up our air is through the use of hydrogen fuel, which produces no carbon monoxide, carbon dioxide, hydrocarbons, or particulate emissions. Hydrogen could be produced in offshore fusion power plants by breaking down water molecules directly into hydrogen and oxygen, bypassing the intermediate stages of electricity generation and electrolysis.

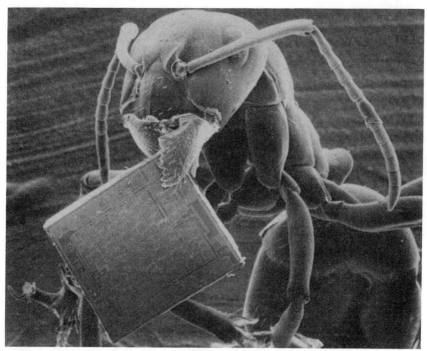

Electronic microscopic photo by Philips of mite holding computer chip

27.   A combination of fiber optics, cameras, and lasers invented by Garrette Lee at the University of California at Davis allows him to poke a fiber optic hair down a clogged artery, see what needs to be removed, and burn it out with blasts from a laser shot down another fiber. This could prevent death from arteriosclerosis, the number one killer in America (causing heart attacks, strokes, and gangrene). IBM has developed a pulsing ultraviolet laser that allows an eye surgeon to precisely etch the surface of a patient's cornea in less than a minute to restore perfect vision. This could give us a total population of perfect vision, replacing the entire eyeglass and contact lens industry.

28.   Artificial intelligence (AI) or "expert programs" can be thought of as computer programs that mimic human responsiveness to questions in a dialogue mode and that replace the need to visit the expert in person. By 1989 there were 10,000 AI programs with as many as 100,000 copies.

By the 500th anniversary of Christopher Columbus's discovery of the "New World," Japan's Fifth Generation Project expects to have a new world of computers that can put all the expert knowledge into a personal computer with the capability of the top military supercomputers of the mid-1980s. Now Japan is beginning to talk about a Sixth Generation Project that sounds very much like Conscious Technology.

29. Dialogue, Chemical Abstracts, The Institute for Scientific Information in Philadelphia and other such scientific data banks can do literature searches so fast that it will speed scientific inquiry as a whole. These would be just some of the data banks available via your TOK.

Most newsletters, newspapers, magazines, books, and miscellaneous reports are in a word processor at some point and could be sent via data telephone lines to such places as the Library of Congress. The Library of Congress could send it all up to a satellite, which could send it to other satellites, which could send them to the entire world simultaneously.

Any individual could go to his or her library computer terminal or TOK, type in a string of key words, and return the next day to read a list of possible document titles and briefs that matched all the key words. After picking the one or two abstracts that seem right, the person would type in the corresponding numbers and go home. Returning the next day, he or she could pick up a printed copy of the full text of the documents, pay the local library for the document, which in turn would pay a percentage to the Library of Congress. The Library of Congress in turn would pay a percentage to the original publishers or authors.

This is fine for documents in the works, but what about the vast number already in the Library of Congress? Kurzweil Computer Products, a Xerox company, has produced a set of machines that can Xerox a page directly into digital form regardless of old-style type. As a result, the old texts can be easily added to our Library of Congress data bank for continuous worldwide access. Some scanners can even take the Cyrillic alphabet and put it in digital form for subsequent computer translation from Russian to English.

If the Ku band was used on the Tracking and Data Relay Satellite System (TDRSS) at its transmission rate of 85 million bits per second, then all of the volumes of the Library of Congress could be rained down on the entire earth six times per day.

30. Human eggs will be frozen, fertilized later, and brought to term in artificial wombs for those beyond childbearing age.

31. You may fly in a future airplane that uses jet engines to take off down a runway and then switches to rocket engines to put you into orbit. Laser airplanes could be "fueled" by a laser beam from a solar satellite that hits and tracks the plane's heat exchanger, heating the inflowing air to over 1,000 degrees Kelvin, which expands out the jet's engines. If you do experience some life extension, then you may fly to outer space in such propulsion systems as ion drive with afterburner, laser-pulsed fusion drive, Orion Project nuclear explosion "putt-putt," anti-matter-annihilation drive, magnetic linear induction or mass driver, focused sunbeam explosion of reaction mass, solar sail, or using heavenly bodies as a propulsion system by whipping around mass or black holes for acceleration.

32. Micro-space will be as much a frontier as outer space. Nano technologies and micro-manufacturing have become so precise as to allow manipulation of materials on sheets of gallium arsenide crystals that are only one atom thick. A single atom can now be implanted at a specific point within a crystal and the whole process can be monitored atom by atom with a scanning transmission electronic microscope. This makes it possible to put vast amounts of information on a single computer chip the size of a pencil point and place it in everything from the human nervous system to irrigation systems.

33. Computer structural analysis of proposed synthetic chemical compounds, or genetic engineering, will become a standard method to cut experimental lab time and forecast results with less actual chemical or biological experimentation. Lab animals will be happy to hear about this!

34. We will learn how to increase everyone's intelligence. Currently we know that IQ can be enhanced by diet, exercise, pills, diverse stimulation at an early age with consistency of love, and holding the breath to increase carbon dioxide in the blood, which in turn increases the capillary complexity in the brain and has a high correlation with an enhanced IQ.

More futuristic methods will develop such as that of Dr. Ross Adey of the VA Hospital of Los Angeles, who has demonstrated that primate learning can be increased by specific doses of radio energy directed at the brain.

35.   Food will be condensed into paper-thin sheets and rolled tightly for economic storage. Instead of freezing food, we will hit it with a dose of gamma rays from Cobalt 60 or Cesium 137, killing the micro-organisms that cause spoilage. This process will cost only a few cents per pound and its effect will be to produce more available food, given that nearly one-third of the world's food is lost to spoilage by pests or micro-organisms. This radiation process reduces food poisoning, eliminates the need for nitrates in food preservation, and will make for long shelf life suitable for storage for disasters. It is quite an advance since the days when food was canned for Napoleon's troops.

36.   Architecture will draw more from the structural properties of living organisms. Today we build only with the skeletal assumptions, rather than integrating tendons, ligaments, and muscles. The suspension bridge is an early indicator of the assumption of both bone and tendon. We will free our current design limitations with these new assumptions constructing magnificently sculpted structures that take forms unimagined today.

37.   The "Frozen Zoo" of gene banks has been set up at the San Diego Zoo for rare or endangered species so that they could be mass produced later. We may get enough undamaged DNA from frozen ancient remains to clone. If so, we may one day visit zoos with wooly mammoths, saber-toothed tigers, and a few dinosaurs.

38.   Superconductivity will make electric transmission far more economical and allow for new possibilities in all areas of life. A superconductor is a substance capable of allowing electrical current to pass through it without resistance. Two IBM scientists, Alex Mueller and Georg Bednorz, discovered that a class of ceramic insulators becomes superconducting at warmer temperatures than ever achieved before. Instead of having to achieve ultracold temperatures working with liquid helium, we can now use less expensive liquid nitrogen, which can be stored in simple vacuum jars. IBM says that these new ceramics "may do for science in the 1990s

what the transistor did for the 1960s." For example, superconductivity could make it commercially possible to have magnetically levitated and high-speed railroads traveling 300 to 500 miles per hour. Vastly reducing energy inefficiencies in transmission will mean that far less use of fossil fuels will be required to provide for electricity consumption. This reduces the CO_2 going into the atmosphere, which in turn reduces the build up of the greenhouse effect heating the earth.

And on it goes . . .

The future of science and technology is driven by ideas. How we manage ideas determines the rate and quality of scientific discovery. In the future an ideonomic data bank where ideas are systematically organized into a science will make management easier. Whatever new integrations of thought may occur, the linking of future ideonomic data bases to international computer networks will dramatically speed the generation and analysis of new ideas—like . . .

- resetting the DNA clock, and new substances and methods to slow aging;
- the fifth force to counter the eventual decay of the universe;
- space migration, when science will have to reinvent life so that it is able to leave the solar system and survive.

The day will come when we'll use chemistry, forms of self-hypnosis, and electrical impulses to design our mental behavior. The Conscious Technology approach will encourage us to take advantage of the intensity of life while managing its greater complexity.

Chapter Seven

Futuristic Views of Science and Technology

The future of science and technology is driven by ideas. How we manage ideas determines the rate and quality of scientific discovery and technological applications. The systematic organization of ideas into a science with laws of ideas called "Ideonomy" is currently being developed by Patrick Gunkel under the sponsorship of the Lounsbery Foundation. Gunkel defines the basic and unending task of the Ideonomist as

> The progressive discovery of all of nature's fundamental, universal, and orthogonal combinatorial dimensions; the identification of all of the continuous bases and discrete elements of these dimensions; and the formulation of these elements, bases, and dimensions in ways allowing the exploration, generation, and use of all possible ideas with respect to any subject, problem, phenomenon, thing, or possibility.

Gunkel recognizes 320 main ideas or concepts, giving Ideonomy 320 divisions so far. A list of examples is generated for each concept or division. Then a list of types is generated for each example. And finally lists of genera and species are listed for each type. After five years of research, Gunkel has developed an enormous set of lists. Once these lists are completed and computerized, anyone can use this idea data bank to cross-reference such lists through new kinds of formulas and weightings to generate new lists of potential ideas. Such an ideonomic data bank will eventually be available via the TOK.

John B. Calhoun, recently retired from the U.S. National Institute of Mental Health, has studied rat survival relative to various assumptions since 1946 and comes to a different approach to the same issue of how to structure what he calls a "brain protheses." He predicts that "computer-like devices and interlinked systems of them will simulate biological brain function to manipulate more effectively thought products of the human brain and process them for return use in human reflection."

Rather than developing lists of words and descriptive phrases as Gunkel does, Calhoun grouped 7,500 highly condensed paragraphs from a variety of experts into 33 areas representing pillar concepts for survival in a set of geometric relationships. This set of relationships forms a model explained in Calhoun's book, *Environment and Population: Problems of Adaptation.* The intention of this model is to stimulate judicial choices as to next steps in research or thought.

Many other approaches are being developed to create idea machines that can produce intelligence and wisdom in partnership with humanity. Major breakthroughs seem inevitable that will accelerate scientific inquiry and the intelligence of society in general.

What kinds of new scientific speculation might occur with the aid of these new kinds of thesauri or dictionaries of concepts with a universal taxonomy of ideas? Will we decide that the purpose of science and technology is to reinvent life suitable for space migration? Or interpret the tenets of relativity and apply them to psychology for the "Einsteinization of consciousness?" Or conclude that life is simply an electromagnetic wave in a medium of protein semiconductors? Or that time is the reaction mass for the motions of matter and energy? Whatever new integrations of thought may occur, the linking of future ideonomic data bases to international computer networks will dramatically speed the generation and analysis of new ideas. The rest of this chapter discusses such speculation.

Forging a New Partnership with our DNA   One of the basic issues in the pursuit of reinventing life is the unravelling of the mysteries of DNA. DNA makes us and increasingly we will remake DNA. In a similar fashion, we make computers and robots that are remaking us. One could speculate that DNA creates humans to keep DNA going indefinitely. Humans may create computers and robots to keep humans going indefinitely. Computers and robots in turn might create mass and energy systems to keep computers and robots going indefinitely. Mass and energy systems seem to have given rise to DNA. Now, if it turns out that we humans *do* go off into the galaxies, and maybe breed with extraterrestrials, and figure out how to rig the universe so that the implosion never occurs for the next round of the big bang, then we will have completed the cycle, that is, mass and energy systems going on indefinitely.

Another speculation also relating to DNA is Dr. Timothy Leary's view of history as the conversation between the central nervous system (CNS) and DNA. During correspondence about this book he wrote that he believes that when people are speaking about mystical experience, they really mean neurological or experience within the CNS. And when people are talking about technology, they really mean DNA. DNA builds structures. The central nervous system is one of the structures that DNA built. He prefers to view all external technology as DNA produced, since it originates as extensions of some anatomical or neurological process. Once the mystically inclined or CNS-inclined people realize that technology is organic, in that it is DNA designed, they can get over their fear of technology. Leary points out that the spinal column was hardware technology to the amoeba. "Amoeba Naderites 100 million years ago were shouting BAN THE BONE!"

A playful and potentially serious speculation about DNA is hearing what it has to say. For example, Dr. Susumu Ohno at City of Hope Medical Center in Duarte, California, gave a lower musical note to the heavier molecules in DNA and a higher note to the lighter molecules that make up DNA. He was then able to write music based on the sequence of the four molecules (adenine, thymine, guanine, and cytosine) that make up every DNA on earth. The sequence of these four will be different for a cancer gene than for an enzyme that breaks down sugar.

Dr. Ohno found that the music created by translating these DNA codes corresponded to what these chemicals of life created in reality. The cancer-causing gene sounded chaotic and deathlike, whereas an enzyme that breaks down lactose sounded sweet. Why? Is there some new principle to be discovered and new technological application?

"If you want to study, for example, which genes are for certain anti-bodies, you can look at the sequences and put them into a computer and compare. That's boring," says Dr. Ohno. "But what I am hoping, instead, is that one can put them into music and by listening you can figure out what the gene is for." Could we all learn what the DNA music would be that increases our intelligence? And play that in public places? That would be a fine example of Conscious Technology.

Life Extension   Another major topic that will gather many people's attention as the baby boomers age is gerontology, longevity, and aging theory. It is reasonable to expect that as baby boomers move into the market to buy anti-aging medicines, medical research in this area will get great infusions of investment capital.

The big gains in life expectancy statistics between 1900 and 1950 in the United States were caused by more babies surviving the early years, not with people aging later. So the big gains to be made by the new technologies mentioned in the preceding chapter have not yet had their impact.

Average life expectancy of all Americans according to *Vital Statistics of the United States, 1985* of the U.S. Department of Human Services were:

1900	47.3	1982	74.5
1920	54.1	1983	74.6
1940	62.9	1984	74.7
1960	69.7	1985	74.7
1980	73.7	1986	74.8
1981	74.2	1987	74.9 (est.)

There are several theories about how we age. The Zhores Medvedev Theory asserts that the increasing errors in your DNA's ability to correctly roll out RNA is the culprit. The enzymes don't get the proper programming to reproduce cells, tissues, organs, and systems correctly so they slowly fall apart. Another theory by Medvedev is that we have gene redundancy in our DNA, which normally fills in for damaged genes. These extra genes get used up as we age and hence we are no longer able to keep all of our systems in full operation. A third explanation is that age is programmed into DNA. Imagine a built-in clock in our DNA that rolls out

RNA instructions to make us just a little older as we go along. We may discover a "death hormone" in the pituitary gland and neutralize its effects chemically.

In this theory, DNA is running the show and only sees organisms as testing grounds for what works and then merges with another DNA in another organism that finds another set of things that work. In this way the new offspring DNA is the living continuity of past DNA only with the better surviving skills. Death and aging of organisms may have been necessary to keep the improvement of DNA going. Thus, there is genetic pressure for us to get to reproduction and childrearing to keep DNA going, using humans as "throughput." If this built-in clock theory is correct, then we might find out how to reset the clock. If the first two theories are correct, then we might find out how to repair damaged DNA and maintain the back-up DNA.

Currently, we will be extending life via improved standards of living, medicines like Interferon, vitamins and minerals, exercises, diet, transplants, bionics, regeneration, cloning, cryobiology, hibernation, and various forms of genetic engineering. A new group of substances for slowing the aging process in warm-blooded animals by 20 to 100 percent are called geroprotectors. The Soviet publication Sputnik claims that "The drop in temperature of man's body by a mere 2.5 degrees could add 50 percent to his life span" and that enterosoption "purifies the blood of old animals [which] slows the rate of age-related changes." Maybe we will learn how to alter our hypothalamus, which controls our body temperature, and reset our biological thermostat a few degrees cooler.

American research has long demonstrated that limiting the diet in lab animals extended life by 50 to 150 percent and that there is a high correlation between getting up early in the morning and living longer. Antioxidants and microenzymes help keep our molecular structure together. We may develop quick-freeze clothing that automatically lowers our body temperature in case of an accident. We will also select the best techniques of living from among all the world's cultures and integrate them into a new culture for improved living, such as T'ai Chi exercises, which the Chinese claim prolong life. All this makes us more sensitive to our systems and helps us learn what to avoid that is degenerative to our lives.

Artist's concept by Champion of future old age couple.

FUTURISTIC VIEWS OF SCIENCE AND TECHNOLOGY

We may grow specific body tissue drawn from our own DNA to replace our worn-out parts. In the meantime, we might keep parts from dead people, or grow "neomorts," or freeze organs for later implantation. New stimulation techniques indicate that we may be able to regenerate whole organs and limbs. Dr. Stephen Smith of the University of Kentucky Medical School applied electric current to regenerate frog legs. Red blood cells return to a primitive state called blastema to reform into what is required for regeneration.

Since the immune system is a key to general health and we are learning how to extend its function, it is reasonable to think that this alone will be a major factor in increasing our life span. The rapid growth of international AIDS research into the immune system should lead to breakthroughs here.

Another addition to public places might be a biotuner in doorways. Currently, we are able to distinguish healthy from diseased tissue by the difference in heat or infrared radiation. Eventually, we may be able to do the same with other portions of electromagnetic radiation in the radio, microwave, or ultaviolet frequencies. Infrared might be the best for one kind of tissue; radio frequencies might be the best to diagnose another kind of tissue. If so, then we could chart all the locations in the body, assign the healthy range and type of electromagnetic radiation for each location, and store these norms in a computer. Then imagine a diagnostic machine that can read your body's emissions from top to bottom recording each part's radiation.

Next the computer could match what is healthy and what is not. It could determine how much of what energy should "tune" the part to move it closer to a more healthy condition. A little zap at the heart or a little buzz in the lower lungs might be the sufficient preventative maintenance to keep you in a more healthy state. Imagine such a system modularized into a solid-state device and put into the doorways of public places and in walk-through metal detectors in airports. Such biotuning devices could also buy time for emergency care in case of a serious accident.

Plant physiologist Rupert Sheldrake speculates in *A New Science of Life* that since each plant has its own "morphogenetic field," a change in one field affects the general field of another of that type. A plant acts in part because of the interplay of others' fields. If this is so for plants, then why not for us? If it is, then as more people increase their life span, they may have an effect on all human life spans.

Some will argue that the slow loss of brain cells could constitute the limit to longevity, but this can be addressed by neuron transplants specifically grown for this purpose, not to mention such mechanical solutions such as our future merger with computer technology. The more one examines the future possibilities of life extension, the more it becomes clear that one day we will control our life span and die by choice.

There are a variety of research streams and improved cultural norms that make it seem that our life expectancy may go up 10 or more years within the foreseeable future. During those added 10 or more years, medical research will continue and new advances may occur that will give us another 20 years. During those next 20 years, research will continue and more startling advances could occur to give . . . well, who knows, but this is the first time that we can actually talk with some reason about the potential of indefinite life expectation.

Subatomic Physics and New Views of Reality

The big excitement in subatomic physics is over the idea that we may discover how the four known forces of the universe could be related into a united theory. These four forces are gravity, electromagnetism, weak forces (those involved in radioactive decay), and strong forces (those that hold the atom together). The idea is that all the forces must have been one in the moment of the big bang that started what we call the universe. Now we can distinguish four forces and are beginning to discover how they interrelate.

But are there only four forces? Throughout the history of science, we have often found more to nature than expected. Maybe we will find a fifth force—a force that has to do with intelligence, the mind, consciousness, or life. We know that the four forces are entropic, they run down, dissipate, and become less organized. Intelligence and life seem to have some ability to be antientropic. For example, an organism produces a seed—seeds organize matter and energy into a new organism. One seed produced the brain that reflected on the universe and organized ideas to explain entropy. Intelligence can give organization to vast arrays of data and invent robots to build machines that produce synergistic effects in society. Could intelligence be a fifth force to counter the entropic nature of the other four?

Astronomers give use two long-range futures. Either the the universe continues to expand to a final cold entropic death or it contracts until it repeats the big bang for endless bangs and contractions. A third possibility might be a continuous big bang and implosion of the universe. Since for every action, there is an equal and opposite reaction, there must be something coming in at the big bang simultaneously as something is exploding from the big bang. In this view the universe is continually and toroidally expanding and contracting.

These three futures for the universe doom intelligence to a futile and momentary position in the cosmic scheme of things. But what if we do migrate beyond the solar system, the galaxy, and eventually populate the universe? What if we do meet and mate with other life forms and permeate the universe with intelligence, as the four forces permeate the universe today? Will intelligence build a conscious technology sufficient to prevent either the entropic expansion or contraction of the universe? If so, then indeed intelligence is a fifth force of the universe. We've got about a 15-billion-year drama in front of us: will intelligence grow stronger than the first four forces and beat the entropic death or will intelligence fail to rise to the occasion and secure its fate as a cosmic tragedy?

Some look at consciousness and intelligence as being a force in the universe from a different perspective. A leading theoretical physicist, Freeman Dyson, in his recent book *Infinite in All Directions,* bluntly states that matter is "an active agent rather than an inert substance." Many believe there is a "life force" today that already permeates the universe. If so, then this would be a key Conscious Technology bridge between the mystic and physicist that books like the *Tao of Physics* have tried to build.

Some research seems to point to this possibility. Dr. Robert N. Miller summarizes research into such a possibility in an article entitled "Para-electricity, A Primary Energy," in *Human Dimensions:*

> The results of the experiments described in this paper indicate that a primary energy, different from the energies recognized by modern science, is emitted by magnets and

by the hands of healers. The energies from both sources cause decreases in the surface tension of water, change the structure and color of crystals from cupric chloride solutions, change the hydrogen bonding of water, and accelerate the growth rate of rye grass.

We may be a long way from finding a fifth force in the universe, but we have just begun to examine the marvels of the world of subatomic physics and already new theories are being developed that are radically different from our current views of reality.

For example, John S. Bell has theorized that all of the possible subatomic reactions *do occur* and we are only aware of and exist in the world of one of the occurrences. This means that the "universe" continually branches off into other "unseen" universes from the one that we experience. If this theory were true, then there are are so many worlds created every moment that it is impossible to comprehend the whole of life.

Even our previously limited 20/20 eyesight of the visible spectrum has been expanded by 10 to the 36th power. We can see through our telescopes out to a distance of 10 to the 18th power of magnification and through our microscopes "in" to 10 to the -18th power of magnification. We have yet to digest the enormity of this reality, which is only the light part of the electromagnetic spectrum.

We will see the universe differently through new kinds of eyes in space. Our satellites will let us see the universe as a combination of light, infrared, radio waves, micro waves, ultraviolet, X-rays, gamma rays, and cosmic radiation. What effect on our consciousness and view of reality will there be as we are able to see the universe through such diverse "eyes?"

Just as the two-dimensional shadow gives a hint of the three-dimensional object, so too the individual slices of the electromagnetic spectrum give us a hint of our surroundings. But just as the three-dimensional object gives an excitingly different sense of reality from its shadow, so too the universe and our earth as seen through the full range of the electromagnetic spectrum will permanently alter our view of things.

Now consider that electromagnetism is only one of four known forces of the universe. Imagine that you could actually see gravity and the other forces. We see the universe in terms of the visual spectrum because our satellites have sensors that respond to those electromagnetic frequencies. We will see our environment in terms of X-rays because we will have satellites with sensors that respond to X-rays. Will we have satellites that respond to gravity? Or microscopes that will respond to the strong and weak forces? And what if there is a fifth force in the universe? A life force? Is our mind the sensor that responds to such a force? Whatever the case, advances in sensory technology and subatomic physics will make our 21st-century view of reality quite different from ours of today.

Brain Research

Brain research is another major area contributing to our Conscious Technology future that forces the old questioning: is the mind a product of the brain, or is it in the brain like software is in the computer, or is the mind a node in a universal mind network? As discussed earlier, these views need not be contradictory.

We know that the mind can affect the brain as we focus our attention in meditation, decide to ingest psychoactive agents, or give up smoking through self-hypnosis. All of these activities alter neural firing in the brain. And such cerebral activity alters our mind. The mind and brain are mutually affective.

Science has neither proven nor disproved that there is a universal mind that interacts with individual minds, leaving aside for the moment that we are building a technological universal mind through computer networks to interact with individual minds. Those who believe in the universal mind accept that sensory data affects the brain and in turn, affects the individual and universal mind. They simply say that the sequence can be reversed as well, that the universal mind can affect the world through the individual.

If the universal mind is false, then there is no impact on the first two views. If it is true, then it does not contradict them, but simply enriches them. Hence, one could believe in all views. But regardless of which view or combination of views we believe, the future applications of brain research will alter the mind.

The brain is composed of billions of neurons or nerve cells that briefly let potassium and sodium mix to make an electrical impulse, after which the nerve has to replenish itself. Beyond this, we have little agreement about how the brain relates to thought, memory, and feeling. But the explosive growth in brain research and computer neural network design will no doubt spew forth a rich array of future scientific speculations about how the brain works.

In the classic modern cybernetic models of McCulloch and Pitts, the brain consists of a neural network in which each element is conceived as delivering a binary logical operation on its predecessors to its successors. Critics of this view point out that combinations of these operations become immediately too complex for analysis and the concept does not account for discrete thought.

Maybe Hebbs has a better concept with his "interacting cell assemblies model," which accounts for discrete thought. Or Karl Lashley at Yerkes Laboratory and later Karl Pribram, who believe wave-front interaction in the brain makes perception like a hologram. The wave fronts in their theory are caused by many neurons switching on and off.

We know that the brain contains a set of chemicals like endorphins, encephalons, serotonin and norepinephrine. These chemicals are neurofacilitators or transmitters that seem to explain such behavioral changes as alertness to passivity.

For example, a substance called "PDH" may be the "stuff" of memory in the brain, since we remember more when we take PDH. Serotonin is one of 30 known chemicals in the brain that is secreted by nerve cells. As serotonin is metabolized, it breaks down into 5-HIAA, which can be found in low levels in the urine, blood, and cerebrospinal fluid samples of aggressive, maladjusted, or psychotic individuals. Could we simply make 5-HIAA and give it to such troubled individuals? The currently available tranquilizer called lithium helps increase serotonin, which in turn creates more 5-HIAA.

Vasopressin helps restore memory with 15 weeks of nasal spray. Parkinson's disease due to the brain's insufficient secretion of dopamine has been altered by transplanting nerve cells that do secrete dopamine into the brain. Such new discoveries are occurring at a mind-boggling pace.

It does seem that we are nearing the day when we will know enough of the brain's chemistry and corresponding behavior that we will consciously design our mental activity. For example, you might want to have your mind passive for reading in the morning but active in the afternoon for writing. Far-fetched? Who would have believed a century ago that half of the children in America would have "perfect" teeth today? The four-minute mile was seen as the limit of human capability, yet today with improved training, nearly all college runners beat that limit regularly. It is not far fetched at all that we will develop near-"perfect" memory and intellectual superior minds for all in the 21st century.

Durk Pearson and Sandy Shaw in *Life Extension* have documented that the drug hydregine improves memory and intelligence. As we age, adenosine triphosphate or ATP volume declines in the body. Piracetam stimulates a chain reaction to produce ATP in the brain and improves activity between the cerebral hemispheres. Dr. Ferris of NYU found that piracetam in combination with choline significantly improved memory and alertness. Lecithin, phenylalanine, and prescription drugs like Deaner and Diapid improve general brain functioning. We also know that meditative and motivational techniques have improved mental behavior. What gains can be made by using both consciousness techniques discussed earlier and chemistry together?

We are learning that we can program our brain the way we program a computer. Self-hypnosis is one example. Another is by listening to tapes with specific messages while we are asleep. Culture itself programs us. For example, we are told that to be kind is good, to be clean is good, and to tell the truth is good. Storage in the brain of all these ways to be good could be called the conscience. If we listen to our conscience and do what our brain has stored as good, then we feel good. In this way our culture has programmed us to act so that our brain rewards us by producing chemicals that make us feel good.

According to John Lilly in *Harper's* magazine, humans can control the course of a mule carrying materials to difficult areas by manipulating electrodes implanted in the negative reinforcing area in the mule's brain. Delgado has stopped a charging bull dead in its tracks with an impulse to an electrode implanted in the bull's brain.

There is no reason to think that the pace of such discoveries will slow down. Research funding is continuing to grow and computer-assisted analysis and communication is speeding the applications process. Hence, the day will come when we will use chemistry, forms of self-hypnosis, and electrical impulses to design our mental behavior. These approaches, coupled with C-T exercises and technological additions to the body, are the tools that will make the human consciousness of the 21st century.

Space Migration   No single enterprise will stimulate science, technology, and consciousness more than space migration. The late NASA scientist Krafft Ehricke likened the earth to the womb of humanity that will give birth to our progeny throughout the universe. As it is difficult for the embryo to appreciate its eventual feat of walking the earth, so too it is difficult for us to appreciate the magnitude of our inevitable migration to outer space. More than peace on earth, space migration will renew our faith in progress, release our human potential, and resolutely defeat Malthusian economics.

The purpose of science in this scenario will be to understand how to reinvent life so that it is able to leave the solar system and survive without near starlight. As we migrate to new areas of the galaxy, our sense of space will alter. Since time and space is a relative continuum, our sense of time will alter as well.

Because the financial commitment is enormous, we will begin the process of space migration in earnest only as quickly as the public will allow. Eventually, the public will come to understand that we will go to space because (1) we are curious—which will be positively reinforced by the TOK, (2) we need an insurance policy that if we blow it here on earth, human life will still go on in outer space, (3) great wealth is to be made (explained later in the business chapter), (4) we are sitting ducks on earth if more advanced but hostile extraterrestrial civilizations find us first, and (5) the military of both the U.S.A. and the U.S.S.R. are already building permanent occupancy of space today. It is even the official Soviet civilian policy to migrate to space. And President Reagan's 1988 space initiative included "Project Pathfinder" to lay the foundation for the expansion of human presence throughout the solar system. So, the issue of going or not going to space is a dead one. The only issue is how.

Although the early efforts have been nationally oriented, the second age of space will be marked by the increasing internationalization of space programs. Both the Soviet Union and the United States are increasingly bringing citizens of other nations aboard their space probes and 13 European nations have formed the European Space Agency. Eventually, all nations and citizens will be able to invest in an international space program similar to what INTELSAT has created for communications. In the meantime, space chauvinism is still very much the order of the day.

Unless something major occurs to change current trends in technology and politics, the Soviet Union will be the first to land a human being on the planet Mars before the year 2000. This will fix in our brains more than the moon landing or Sputnik that we are destined to leave the earth. Even though the Soviet Union has orbited eight space stations and the United States has orbited one, this has insignificant public impact compared with what the first human on Mars will have. There is a move afoot to create a Soviet-American joint mission to Mars, but the politics of this makes it too uncertain to predict at this time. After all, why should the Soviet Union share the greatest public relations event in Russian history?

It might, if it perceived the risk of cosmonaut death as too high. If the Soviet Union goes alone and something goes wrong, then the world will see the Soviets as brutes willing to kill their people in an attempt to beat the Americans. The Politburo might see the risk of such a world backlash as too high in a post-Afghanistan period. Alternatively, it might decide to go with the Americans, reasoning that it is better to show parity with America in either success or failure than to risk the public relations fiasco of being the first to kill humans on the way to or from Mars.

In either case the sheer economics of future large-scale space migration beyond that of a simple mission to Mars is beyond any nation or corporation to "go it alone." President Reagan already committed America to the first truly international space station. The United States will pay $16 billion, the European Space Agency will pay $4.5 billion, Japan $2 billion and Canada $1 billion. Construction in orbit is expected to begin in 1995 and be completed after 20 shuttle flights in 1998.

The following lists some early steps to migration:

1987   First successful test of heavy lift vehicle *Energia* suitable for space shuttle or mission to Mars (USSR).

1988   Missions to Phobos (Martian moon) to see if there are sufficient resources for temporary life support as well as for the manufacture of return fuel to earth (USSR).

1988   Weightless human test 366-days demonstrated that humans can make it to Mars, restabilize biological functions with gravity on Phobos and Mars, and then weightless return to earth (USSR).

1992   Joint robotic missions to Mars via the Martian moon, Phobos
or   (based on signed agreements among USSR, France, USA).
1994

1998   First Internationally Controlled Permanent Space Station in low earth orbit. (USA lead nation).

1999   First human landing on Phobos, followed by shuttle craft with humans landing on Mars and return to earth (USSR or joint USSR and USA).

2006   First international lunar base (US lead)

2010   Geostationary Orbital International Space Station

2015   If no joint Mars landing with USSR, then second nation to land human on Mars (USA)

2020   Moons of Jupiter and asteroid mining

2025   Geostationary Space Community of 5,000 citizens

A more optimistic alternative scenario is put forward by Richard Hoagland in *The Monuments of Mars.* He contends that photographs taken during the 1976 Viking Mission to Mars have been reanalyzed and give reason to believe that there are structures that housed a visiting extraterrestrial species on the surface of Mars 500,000 years ago. The scientific gains from decoding such artifacts are incalculable. If better photographs by the United States and the Soviet Union to be taken in the early 1990s verify this hypothesis, then the Second Age of Space will take off like a rocket.

If the race to find evidence of extraterrestrial intelligence on Mars proves unfounded, then there could still be some large economic returns. Phobos seems to be full of rare metals like platinum.

Meanwhile, Richard Berenzen, President of The American University, sees a great future through the eyes of new kinds of telescopes that will lead to revolutionary thinking about the universe. He points out that we will have interferometer radio telescopes on the moon and Mars for distant seeing, bigger orbital telescopes, an optical observatory on Mars, gamma ray telescopes, radio telescopes, and cosmic ray telescopes.

Previous equipment gave us the surprise that the universe was not perfect when Galileo showed pock marks on our moon and other moons orbiting Jupiter. And it was the surprise of Halley's comet that completed Netwon's and Halley's calculations of celestial mechanics. More modern equipment surprised us with evidence of the extraordinary energy of supernovas. In the same way, Dr. Berenzen points out, our future electronic eyes will unveil surprises that will revolutionize our thinking about our universe and ourselves.

Policy Implications

In the past, science was largely an individual effort. As it became more complex and equipment become more expensive it became more of a group effort. Today it has become an international effort involving both governments and the private sector. Increasingly it will become augmented by partnerships with intelligent machines. This means that the speed and ease of scientific inquiry will radically increase in the 21st century. As a result the human role of setting direction will become far more critical than in the past. This means that consequences of poor or haphazard science policy will be more disastrous than in the past.

This book argues that the central thrust of science and technology policy should be to pursue science and make technology that enhances our consciousness. The details of this policy can be identified by imagining how current technology could be made to become more immediately responsive to our minds, seem more conscious itself, and enhance our consciousness.

Conscious Technology as a Technology Assessment Criterion

Conscious Technology should be a key criterion for technology assessment in the same way that environmental impact is a criterion for technology assessment. To apply Conscious Technology to technology assessment we would ask questions like: does the technology (1) reduce the time lag from thought to response? (2) improve brain functioning? (3) stimulate aesthetic response? (4) integrate with physiology? (5) lend itself to being applied in such a way as to bring the unconscious to the conscious, as an individual, group, species, and eventually among species?

For example, animal testing violates point 3 above. About 60 percent of all biomedical research uses animals and 70 million animals die each year. We can substitute animal experiments with computer modeling or simulations, better research coordination via the TOK data banks to avoid unnecessary duplications, chemical analysis, more use of cell tests, tissue cultures, and micro-organisms, and even cell cultures from cadavers. Increasing these approaches should drastically reduce such animal carnage. This would be a more conscious use of technology for medical research. It is our policy to do as much by these means as possible since it helps no one's consciousness to sit and behead mice all day in the lab.

About 3.4 percent of the U.S. work force are scientists and engineers and 70 percent of the federal research and development budget is for defense. If progress continues in disarmament and we move toward some of the new approaches explained later in the defense chapter, new directions for science will open. Conscious Technology policy could then play a more central role.

We have had agricultural technology for the agricultural economies, industrial technology for the industrial economies, and information technology for information economies. Next we will have conscious technologies for the Consciousness Technology economies. We can now see the day when both agriculture and industry are nearly 100 percent automated, leaving the mind as the next economic frontier.

The focus should be on the invention of tools that make happier and healthier minds that come to "know thyself" and make for a more smooth continuum between consciousness and technology in general.

Apply C-T Exercises to Science and Technology

Some of the C-T exercises explained earlier lend themselves well to assisting market analysis and product design. One could visualize or pretend that the current product is talking with them and then identify what engineering is required to make the visualization real. Such C-T exercises bring our unconscious desires to our conscious mind. Since we want our technology to be more responsive to our thought, our unconscious may have some good advice for us.

A Futures Wheel could be done with the current product in the center and each spoke of the wheel could show a different variation of how the product could be designed to seem more "conscious" and more immediately responsive to our thoughts. Each new product idea could have spokes that identify what new elements need to be incorporated in the new design.

In the Futures Wheel below of a video cassette recorder (VCR), the new designs would include voice activation so that you could tell it what to do. This implies that a microphone and voice recognition program would be added to future VCRs. The future VCR might also search TV programs or remote visual data banks via computer communications and match your previously computer-stored preferences. If a fee were involved,

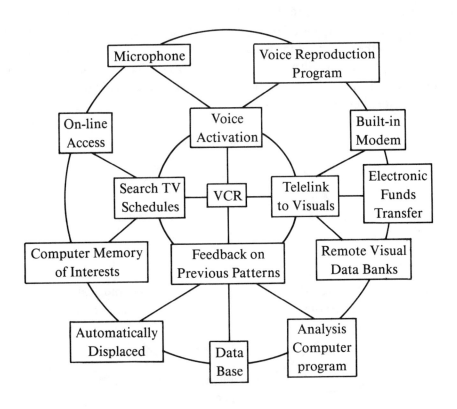

payment via computer communications and electronic funds transfer could be done. The VCR could also be equipped with a computer program to analyze your viewing patterns and make recommendations. The above futures wheel shows the more "conscious" technology VCR of the future.

Another kind of C-T exercise is called Synectics. It involves a series of group brainstorming sessions to make the familiar strange and the strange familiar. This altered point of view of the participants makes unconscious activity and creativity more acceptable. One group was assigned the task of coming up with an idea for a new can opener. They came up with the very successful innovation now known as the "pop top" can. This new kind of can opener is more immediately responsive to our mind, since it cuts out the steps of finding and holding the can opener.

Similarly, in the scientific method, we could use C-T exercises during the observation and hypothesis-formation steps to guide us more directly to questions that point to the key links between consciousness and technology. Science has long paid homage to the value of insight, but it has not developed the science of insight as it has with the sciences of physics and chemistry. As explained earlier, feelysis and mystic logic can complement the scientific method of analysis and be added to the classic research and development cycle as diagrammed below:

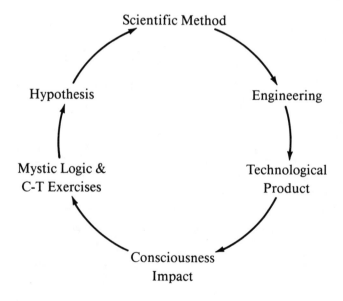

Society is becoming far too complex for people. Our environment is not as immediately responsive to our minds as would be necessary to simplify our lives. We will have to make technological advances in such a way that cuts out as many steps between thought and technological response. The pop-top can is an example. Unless we consciously design our technology to reduce steps between thought and response, our lives will become too complex and put individuals at the mercy of larger and impersonal systems. The Conscious Technology approach will encourage us to take advantage of the intensity of life while managing the complexity.

Toward the end of the first section on consciousness, various C-T exercises were explained to help the unconscious and conscious minds get together. Now we turn to the notion of the use of global technology to help the species unconscious and conscious get together. What is required is the creation of events for the species to respond as a whole. This has been possible only recently in human history with the advent of global communications technology. Events can now occur that stimulate our species consciousness—nearly simultaneously.

But there is the danger of future electronic Hitlers. Hitler took over the minds of some of the most educated people in history through mass rallies and quasi mass hypnosis, as evidenced in the film *Triumph of the Will.* Can similar "mass-mind" techniques be used in our rush to expand our consciousness through computer-guided imagery? Yes, if we lose a free press, forget to make such events interactive via the TOK, if individuals forget to balance their mystic selves with their technocratic selves using C-T exercises, and if we don't follow some of the suggestions in the following chapter on government and politics.

With this warning in mind, global conscious technology events are intended for occasional stimulants to help the species become mindful of itself as a whole.

There may well be a subconscious consensus about the future. It is just now beginning to solidify. When it does, I believe it will be the Conscious Technology view. In the meantime, we will need the deliberate manufacturing of events to bring the species perceptually together. Some events have already occurred.

The first event was the success of Sputnik. The subconscious consensus was that the species had entered a new age. The second event was seeing the earth from space. The subconscious consensus was that the species saw and loved the planet as a whole. The third event was the moon landing—humanity could do anything if it put its mind to it. And the fourth event was the nuclear melt-down near Kiev—we could blow it all.

These events began the process of putting our species consciousness and unconsciousness together. Many of us may have unconsciously held the above notions, but these four events forced our simultaneous acknowledgment that we have entered a new age, which involves the love of our planet as-a-whole, knowing that we can do anything if we put our minds to it, and that we could blow it all.

Global events such as the World Soccer Cup or the First Earth Run should include species-significant sounds and images flashed worldwide. The sounds of a newborn baby or the image of the earth from space could stimulate us to free associate and share these associations randomly via interactive global telecommunications to reinforce species bonding among diverse cultures.

The TOK could facilitate transcultural C-T exercises. Through the computer matching capability, exercises could be created and carried out among peoples from diverse situations. People are already organizing around interest rather than geography through global computer communications. The TOK adds a broader set of media such as graphics, video, and sound to the print medium. This creates more stimulus for a fuller unveiling of the unconscious response to species-wide events.

Another area of the future science and technology policy is Isaac Asimov's three laws of robotics published in *Opus 100*:

1. A robot may not injure a human being or, through inaction, allow a human being to come to harm.
2. A robot must obey orders given it by human beings except when such orders would conflict with the first law.
3. A robot must protect its own existence as long as such protection does not conflict with the first or second law.

The laws seem straightforward, but they have a fascinating implication when you consider that we are merging with technology and becoming cyborgs: we would be programming into this merger our peaceful, nondestructive future—this is truly a fine futuristic view of science and technology. But now it is time to turn to the political mechanics of all this.

Neither mystics nor technocrats are appropriate leaders for a free people in a complex culture. Old-style politicians show little understanding of new technology and human consciousness, and are unlikely to change through building coalitions in a political hierarchy or as lawyer/technocrats. When the gap between our new abilities and political leadership widens enough, the new politicians are likely to come from business, science, or the arts. Expert computer programs may replace lawyers for more simple matters like contracts, wills, and divorces. Instead of adversarial debate, we need speakers, listeners, and fair witnesses to try to enlighten all comers. Some problem areas to watch. How we can build a new world court that can enforce its decisions. An International Space Corporation described. Participatory democracy, in which citizens make decisions directly, rather than through elected representatives. Electronic town meetings which could be worldwide through host computers linked to a World Court. Bureaucratic change and the Strategic Analysis Grid.

*"He who cannot change the very fabric of his
thought will never be able to change reality"*
ANWAR EL-SADAT

Chapter Eight
Government and Politics

Although the nation-states will become more effective, other centers of power will grow faster. This will leave the nation-states less powerful in the 21st century relative to the growth of corporate, media, and individual power. Just as royalty is still a factor in the United Kingdom but lost power relative to the growth in parliamentary democracy, so too nation-states will remain, but their autonomy will continue to erode.

As a result, nation-states may have to accept new institutional arrangements, such as the New World Court explained below to stay in the international power game. Otherwise, they may become withering artifacts of autonomous power, much like what happened in England.

We have seen corporations evade trade embargoes with Cuba by using Mexico as a middleman. Corporations in South Africa are completing products in Swaziland to get around international trade sanctions. Since corporations can move faster than governments and are not bound by geography, it is only a matter of time when they eclipse government power. Nation-states will have to come to terms with these changes and may have to offer the prestige of including them in new international arrangements.

International media is also chipping away at government control of information. The news media was instrumental in breaking the Nixon government in America, making the Aquino government in the Philippines, and initiating the Camp David process for the Middle East. Its power broker role can only increase with advances in telecommunications.

One might have thought that the United Nations would have become the center of global political power, but it has become a bureaucratic dinosaur in comparison to its tasks. Granted, it made possible the coordination necessary to eliminate smallpox from the face of the earth, and it may one day reduce the impact of the Greenhouse Effect and become more accepted for peace keeping, but compared with its cost and scale of lost opportunities, it seems a sad organization.

For example, in 1969 Secretary General U Thant devised a clever plan to have the U.N. begin to help coordinate international policy. The first step was to get nations to state their national policies on environment, food, employment, technology, space, and so forth.

His tactic was to hold a series of U.N. conferences to get nations to state their positions or lack of positions on these issues. Then the U.N. Secretariat was to analyze these conferences and make recommendations for U.N. coordination. This could have made the U.N. a political force with real leadership. But sadly U Thant died long before the conferences got underway and no one at the U.N. Secretariat followed the strategy. The only analysis of these series of conferences with an eye to potentials for coordination was a diligent attempt by the American think tank called The Futures Group, which produced *The United States and Multilateral Diplomacy* in May, 1984.

The New Politicians

Unfortunately, the current crop of politicians has little vision and collectively seem at a loss to handle the increasing complexity of issues today, let alone those of the future. This might seem to argue for a technocracy ruled by technocrats. But that flies in the face of both representative and participatory democracy, because such social and technological managers of society would eventually be accountable only to their own "experts." There would be little incentive to include the "unwashed public" in their deliberations and to make issues clear to the average citizen. The result would be to eventually create an unstable cleavage in society.

The more mystically inclined have shown little competency in matters of technology, which increasingly shape political options. They tend to be romantics looking for the one simple solution to every complex problem. Neither the mystic nor the technocrat is the appropriate leader for a free people in a complex future.

If necessity is the mother of invention, then one day, maybe by the year 2000, we will see the beginnings of a new kind of politician. Not all politicians in the future will arise to the challenges facing us, but inevitably there will be some who comprise a new breed of politicians for the Conscious Technology civilization that will be in bloom between 2025 to 2075.

Where will these new politicians come from and why will they exist? They are not likely to come from within the ranks of politics. History shows that major innovations tend to come from outside the area that is innovated. Also, the process of rising through political hierarchy tends to exhaust truly bright innovators by the time they have reached prominence. Too many compromises in the process of building political coalitions tends to water down genuine originality. Our new politicians are more likely to come from the worlds of business, science, and the arts. But we will know for sure only when this new kind of leadership emerges.

New politicians will exist because the old-style politician is slowly but surely failing to manage his or her responsibilities and shows little understanding of the new powers being developed in technology and human consciousness. When the gap between our new capabilities and political leadership gets wide enough, then the citizen will be ready to hear from our new politicians.

The key characteristic of the new politicians will be their ability to see the world as the synthesis of the mystic and technocrat, as did some of the American Founding Fathers such as Washington, Jefferson, and Franklin. They understood that the way of the heart and the hand must be joined to become the way of leadership. Like these unusual politicians, our new politicians will seek technological solutions that enhance consciousness and will share consciousness that simulates improved technological design. They will be much different from the lawyer-technocrat of today and they will not resort to the ways of the occult high priests of the past, who calcified mystic insight into a set of political rules.

There is no way of knowing how many "closet mystics" are in government. It has not always been politically smart to show this side. But one American Congressman, Charlie Rose, showed his colors when introducing the Dalai Lama of Tibetan Buddhism on his first visit to Washington:

> Enlightenment starts with individuals. And if America is to cope with its current level of dilemmas, it must reach a higher level of consciousness than the level on which our problems were created. And the belief of Tibetan Buddhism in the evolution of the individual is harmonious with the desire of a growing number of our citizens for spiritual growth to reach higher consciousness . . . Let us seek the path of love and higher consciousness and personal transformation. His Holiness is a guide to enlightenment.

It has been well documented that the founding fathers of the American Revolution were mystics and some belonged to occult groups. Both sides of the Great Seal of the United States are full of mystic symbolism. The side with the pyramid states that the American goal is enlightenment in a new order of the ages. And the American motto *E Pluribus Unum* could be translated as Zen, if Zen is that sense of many becoming one. The above Latin phrase translates as "from many one." This is a clear statement of mystic vision. Even though this is all bluntly written and illustrated on the back of every one dollar bill, politicians have tended to shy away from expressing their mystical selves and inclinations.

Old politicians or the lawyer-technocrat will be seen as increasingly shallow or barren. Anything that can be made complex will be made complex, if two or more lawyers have anything to do with it. The old politicians had the idea that they would do it for you and had little or no interest in making it simple enough for you to do it yourself. The new politician will seek to simplify the complex. He or she will be a public educator who identifies the future consequences of policy options. His or her intent will be to facilitate the empowerment of the individual.

The line of demarcation between the old and the new politicians will be their simplification of law for the citizen. They will encourage the use of expert computer programs to replace lawyers, as much as possible, for the more simple matters like contracts, wills, and divorce. There would be menu options on one computer program that could be used many times at less than the cost of one visit to a lawyer for one problem. This expert computer program could be used over and over for many problems.

We know that when the price goes too high, the market goes elsewhere. The price of lawyers will drive people to alternatives like computer programs to get their counsel. Our new politicians will lead people in this new direction.

Law is based on past precedent and agreements. It is by its very nature not a particularly future-looking enterprise. However, the new politician will encourage the development of computer banks of issues and options that could arise, so that future judges will have a reservoir of thought to call upon. For example, what if a person is put in cryogenic suspension today and is brought back to life 25 years later? Does this person get to reclaim old property now owned by others? What rights do such people have?

Rather than having a court approach these matters under public pressure as in the surrogate mother cases, a body of thought could be developed over time and made available when the issue arises. In this way, we may be able to avoid a legal policy flow crisis, as the issues become more complex with decreasing lead time for analysis.

Who pays for this service? And who owns the data? The American Bar Association or a private data bank corporation could receive initial funding from the Department of Justice. Judges, lawyers, writers, universities, or the Department of Justice would pay for access. Our new politicians will lead by stating their options on future matters that will become part of the record of opinions. Ordinary citizens could also add to this data bank via their TOK; however the entity that owns the data bank will have responsibility for editing and quality control.

New politicians will also work to get beyond the adversarial approach to political debate. One approach is Tibetan debate. It could be thought of as a Robert's Rules of synergistic discussion. Unlike adversarial debate, with two sides each trying to prove the other is wrong, Tibetan debate's objective is to enlighten all participants. There are not two sides, but three roles that can be played at different times by all. As a result, no "one" wins, they all learn.

The three roles are speaker, listener, and fair witness. A speaker begins by stating the essence of the truth and claps hands to underline the crescendo of that insight. If the listener is so overwhelmed by the insight that he or she doesn't counter or say that is already well known, then the speaker continues and free associates beyond the previous insight. If the listener is not overwhelmed and does counter within two seconds and the move is acceptable to the fair witness, then the listener becomes the new speaker explaining what is a more overwhelming insight.

If the fair witness disagrees with the move, then he or she becomes the new speaker explaining a more inclusive truth. The fair witness can also choose to silently enhance the speaker's words of wisdom. This triangular debate allows for roles to be quickly changed, until it becomes clear that no one has the whole truth and that each can contribute to the enlightenment of all. This is a far cry from the technocratic zero sum debate in our legislatures today.

New politicians will include spiritual force in their methods of leadership and problem solving. For example, had a new politician existed during the Iranian takeover of the U.S. Embassy in Teheran, he or she might have begun working with the Islamic Center in Washington, D.C., in addition to other approaches. This center is the "embassy" from the Islamic people to the American people, in a similar fashion that the Roman Catholic Church has an embassy in Washington. The crisis in Iran was also a crisis in the Islamic community. This community could have been enlisted at the early stages by holding negotiations at the center.

Such an addition to economic and military force lets Moslems in Iran and elsewhere know that the U.S. welcomes Islam, but not the holding of hostages in embassies. It would have shown an understanding that the U.S. Embassy takeover was also an expression of a crisis in Islam that Moslems had some responsibility in healing or solving in cooperation with America. Instead, President Carter held a prayer meeting in the National Cathedral, not realizing that he had ignored the proper spiritual diplomatic channels at the Islamic center.

As everything gets more complex and information overload becomes endemic, intuition will become more necessary for coping effectively, let along keeping ahead. Intuition is improved by bringing the unconscious to the conscious mind. The C-T exercises explained earlier help this process. Hence, our new politicians will use C-T exercises as one element in their strategy to manage complexity.

Some Issues to Worry About

Unlike our old politicians, the new politicians will not avoid difficult problems with entrenched and conflicting interests. Many of the environmental problems fit into this category. The environmental futurist Lester Brown summarized the key environmental issues to worry about in a briefing in December 1987: "Over the past year, I see a world where forests are getting smaller, deserts are getting larger, ozone is depleting, top soil is eroding, and the atmosphere is warming up." We are losing 20 million to 50 million acres of rain forest a year. The American science fiction writer Robert Prehoda once said "A problem avoided turns into a crisis, and the crisis not mastered can turn into a cataclysm farther down the road." New politicians will distinguish themselves by following this sage advice.

For example, water will become an increasingly critical problem in the future. According to the Global Tomorrow Coalition in the United States, the per capita water availability will drop by 50 percent between 1975 and 2000. Meanwhile consumption in the United States went from 89 billion gallons per day in 1980 to more than 100 billion today. New politicians in America and elsewhere will see this problem as an opportunity to create new value. Waste treatment plants could be run at a profit if they were designed to produce shrimp, methane, and fertilizer. Water needed in industry could be recycled. Armco in Kansas City uses 5 to 10 percent less water to produce steel by recycling water. A paper mill in Israel saves 10 percent by recycling. And six oil refineries in the Soviet Union have closed water systems.

Chemical pollution will also increase. The United States produces 65,000 chemicals and 1,200 new ones each year. The implications for waste treatment and seepage into the ground water are staggering. According to the U.S. Environmental Protection Agency, 16,000 landfills have dangerous chemicals percolating into ground water. As many as 260 million pounds of toxic chemicals per day are disposed of unsatisfactorily.

We might get complacent because the air and surface water have improved since the mid-1970s. But the new politicians will teach us that there are still many problems and they are growing daily. Greenpeace claims that 300,000,000 tons of hazardous waste each year are not properly disposed of and only one-sixth of this is subject to EPA controls. Greenpeace further points out that 80,000 pits, ponds, and lagoons with hazardous waste threaten 90 percent of U.S. drinking water supplies. New politicians will call for research in chemical treatment systems to convert this danger into a new resource, just as wastes from oil refining produced plastic. They will also push genetic engineering to produce new plants that will resist pests and hence reduce water pollution from insecticides.

But the most complex and possibly the longest term problem facing the new politician will be the biological effects of electromagnetic radiation. This is one of the greatest unknowns facing the future. In the 1940s we began the big industrial/chemical commercialization, 20 years later we began the push to clean up its biological effects. Now we are beginning the big electronic commercialization. What biological effects will we find in the next 20 years? the next 50 years?

All electronic devices add electromagnetic radiation to our world. How will we be affected by these new sources of energy? What will their interference patterns be with naturally occurring electromagnetic radiation? What effects might there be from their acting synergistically with other agents?

One area of concern in the merger of technology and human biology is the interference with internal electronic devices as we become cyborgs. Digital thermometers have given false readings in hospitals that were next to radio stations. Heart pacemakers have been jammed by electromagnetic energy. These problems can be fixed and have been fixed, but we will have to be alert to such problems as we miniaturize our technology and merge it with our biology. All of a sudden our bodies and thoughts may respond to changes in our bionics induced by electromagnetic radiations that haven't been made compatible. We may experience effects from the interference with our internal electronics.

Normal magnetic strength on the earth's surface is about 0.5 Gauss, but when you handle a hair dryer, food mixer, or an electric drill, you experience 20 to 40 Gauss. When you get 100 Gauss you can experience very uncomfortable reactions and sensations of flashing light in your eyes.

Peter Semm, a West German scientist, demonstrated that our pineal gland is sensitive to weak magnetic fields. Peter Ossenkopp of the University of Western Ontario has shown that the opiate levels in the brain are altered by changes in slight variations in magnetic fields. This is all indeed complex, but our new politicians will be scientifically literate and will seek new ways to educate the public.

Early in this book, we looked briefly at the consciousness techniques that we may need to develop to help us avoid the negative mental effects of electromagnetic energy in certain situations. The current state of research in this area is quite spotty and it is difficult to do any comparative analysis at this time.

The complexity of analyzing the environmental impact of electromagnetic radiation will be far more than was the case with air and water pollution of the past. But it can be made simpler if we insist on standards of information on this topic. Five variables are required before any comparisons of data can be made:

1. Cycles per second of emission
2. Amplitude or strength of energy from the emission
3. Distance the object is from the emission
4. Time lapse of the object's exposure
5. Resonance of the object exposed to the emission and its dosimetry (how much energy is actually absorbed by the object)

If any one of these variables is missing, we will always be comparing apples with oranges and get hopelessly confused when trying to put together the proper picture of the whole range of the electromagnetic effects on life.

For example, the National Academy of Science in cooperation with the U.S. Navy in a research report on biological effects of extreme low frequency (ELF) cites research conducted by Heller and Teixeira-Pinto showing that garlic root tips exposed to pulsed radio frequencies at 27 MHz for 5 minutes induced chromosomal aberrations in growth. But at what distance and how much energy in the field?

The same source goes on to say that "The release of calcium ions from cat and chicken cerebral cortex was reported to be reduced by environmental fields with intensities of 10-56 V/m [volts per meter] and frequencies of 6-20 Hz." But for how long and at what distance from the source? The same variables are left out when the same report notes that monkeys' interresponse times were shortened when exposed to 1-100 V/m at 7-75 Hz.

James D. Grissett, of the Naval Aerospace Medical Research Laboratory in Pensacola, Florida, commented on this report:

> It was clear that ELF fields would generate electrical activity in the central nervous system that would be relatively small compared to electrical activity generated by normal functioning of the nervous system. Classical research in neurophysiology provided no basis for predicting an ELF effect on neural activity; however, some neurophysiologists are developing complex theories on the ultrastructure of nerve cells, that are compatible with classical neurophysiology and that also proved a rational basis for predicting that brain nerve cells may be susceptible to electrical influences far weaker than those which directly elicit firing of nerve impulses.

So we know there are effects, but data on what is proven to be dangerous is still incomplete, and no agency seems to be compiling the whole picture.

A very controversial area is reported on by Bill Bise in Oregon. Pulsed 10 Hz ELF frequencies skipping off the atmosphere from Soviet radar in Siberia may be affecting the central nervous system of the public in the American Northwest. The EPA went to Portland to check this out and found that the strength of the field was only 1/10 V/meter at the peak of the pulse. This is nowhere close to the 10-56 V/m at 6-20 Hz that correlated with the release of calcium ions in the cerebral cortex of chickens and cats reported above. But then again, we don't have long-range studies to show any effects from years of exposure.

Jack Calhoun of NIH claims that research in Gulf states shows that the incidence of coronary attacks increases 30 minutes before a storm front. He says this is caused by long wave lengths or ELF. This gives us an approximation for the first variable, nothing for variables 2, 3, and 4, and we can look up the resonance of heart tissue.

Our new politicians will identify a government agency to track all research on electromagnetic effects and have legislative bodies set the general goals. But they will need scientific establishments to set the standards, rather than do that in a political environment. The National Academy of Science would be the appropriate body in the United States to set these standards.

Along with these environmental problems, our new politicians will face the impact of an aging population boom. For example, 5.3 percent of the GNP in the United States in 1960 was spent on health care. In 1970 it rose to 7.6 percent and in 1988 it was 12 percent. With the baby boom population bulge not yet in retirement, this is likely to increase dramatically, even if the cost per person stays the same. The economics of this will be discussed later in the book.

Our new politician will come up with strategic but simple changes. For example, the United States pays $175 billion for German and Japanese defenses, which is more than the federal budget deficit. Certainly these two countries have enough American dollars to pay their way. And the United States is also paying for defending many countries' oil supply in the Persian Gulf. Granted America has a defense policy in its own interest, but when it is a shared interest, the partners that can afford to should pay.

Another example was suggested by Michael Michaelis, former director of the Washington office of Arthur D. Little, Inc., to make it a rule that all government reports have a final section that states the unresolved questions and future agenda for the subject of the report. These final sections could be cross-referenced in a data bank for use in the future legal issues data bank. They could also be used to compare with recommendations before congressional hearings. Future government reports and contracts would have to address these sections so that there would be an accumulative effect in government policy, much like we have experienced in science.

Another simple idea, but more difficult to carry out, is to divide government budgets into three sections: first year, third year, and sixth year. This immediately forces long-range considerations for every budget item, a problem that has long plagued all politicians.

The new politician will also seek bold applications of science to solve problems. For example, nuclear waste could be put in special insulators and shot to the sun via linear magnetic induction accelerators or mass drivers, instead of in salt mines or in undersea containers that might get disturbed over the thousands of years necessary to render the waste safe. Granted, old politicians will occasionally learn and support bold scientific applications, but this is the exception, not the rule, since few have ever had strong science advisors.

First public demonstration of the Linear Induction Accelerator or Mass Driver

Another bold application of scientific understanding on the part of the new politician might be the use of high-powered laser beams to "patch" holes that cyclically grow each spring in the ozone layer over Antarctica. Ozone is created by photons from the sun hitting oxygen in our atmosphere. We can speed up this process by pointing ground- and/or satellite-based lasers at the damaged areas.

A marvelous opportunity was lost by old politicians when the moon landing was played as a nationalistic victory with no follow-on program. The new politician would have heralded the event as a human achievement, claimed victory in the first age of space competition, and then invited all the world to join in the second age of space marked by global cooperation. A new approach for a global space program will be discussed later in the chapter on business.

The Soviet politicians have always understood that science and technology are important instruments of state policy. For example, Vietnamese fighter pilot Phamtuan became the first space traveler from a Third World country when he blasted off with Soviet Cosmonaut Viktor Gorbatko in the Soyuz-37 space ship July 23, 1980, to link with the Salyut-6 space laboratory. This was a dramatic signal to many in the Third World that the U.S.S.R. was ahead of the United States in both technology and the sharing of the frontiers of science.

Old politicians may well want to solve many of the difficult problems discussed above but give up because they are hopelessly disorganized. The new politicians will organize and manage their offices as situation rooms and because they grew up in the computer age they will personally use the TOK rather than relegating everything to secretarial help. The fewer steps between the politician's brain and data, information, and intelligence, the better the decision. Secretaries of old politicians too often knew more then their bosses.

New politicians will be truly global in perspective and action. The big jumps in oil prices in 1973 and 1979 opened the eyes of many national leaders to the reality of the global economy. The 1987 stock market panics in New Zealand, Australia, Japan, England, and the United States further awakened national leadership, but they will not have made the transition to truly intelligent global decision making until the late 1990s. Even the American new politicians will be forced to be more international and species-oriented since 50 percent of public high school students will be Hispanic, Black, and Asian by the year 2015, if current population and emigration trends continue in the United States.

It is clear to me from the tombs in the Valley of the Kings in Egypt that people/governments knew what they believed, lived those beliefs, and worked coherently within those beliefs toward goals imbodied in the beliefs. Our contemporary world has not yet finished creating that kind of coherence of belief. New politicians will have this task as central to their political campaigns.

One view that purports to finish that coherence is currently called the "transformationist" worldview. This belief system assumes that when enough people are enlightened, humanity will be totally transformed. The primary thrust of transformationalists is to get people "enlightened," and they tend not to examine the details of conventional political change. Most of what is referred to as "New Age" activism fits here.

Migration to space is another vision of the future. Its supporters see space migration as providing the freedom of movement, economic security, and endless newness to prevent conflict resulting in total destruction. Conscious Technology is a third view that is able to bridge the first two.

Conscious Technology seeks to enlighten by merging human consciousness and technology, be it on earth or in space, whether or not "we all will be changed in the 'twinkling of an eye,'" as said by many of the leading New Age lecturers.

Imagine all the cultural symbols throughout all time, like ribbons of music flowing in and out of your mind.

The new politician will lead the development of a coherence of vision that is multifaceted enough that everyone can see how they fit into the whole, be they baby doctors in Siberia or agroforestry advisors in the Sahel. Conscious Technology is the most likely such candidate future vision thus far.

World Governing Systems

A single world government entity is not desirable. It puts too many eggs in one basket. Nature demonstrates that a complexity of semiautonomous but interlinked systems survives better than single-species systems. An ecology of power seems a more natural evolution for global management. It also means that it is not necessary for everyone to accept the same single government.

However, to make an ecology of power effective, its elements must be viable. Currently, the global judicial function in the form of the World Court is not viable. We need a NEW WORLD COURT.

Imagine a future world court that can enforce its decisions composed of two representatives from each of the global power systems such as the multinational corporations, nongovernmental organizations, nation-states, and the media and chaired by a representative of the Secretariat of the U.N.

In the old World Court, there were no reliable methods or procedures to enforce rulings. In the new World Court, the members are able to enforce their rulings by virtue of their own power bases and self-interests. For example, if a case was decided against a corporation and the ruling included a 5 percent tax on all the dealings by that corporation, then all of the nation-states could enforce the additional 5 percent tax and be happy for the additional revenue. Even the other corporations would be interested to see that the 5 percent tax was enforced to give them the competitive advantage.

If a government decided not to charge the extra 5 percent to attract that corporation's investments, the New World Court could rule that all corporations could raise their prices to that country. It will not be easy to get all the elements of such a global system to run smoothly at first and refinements of these principles will be necessary. But the current World Court has no chance of enforcing its rulings in the present configuration.

How would this new world court be set up? The current membership of the old World Court would elect one international juror who would chair the first transitional New World Court.

The two nation-state members of the new court would be elected by the members of the U.N., just as the Secretary-General is elected today. Possibly the Secretary-General would be one of the two nation-state members to get the ball rolling properly, but then be replaced by a membership vote of the U.N., as the Secretary-General should be too busy to properly fill the additional role on the new World Court. He or she would be available in the future, should the eight-member court arrive at a split decision. This has the disadvantage of giving potentially more power to the nation-states. Alternatively, three instead of two representatives from the Non-Governmental Organizations (NGO) community might be chosen to make it a nine-member court.

The two corporate members would be elected by registered businesses. Each vote would be weighted by the wealth of that corporation; that is, a corporation with the value of $10 billion would be counted twice as much as a corporation with a value of $5 billion.

Since the media is to be the interface between events and the general public, it seems correct to have the two members of the new World Court elected by popular international vote. Such a global election would be carried out via the TOK. Alternatively, media systems could elect two representatives by weighted vote based on their circulation, viewer, or listener statistics.

NGOs could elect their two or three members by having weighted votes based on each NGO's total membership, geographic and content scope, and budget. The NGOs such as scientific organizations, universities, and private voluntary organizations, would elect two or three representatives of sufficient stature, so that they would know who to poll for technical knowledge or scientific advice.

Such organizations might be the Institute of Electrical and Electronic Engineers, InterAction, the International Council of Scientific Unions, or any of the universities. Heads of NGOs should be ineligible so that bureaucrats are not chosen. The intent is to have leading scientific and humanitarian minds on the court and to avoid any particular NGO advantage.

This New World Court would replace the old World Court but remain within the U.N. structure. Its proceedings and agenda would be posted in the international computer systems and made public via the TOK. Citizens could comment on a case via the TOK, but they would not have legal power in the court.

The legislative function of the U.N. only reflects representation by nation-states in the General Assembly and power systems at the end of World War II in the Security Council. A more equitable solution would be to reflect the changes in global conditions. The U.N. General Assembly could be modified to have three factors weight votes: (1) by nation, as it is today; (2) by population; and (3) by GNP. The U.N. dues could also be calculated by the same formula.

One addition to these dues could come from new commercial activities that use what the U.N. has called the "common Heritage of Mankind." Natural resources like oil in Antarctica or materials on the sea bed (Robert Nathan Associates estimate a $45 billion value by the year 2000 in oil, gas, manganese, copper, and nickel from the sea bed) or on the moon should go to the developer, but the developer should pay a tax to the U.N. This might put the UN on a more solid financial footing and give benefit to those countries that do not have the capability to develop these resources.

Another international governing system will be created for the development of outer space. The European Space agency with 13 countries is one model for regional cooperation, while INTELSAT with 113 countries is an international model. These models can be expanded to a proposed International Space Corporation or INSPACECO.

There would be three classes of ownership of INSPACECO with three cost/income centers. The first would be for nation-states. In the beginning it might start with the United States, Canada, the European Space Agency, and Japan. NASA would become a part of the nation-state division of INSPACECO. If the Soviet Union and its allies can come to acceptable terms, they too should be part of INSPACECO. This seems remote under current conditions. However, a successful joint American-Soviet mission to Mars would dramatically enhance the possibilities.

A second division would be for such corporations as Rockwell International, Siemens, and Mitsubishi. And the third category of ownership would be for individual investments. This could include governments or corporations that do not have their own space programs or capabilities as well as individual citizens and NGOs.

Given the budget constraints of the United States, NASA cannot expect to get the funds necessary in the late 20th century to carry out an expanding program into the 21st century. It will be forced to join forces with friendly nations.

Meanwhile, corporations want to industrialize space from a profit perspective. That can be in conflict with national goals. Nations want to land on Mars for national prestige, whereas corporations prefer to build

This is TRW's concept of the first internationally funded permanent space station as proposed by President Reagan in 1984.

solar power satellites and space factories for pharmaceuticals and new materials for sale on earth.

Simultaneously, individuals would like to invest in the development of space for both prestige and profit. Each of the three divisions of INSPACECO would set its program goals and objectives by vote of its membership weighted by stock ownership in its division. The votes of the third division would be sought by both the first and second divisions. Hence, nation-states and aerospace corporations would compete for an individual's support. Granted, many megaprograms such as terraforming Mars will be jointly carried out by divisions 1 and 2, since the interests of both would be served.

NASA photo of artist's concept of space robot

The Communications Solution

As the more mature Conscious Technology civilization takes shape between 2025 and 2050, the human species and its technology will be one continuous whole interconnected via multiforms of communications. Each point in this continuum will have access to any other point. But years before this is achieved, and technically possible today, legislators will have access to quantifiable trends and assumptions made in previous testimony so that more enlightened legislation is possible. Today, there is no systematic tracking and testing of assumptions in politics as there is in hard sciences like physics and chemistry. Manfred Kochen has made useful suggestions in this direction in his paper "Extending the Human Record: A Vision for Function of the Library of Congress in the Future."

The TOK will be the passport to many governing systems and will create political power for the individual. Instead of one entity taking over the world, everyone will be able to create and take over his or her own electronically linked world. Individuals could create international memberships via their TOK for all kinds of purposes, including creating their "network nations," as explained by Murray Turoff, the father of computer conferencing in a book by the same name.

Such network nations could compete to attract new "citizens" from around the globe. Unlike geographic nation-states, these network nations could allow the individual to have citizenship in many nations. The individual could electronically change citizenship quickly and often.

We talk about the world telecommunications system as if it were the nervous system of the globe. But unlike our biological nervous system, which is a two-way system, much of our telecommunications system is only one-way. We can watch the news of starving children in Ethiopia or volcanic destruction in Colombia, feeling unable to directly feedback with help. We know that the melt-down in Kiev means that people will need help, but how to give it while eating dinner in front of the nightly news?

When an organism is continually stimulated without the ability to respond, habituation sets in. We have a global one-way nervous system, which is not connected to a global muscle system or brain to respond appropriately to the information. The global muscle system is really the international corporations and the brain is partly that and partly governments and NGOs.

The TOK will change this situation by making it possible to be responsive. You could see a disaster situation on the television element of your TOK, then switch to the international data networks to find out what organizations are in place and what they need. You could then transfer some money from your account to the organization to help the relief effort, all within seconds of hearing the news. The American government has taken the early steps to make this a reality by using the international computer network called CARINET to coordinate disaster relief with private voluntary organizations working in the Third World.

Another approach is to have television shows on issues with a special number to call and a series of numbers to enter to give your response for quick polls that can be displayed later on the same television show.

Participatory Democracy

Participatory democracy is not the same as representative democracy. In representative democracy there are officials to represent the electorate. In participatory democracy you don't have representatives—instead you participate in the decision-making process directly. One example is the state initiatives or referendums. When enough people sign a petition or statement of proposed law, it gets put on the ballot for statewide election. If it passes, then it becomes law. No representative "did it." The New England town meeting is another example—the whole town discusses the issues and votes.

There have been some processes like Charrettes (that pulse between small groups and the whole) and Syncons (that merge small groups to the whole). These processes involve a cross-section of 100 to 500 citizens discussing an issue or series of interconnected issues until a consensus is reached. There is no legal power to enforce conclusions from such processes, but the information power or public press power can be so overwhelming that these processes have changed previous decisions. *Anticipatory Democracy* edited by Clem Bezold in 1979, documents, some of these social technologies of freedom.

Such social technologies could be formalized into an "electronic town meeting" and be made available on the TOK. In the meantime, computer conferencing applications could be used as discussion forums rather than for voting. The City Council of Colorado Springs, Colorado, became the first governing body to do this, when it voted 7-2 May 10, 1988, to use electronic mail among Council members and accept comments from the general public via either personal computers or publicly accessible computers located in the Pikes Peak Library.

It is interesting to note that computer usage seems neither right wing nor left wing. As a result, a wide range of opinion will be made available on the issues of the day.

Canada is perhaps the prime example of a country that has seriously examined the possibility of using participatory democracy in combination with representative democracy. In the mid-1970s the Canadian Ministry of State for Urban Affairs asked me to design a process in response to Prime Minister Pierre Trudeau's expressed interest. It called for a combination of agency analysis and a national public Delphi survey (a repeating questionnaire that moves toward consensus) conducted by news media of citizens' attitudes about present problems and future possibilities and priorities.

During the first phase, the government prepares policy briefing and options sheets for a participatory process involving metropolitan, province, and federal participants, while newspapers, radio, and television conduct a public Delphi to generate public feelings for the governmental participatory process. The second phase is a one-week intensive participatory process of metropolitan, provincial, and federal representatives to evaluate and synthesize policy options and public Delphi conclusions in order to evolve broad public policy criteria and/or to make policy recommendations.

During the third phase, newspapers, radio, and television disseminate and evaluate the results of the participatory process, and the government does its own evaluation. Next the media prepare and conduct another series of public Delphis in response to public reaction to phase 3. Likewise, the government prepares its issues, briefing, and options sheets from its evaluation of phase 3 in preparation for the next participatory process. And the process continues with computer conferencing throughout for technical and public input in all phases.

The Canadian government changed before the Ministry of State for Urban Affairs could implement this process. Nevertheless, it still serves as a model for integrating both representative and participatory democracy.

One of the potentials of international telecommunications is global participatory democracy as distinct from global representative democracy as in the United Nations. This is a fairly complex issue and there are many ways it could evolve. Here are some key procedures:

1. Each person would have access to some communications tool and host computer of many users.
2. Any person can initiate an issue on a host computer.
3. If enough people on that host computer agree that an issue needs to be addressed, it goes out to the larger audience on other host computers for discussion.
4. If the discussion sharpens the issue suitable for a global vote, and it has the support of some percentage of users of these host computers, then it is put up for a vote on the international data system of the TOK. Everyone gets a vote and if the item is

passed, it is implemented by the authorities specified in the issue.

5. A linkage with the New World Court via the TOK would be used as appropriate.

The account number for a citizen in such an electronic system could be the person's social security number and his or her code or password would be the individual's voiceprint. Voiceprints have been shown to be more accurate than fingerprints, even when you have a cold. There could be a citizen's issues transponder (a device on a satellite that receives, amplifies, and transmits signals) on new satellites for this purpose, so that cost would not be a deterrent to global citizen participation.

Centralization and Decentralization

Both centralization and decentralization are happening at the same time. They are not necessarily contradictory trends. As a system centralizes, it is less able to deal with local day-to-day events. This gives more uncontested power to the local or decentralized authorities. If local decisions add up to bad consequences, the system centralizes again. This occurred as a result of the Space Shuttle explosion. NASA had decentralized. Coherence of Space Shuttle management was cited as "flawed" in the inquiry committee on the explosion. NASA has recentralized its management as a result.

Management via computer communication networks has features of both centralization and decentralization. Because a central authority or headquarters can act through a decentralized network, advantages of centralization can be maintained. The advantages of centralization include systemwide quality control, broad experience brought to decisions, efficient resource allocation, and the provision to all of a sense of direction and how they fit into the whole.

While reinforcing the advantages of centralization, computer networking tends to reduce the disadvantages of centralization. The disadvantages of centralization include top-heavy management, which results in stifling of initiative, slowness of decision making, poor contact with local staff, high travel costs between headquarters and remote offices; and failure to develop systemwide management skills.

In computer networking it is possible for complex information to get around on a timely basis to the appropriate people. It also makes it possible for new staff to watch information flows. This informal approach to corporate cultural training let's them "learn the ropes" more objectively.

Computer networks have demonstrated that they can have the advantages of decentralization, such as stimulating entrepreneurial spirit, cutting time and cost of decisions, and getting the decisions made by the most relevant people with the most relevant information.

This can be done without the disadvantages of decentralization, such as communications delays, duplication of efforts, poor coordination, or weakening central authority. Private corporations have claimed that their telecommuting employees increased their productivity by 40 percent compared with working in the office. Imagine how difficult military management would be without such a balance of centralization and decentralization on its computer networks, or the management of stock market transactions, for that matter.

Strategies for Change

One way to change government is to pay employees on the basis of output. We should index government employees' salaries to their individual and their department's performance. If performance standards are not met within a reasonable period of time, people should be fired. By taking away the power to fire, we have made it exceedingly difficult to truly manage bureaucracies. The current management environment in government makes it "safer" to keep the status quo than to try and do something to improve performance.

Paying individuals by individual performance seems reasonable, but how would departmental output be calculated? Department of Commerce employees would get a salary increase or decrease based in part on the GNP and other indicators of healthy business growth. Department of Education employees would get their salaries altered on the basis of national annual changes in IQ, standard aptitude tests, high school graduation rates, and other similar indicators of student improvement. The Labor

GOVERNMENT AND POLITICS

Department would base its salaries on the rate of job growth relative to the unemployment rate. And so forth. Without a more effective incentive system based on performance for government departments as a whole and for individual employees, political leaders will have little ability to make a difference. Even Ronald Reagan's campaign to revamp government management has had little effect in comparison with the magnitude of the problem of bureaucratic inertia.

A different kind of strategy for change involves an individual who moves faster than institutions can respond. For example, I used to demonstrate computer communications in developing countries before these countries had solidified their international data flow policies by simply doing it—making a long-distance phone call to a computer network overseas in the United States while using a portable computer.

This immediately proved (1) it was technically possible; (2) nothing necessitated a complex legal response, justification, or set of rules; (3) Third World countries could do their own cost/effect analysis, as I paid all costs and showed these costs to government as well as private sector people simultaneously, so that no one one could change the story; and (4) poorer people could make a request through such a network and experience the future of the information and communications economy.

This approach left about 10 countries connected to international data networks and led to their permanent connection via new equipment for less costly local public dial-up access. If I had gone through the normal channels, as I did in one country, nothing would have happened. It was also very much a matter of consciousness. How I walked through the door was a big factor. Just moving fast is not enough. It was a proper balance between my consciousness and my computer technology that allowed this success.

There are change strategies that are more effective than others but are more difficult to implement. The following Strategic Analysis Grid illustrates the range of general strategic approaches. Those who would influence change should consider this grid to help identify alternative strategic approaches. Strategies that fit in the upper left box tend to be easier to carry out but are less effective than those in the boxes in the lower right. But the ones toward the lower right are very difficult to carry out. Moving faster than institutions can respond to create new computer networks is the kind of strategy you would find in the upper right box.

	Change within system	Change from outside system	Create new systems
Information	1		
Positive/ negative reinforcement	2		
Environmental change			3

Let's say the objective was to reduce noise in the library. Cell 1 could be filled in by answering the question "How would I use information to change within a system?" One answer might be to put up a sign on the wall saying to be quiet. Cell 2 would be filled in by answering the question "How would I use positive and/or negative reinforcement to change a system from the inside?" One answer is to give special privileges for resources in the library to the quiet ones, while kicking out the noisy ones. This is more effective than the first one, but more difficult to carry out. Cell 3 would be filled in by answering the question "How would I use environmental change to create new systems?" One answer is to invent a computer network with remote electronic library access—far more difficult to do, but it permanently eliminates the noise in the library.

This grid can help you to see what strategic approaches you have been using in the past and identify the tradeoffs between being more effective versus the degree of difficulty involved. As you mentally try to fill in each box, note which strategies fit your temperament. Then see if you can come up with strategies that are more effective.

As we all become more strategically efficient in social change, we will experience changes in our personal commitments to others. One tactic for keeping effective relations in a changing world is through "weak linkages." Weak linkages are social bonds between and among people that have no institutional force behind them. Occupational linkages have the power of hiring and firing behind them. Professional bondings have peer-group pressure behind them. But weak linkages have only your personal values and the coincidences of time behind them.

Are there people who come in and out of your life for no apparent reason? Kurt Vonnegut called this phenomenon a "Karass" in *Cat's Cradle*. Are there patterns among such people, that might help you to more fully understand yourself and your directions? Understanding your directions helps to eliminate unnecessary complexity. Same with nations. With no direction, complexity and hence irrelevancy takes over and the nation falls.

Another strategy for change is citizen diplomacy. Private citizens of two or more countries work out new relations among themselves to foster changes in international relations. This is an application to the strategy of moving faster than institutions can respond. Such citizen diplomacy has become noticeable between groups in the U.S. and U.S.S.R. Radio, television, and conferences with Americans and Soviets to explore new ways to reduce conflict are occurring with increasing frequency.

Crime

Fostering the genuine attitudes of the mystic will contribute to the reduction of crime, as discussed in Chapters 2 through 4. New early warning technology will also act as a deterrence to crime, as discussed in Chapters 6 and 7. But a combination of both technology and consciousness education has the greatest promise of making fundamental changes.

We will eventually reach the day when the vast majority of all children will not only be desired by their parents, but planned for in advance. The impact of this is difficult to predict, but there is a higher correlation between law-abiding behavior and people born of parents that wanted and planned for them than people born without such planning.

As a child I thought the only way to prevent crime and war was mass mental telepathy, that is if, each individual could read any individual's mind. Even if this were possible, merely sharing what goes through the mind does not guarantee meaning or comprehension; hence, misunderstanding and false accusations with angered counter responses could follow.

As we become cyborgs, we will have sensors that could alert us to increased offensive behavior potential. This would be an early warning system for the individual in a similar way that nations have satellite early warning systems.

Some forms of theft might be averted by installing sound devices with tape recordings that subliminally suggest that people should not steal. Dr. Hal Becker of the Behavioral Engineering Corporation in Metairie, Louisiana has developed such technology to alter consciousness. We could also spray household objects with a very light radioactive trace. If they are stolen, local police could have a device that picks up the trace electronically to locate the stolen objects.

High levels of serotonin in the blood and the colors light pink and green can reduce aggression.

The TOK should play a role in reducing crime. Replacing credit cards with voiceprint recognition on the TOK could reduce credit card fraud, which has reached over $1 billion a year in the United States alone. Burglaries would be reduced.

Tax evasion could also be reduced. Taxes could be paid at each transaction via TOK. Government could give a financial incentive for paying the tax during each transaction.

Conscious Technology as a Policy Analysis Criterion

Conscious Technology should be used as a policy analysis criterion. Having a policy that is not Conscious Technology balanced will be wasteful of human potential. We should ask if the policy, strategy, or tactic under consideration improves the balance of consciousness and technology. This should include the secondary and tertiary consequences as well as the primary ones.

If these consequences do not improve the balance, we should ask what will. If a recommended policy concentrates too much on technology, without concurrent consciousness enhancement, then consciousness will be underutilized and applications of the technology will not be optimal. This has been a common mistake in Third World development—throwing technology at people without transformation of consciousness to go with the new technology. Conversely, if policy concentrates too much on consciousness without concurrent technology enhancement, then the technology will be underutilized and human enlightenment will not be optimal.

The Second Most Important Issue

We all know that the prevention of thermonuclear war is the most important issue, but it is not yet recognized that Third World economic development is the *second* most important problem facing civilization. Consider the following facts:

1. As much as 93% percent of the population crisis *is in* the Third World.

2. The international monetary system *is now threatened* by the mounting Third World debt crisis.

3. The debt in the Third World can be repaid only by the growth of its members' local small business community.

4. All wars since World War II have been in the Third World.

5. U.S. businesses have saturated the First World market and *are now dependent* for their future survival on developing the Third World market.

6. The current illiteracy, disease, and poverty in the Third World means that U.S. businesses *cannot grow sufficiently* to keep *our* own economy on the move into the *21st* century.

7. Eight of the ten largest cities on earth will be in the Third World by 2000 according to U.N. projections:

1.	Mexico City	26 million
2.	São Paulo	24 million
3.	Tokyo-Yokohama	20 million
4.	Calcutta	17 million
5.	Bombay Metro	16 million
6.	New York Metro	16 million
7.	Shanghai	14 million
8.	Seoul, Korea	14 million

9.	Tehran	14 million
10.	Rio de Janeiro	13 million

As a result, it is now time to give Third World economic security as much attention as First World military security. Although global economic threats to peace and plenty are not as imminent or visible as political or military threats, they are still just as fundamental.

Government and politicians must focus on creating rapid development forces with the same sense of seriousness and emergency as they have for military strike forces. The weak point is the formation of very-small-scale to medium-scale businesses. Successful small businesses in America is how the U.S. economy got going in the first place. All the foreign aid for other purposes is nice, but the heart of the solution to the second most important problem facing civilization is the development of small business in the Third World.

This is so important that a U.N. General Assembly resolution should be passed to the effect that (1) foreign aid expenditure should be assessed of each nation as a percentage of military expenditure; (2) developed countries should have to spend that assessment in economic assistance for poorer countries, whereas Third World countries have to spend that assessment on their own development; (3) the U.N. monitors compliance; and (4) infractions are taken to the New World Court (as expained earlier).

The idea is that if the United States has three times the military budget of France, then the United States should have three times the economic aid budget of France. The 1988 military expenditures worldwide were about $1 trillion.

Since this is such an important topic, a separate chapter will explore new approaches to Third World economic development.

Although providing for the common defense is the primary responsibility of government, I have put the Conscious Technology implications for defense also in a separate chapter that follows.

Perceptual warfare. In the information age, the superpower objective will be mind control and the linking of nuclear reductions in the 1990s to similar reductions in conventional arms. Joint U.S./Soviet development of outer space and the Third World could provide profitable new uses for military industrial bases and personnel. Computerizing the U.S.S.R. will make the K.G.B.'s domestic surveillance easier, and computer communications is the least costly way to spread disinformation around the world. A good defense would be to forecast expected ploys from models of Soviet disinformation, and then to pre-empt them.

(JASS) Jam All Strategic Systems. Computer viruses and other jamming techniques would be both a deterrence and a defense strategy, as an alternative to S.D.I. and M.A.D. Joint terrestrial space programs that all nations could support, could be the third leg of the future defense triad along with perceptual warfare and JASS. Integrating communications systems would be to future development what canals and roads were in the past. Stronger moves to counter increased terrorism.

Chapter Nine
Defense

The likelihood of thermonuclear war between the Americans and the Soviets is decreasing every day. The Soviets believe enough in the "nuclear winter" scenario to make them unsure of their own survivability, not to mention blowing holes in the ozone layer and the effects of radioactive fallout. Even if the United States didn't return fire, the risk to the Soviet infrastructure from the effects of their own weapons is too great compared with any benefits from the use of their nuclear weapons.

Nuclear deterrence is only real if people believe there is a possibility of the use of nuclear weapons. Because neither side believes the other will use them, such weapons are no longer a credible deterrent. Most American military analysts are loath to agree with this position. They argue that the nuclear deterrence has kept the peace so far. Since we really don't know Soviet intentions and since a new deterrence is not yet in place, it would be foolhardy to discredit nuclear deterrence. But the fact remains that a full first strike will yield a combination of environmental consequences for the aggressor that could destroy their civilization, even if return fire never occurs.

This leaves nuclear deterrence in a contradiction. If a power is insane, there is no way to ensure it will be deterred from a first strike. If a power is sane, it will not start a nuclear war. If powers will not use their strategic nuclear arsenals, then nuclear deterrence is not credible.

Former President Richard Nixon came to the same conclusion in his book *1999: Victory Without War:*

If war were to break out, an American President would be left with the single option of ordering the mass desruction of enemy civilians, in the face of the certainty that it would be followed by the mass slaughter of Americans. That is unacceptable and not credible.

Hence, the next drama will be to see how good a deal both superpowers can get for eliminating their investment into obsolete nuclear weapons. The 1990s will be the decade of nuclear reductions that should be linked with conventional arms reduction. A conventional arms reduction treaty should be signed before the proposed 50 percent reduction in strategic nuclear forces; otherwise, the Soviet incentive for reducing conventional arms may be lost. We may even see direct negotiations between NATO and the Warsaw Pact military leaders on conventional weapons.

As this drama unfolds, new uses for the military industrial base and personnel will be found in joint development of outer space and the Third World. These new uses could and should be tied to strategic and conventional arms reductions, including chemical (1925 "Geneva Protocol" banned usage, but not production. The United States unilaterally stopped production in 1969 but began again in 1987), biological (the 1972 treaty between the U.S. and U.S.S.R. to ban biological weapons should be reviewed in this new context), and environmental warfare systems.

Some potential first steps could include an integrated global monitoring and communications system, fusion energy development, orbital manufacturing facilities, a joint mission to Mars, disaster relief, the solving of environmental problems like the "Greenhouse Effect," or large-scale Third World infrastructure projects. Space industrialization as well as Third World economic development can be carried out in such a way as to begin to return income to both American and Soviet treasuries.

As explained in the next chapter, national investment into space shows a net income from increased economic stimulation and hence tax revenues. Third World economic growth also simulates First World growth and hence tax revenues. The combination of increased economic stimulation and reductions in arms development and support will yield some relief to national treasuries. Soviets are aware that Japan's 2.5 trillion GNP surpassed their 2.2 GNP in 1987. They can't get superpower recognition with a third-rate economy. The process of conversion from arms to Third World and space development will be slow, taking years before financial gains are reflected in national budgets.

Historians may one day identify the November, 1985, Summit in Geneva as the beginning of the constructive dialogue between the United States and the Soviet Union that marked the turning point away from the path toward nuclear destruction. In the meantime, we are engaged in a related but far different kind of warfare.

Information Age Warfare

With the world becoming an electronically interconnected system of Conscious Technology, it will be increasingly difficult for any power to mount a surprise attack. Surveillance satellites have played an important role in keeping the peace by giving early warning and enforcing arms control and reduction treaties. This tends to prevent aggressors from believing they can secretly prepare for an attack. The faster aggression and other problems can be identified, the more time one has to act to prevent the outbreak of war and to develop friendlier relations.

As we increase the globalization of consciousness, there will be less drive for one country to take the land of another. Each age has its own kind of warfare. In the Agricultural Age the objective was to control land. In the Industrial Age the objective was to control productive capital, as Russia did with Eastern Europe. In Information Age warfare the objective is to control minds. It is perceptual warfare. According to President Reagan in his 1987 and 1988 reports, *National Security Strategy of the United States,*

> We are faced with a profound challenge to our national security in the political field. This challenge is to fight the war of ideas and to support the infrastructure of world democracies . . . To accomplish this we must be as committed to the use of the information aspects of our diplomatic power as to the other elements which comprise it.

If you can make the world think differently, then there is no need to invade with a land army. This is not to say that there will not be any more Industrial Age wars carried out in the Third World, but that perceptual warfare will increasingly be the issue between the superpowers.

The United States' military build-up during the 1980s and its resolve to develop SDI (the Strategic Defense Initiative) convinced the Soviet Union that the next arms race will be too expensive to win. The American economy is too strong to be beaten in a cash war. In addition, the Soviets like the Americans are caught in the nuclear dilemma of no response or total response to confrontation. The intermediate response of conflicts in the Third World is also proving unsuccessful.

This is the basis of the new public relations moves from the Kremlin. They will try to sell to the world the perception that they are the good guys and the Americans are the bad guys. Every technique at the disposal of marketing and public relations will be employed. Handsome Secretary General, fashionable wife, Soviet rock 'n' roll, bureaucratic reforms, Glasnost, and new peace initiatives will mark the new humanism of the Soviet Union.

The Soviet threat tends to unite Europe. As the nuclear disarmament continues, we may see European unity falter. There will be pressure to dissolve NATO and the Warsaw Pact. If nuclear and conventional war is not the future form of warfare and information warfare is, then maybe NATO and the Warsaw Pact should be dismantled or their posture converted to one of perceptual defense or joint space industrialization and Third World economic development.

It may be that the Soviet Union is serious about Glasnost and the general democratic reforms, not only as a strategy in information warfare, but as the next step in their sociopolitical evolution as well. They know that they will not be accepted as a legitimate world power as long as they have a third-rate economy. And they have seen the Japanese economic alternative to military power gain great influence in America. Hence, the strategy of Glasnost to modernize the U.S.S.R. and the communist goal of world domination are not necessarily contradictory.

It should be remembered that Chairman Mao said that the Chinese Communist revolution had developed far enough to open the system and allow for a "thousand flowers to bloom." When he was satisfied that all the critics had exposed themselves, he got rid of them.

Whether the Soviets will repeat this method of consolidation is not clear. But if they don't, then another possible scenario is that the reforms could get beyond the ability of the state to control. After all, the first Russian revolution occurred many years after the Tsar began opening the political economic system.

After approximately 160 million deaths in communist revolutions around the world (less then one third of that number died in all of World War II) and nearly 500 million displaced persons or refugees, the Soviet Union has not succeeded in selling communism to the the First and Third World. Physical force was also used to put down rebellions in Second World countries such as East Germany in the early 1950s, Hungary in 1956, Czechoslovakia in 1968, and Poland in 1980. The Soviets will have to change.

The Soviet Union is adjusting tactics by using the perceptual warfare technique of calling communism something different. The surrogate international Soviet sales forces in the Third World are beginning to say that they are not communists, but humanists. Hence, all the bad associations with the word "communism" are now sidestepped, as the attempt is made to usher in the new humanism for the Third World. Naturally, when people hear new terms, they think words refer to things, but in information war, they don't.

Meanwhile back in Moscow, the Communist Party cannot afford to change terminology, since it is that terminology that gives them the right to hold power. Ranking officials go home at night worrying about what the other Soviets think who did not get their promotion simply because they were not members of the Communist Party. The party loyalists may accept all kinds of change, as long as they keep their position and terminology. Hence, we can expect many new interpretations of Soviet communism. But we should not be fooled into thinking that the authoritarian nature of Soviet politics will give way to freedom, as it is understood in the West, until the Communist Party relinquishes control over all appointments and lets the government be directly responsive to its people.

It has become fashionable for the West to believe that as the U.S.S.R. computerizes its society, it will necessarily become more democratic. This is naive and wishful thinking. Computers make the control of information and intelligence far more effective than thousands of KGB agents. Computer programs can be written that list sensitive words. When these words are transmitted via computer communications and tapped, the program can activate recording equipment and even alert live monitors. This gives far superior and cost/effective monitoring of the thoughts of Soviet society than in the past, as they communicate rather than travel to their surveillance.

But a more sinister possibility for the use of computer communications in information warfare is possible. One person acting alone in Moscow or anywhere in the world could buy accounts in 100 different international computer networks. That individual could write a disinformation piece on a computer and enter it into all of the 100 networks in the morning. In the afternoon the person could change his or her network identification and respond to the morning bulletin as if he or she were a second person. Then in the evening the person could once again change electronic identity and respond to his or her first two planted misinformation pieces making it seem that this has become a hot topic in 100 international computer networks. The next morning international news services might run a story that a rumor is going around that . . . and that afternoon the disinformation agent in Moscow could enter the news story in some of the international computer networks, further stirring the pot and giving the original fantasy an increasing sense of reality to the world. Computer communications is the least costly way to deploy disinformation around the world.

There is a Sufi story of a woman who told a lie, felt remorse, and went to the Sheik at the Mosque to get advice on how to correct her sin. The Sheik told her to come back with a pillow. When she did, he took her to the top of the minaret, opened the pillow, let the feathers fly out all over the city, and said, "You will be forgiven when you bring back all of the feathers to me."

One person acting alone can spread disinformation very effectively. It takes far more time to clear up the disinformation than to spread it. A Soviet agent could go to a Third World country and spread rumors for say one month that would take Americans years to clear up. This approach tangles opponents in so many problems that they are not able to make progress on other fronts. The cost/effect of pinning down the Americans with such "information ground fire" must be very attractive for a tight-budgeted Soviet Union.

Judeo-Christian ethics teach that if you have to lie, your goals are wrong. It is Marxist-Leninist ethics to tell a lie if it furthers the goal and it is unethical to tell the truth if it inhibits the accomplishment of the goal. Hence, there is an ideological basis for information warfare.

All U.S. and allied policy should be focused to change the criteria for decision in the Politburo of the Soviet Union. Anything less than that will doom the world to power politics and brinkmanship for the foreseeable future. If the new initiates of the Kremlin are indeed fundamental changes in the criteria for decision, then all U.S. and allied policy should be focused on positively reinforcing the change. It may be that the new policy of openness to criticize government so that reorganization can occur in a democratic environment is a new criterion for decision making in the Politburo, but it could also be a common-sense tactic to make the old "world communism" goal more possible. The key element to change in the decision making of the Politburo is world Marxist-Leninism. In either case, we should encourage these new directions and such normal world citizen behavior as the joining of GATT (the U.N.'s General Agreements on Tariffs and Trade) and other international mechanisms as an incentive for genuine internal change. We should have both the olive branch and the cluster of arrows approach.

How to Defend Against Information Warfare

As with any defense, forewarned is forearmed. The same applies here. First identify the logic of disinformation. For example, the most common ploy is to accuse your opponent of what you are doing. So, if the Soviets accused the Americans of infiltrating Third World youth organizations to spread propaganda, you would assume that the Soviets are doing it. Another logic is to positively reinforce those values that erode free market economies. If the values that give strength to free market democracies can be weakened, then Soviet relative strength will increase.

The Russian culture has never been number one in the world. There was a time when Islamic culture was leading in science, mathematics, art, and engineering. And other countries such as Portugal, Spain, France, and England have had their turn at being number one. But the Russians have not had that honor. There may be a stronger Russian drive to be number one than the Soviet drive for world domination. If world domination is no longer a Soviet goal, the Russians might still want world prominence by weakening their opponents' political economic leadership through information warfare with the objective of crippling values.

After identification of the various ploys or logics, Soviet media and actions should be monitored to see what ploys are increasing and decreasing. This will yield a picture of the trends of Soviet information warfare.

Models of Soviet disinformation should be made. Current news could be fed into the model to correct it until its forecasting becomes more reliable. If it turns out that an increasing pattern is for communist Third World shortwave radio broadcasts to accuse the United States of spreading new diseases from airplanes, then a counter move would be to find out what new diseases are occurring and broadcast information about how they began, spread, and can be cured, so that it would be too late for disinformation to have the sought effect on the public. The idea is use information as a preemptive strike.

This requires a far more anticipatory posture for the U.S. Information Agency than it has ever had. Forecasting is a complex and controversial art. There are may ways to take the analysis from here. But this gives you the beginning steps and the general idea of forecasting disinformation in order to counter before the impact in public opinion.

Another approach is for the international media to report each day on the juiciest piece of disinformation as sort of a vaccination of consciousness. This should also be a priority for the U.S. Information Agency.

Since it is often true that the best defense is a good offense, a more positive approach to Information Age defense should be considered as well. Opponents could be challenged to be more open, by stripping away unnecessary obstructions to friendship, becoming more responsive to their people, and sharing information. President Reagan's challenge to tear down the Berlin Wall and President Gorbachev's challenge for the two nations to develop a joint landing on Mars are examples of this kind of approach. President Nixon missed such an opportunity when we landed on the moon. Instead of saying, in effect, gee wiz isn't America great, he could have dramatically invited all nations to work with America to build an international civilization in space.

What agency should lead the Information Age defense? Parts of it should be handled by the Department of Defense, the CIA, the State Department, USIA, USAID, and the National Security Agency. Policy coordination for the President should be handled by the National Security Council, yet what agency should have overall responsibility? There are more parts of the puzzle to consider.

Alternative to MAD and SDI

Mutual Assured Destruction (MAD) meant you would be deterred from attacking because you cannot survive the counterattack from your opponent. Each side was essentially saying "If you shoot, I'll destroy your country." The Strategic Defense Initiative (SDI) or Star Wars meant "If you shoot, I'll destroy your bullet in mid-flight." You would be deterred from attacking because you cannot affect your opponent. The alternative is Jam All Strategic Systems (JASS): "If you shoot, your bullet will not be fired because I have jammed your trigger."

There are a variety of ways to deploy JASS. One is to imbed "dark programs" in the opponent's computers. For example, you could write a computer program to "eat" or destroy all programs in a computer. Such a dark program could be implanted in part of a computer chip so that it is not detectable. The chips with the dark program could be part of Japanese computers sold to the Soviets for their submarine forces. When the command to fire went through the Japanese computer chip on the Soviet submarines, the dark program would be activated and destroy the computer's programming. Alternatively, if hostilities were imminent, a satellite signal could activate the program. (This should not be confused with the 1987 sale of a Japanese computer that could help the Soviets design better turbines for their submarines.)

A variation on this is the use of computer viruses. These came to light in 1988 when a computer virus infected the U.S. Department of Defense's Advanced Research Projects Agency computer network. Although it was a harmless program, the principle can be applied more destructively. Like the above dark program, the virus would destroy the opponent's programs, but unlike the dark program, it would not be implanted on the chip. Instead intelligence agents who have access to an opponent's core computer systems would add the virus when needed.

Another method would be to use agents to put jamming equipment in critical locations in the opponent's military communications links. This equipment could be activated by satellite signals. Similarly, devices could be placed at critical points in national electric grids that could cause shorts when activated by satellite signals.

Won't the opponent find these dark programs and jamming equipment? Yes, but they can be replaced in new configurations, leaving the aggressor unsure of the reliability of attack forces. Hence, aggression would be deterred because of uncertainty. JASS has both the advantage of being a deterrence and a defense strategy.

When you consider how much money goes into MAD and how much is proposed to go into SDI, it becomes clear that for far less money a great deal of JASS can be deployed. And it does seem to be the next logical step in the definition of deterrence.

DOD photo of artist's concept of SDI hypervelocity gun

Defense and Arms Control Negotiating Points

A new triad will begin to take shape: (1) information defense; (2) JASS; and (3) joint projects. Information defense will be increasingly necessary as warfare moves from things to ideas. It is possible that the Soviet Union may one day adopt a less aggressive posture as has its communist neighbor, the People's Republic of China. But until that happens, this leg of the triad will see the most action.

JASS will be necessary for holding nuclear and more conventional attacks within the confines of the aggressor's territory. It is the most forward of forward defensive strategies. Even if we eventually get rid of strategic nuclear arms, the advances in long-range accuracy and stealth technology make a non-nuclear strategic capability possible. JASS is a response to a future "shooting war" scenario, whereas information defense is a response to a perceptual war scenario.

The joint projects leg of the triad has the most potential for transforming destructive behaviors. These are projects that would involve primarily the United States and the Soviet Union, but they could and should involve other major powers as well. Preferred projects are those that would consume capital and labor that had previously been dedicated to purely military purposes.

Imagine a 50-year business plan for the global economy including the development of outer space that is jointly created and coordinated by OECD (the Organization for Economic Cooperation and Development) and Comecon (the Soviet and its allies' common market). Any enterprise needs a business plan. Today we talk about a global economy, but there is no real capability to manage it as if it were an integrated economic system. From such a 50-year business plan, many joint projects could be identified and carried out.

Many scientists and engineers that work on weapon systems are also qualified for work on such potential joint space projects as a mission to Mars, space manufacturing, solar energy satellites, orbital habitats, space farming, and pharmaceuticals production. The Soviets have little space shuttle experience and the Americans have little heavy lift vehicle experience. These two capabilities combined in a single project are necessary for serious space industrialization. Each side will have to duplicate the other's advantages if they go it alone.

The cost of space development is becoming too high for any single nation to keep up the momentum. The United States should create in cooperation with its key allies (Japan and Europe via the European Space Agency) a single allied space program. To some degree this is the case with the current program of the space station, in that plans were prepared together and funding is shared. The Soviet Union is doing the same with its allies. The next step is to create joint programs that all nations can support. The private sector should have it's own international cooperation system that works in concert with these transgovernmental programs.

The United States has repeatedly said that it would share the SDI with the Soviet Union. The Soviets oppose testing of SDI in orbit. An interesting joint project would be to have joint American and Soviet testing of space-based strategic defenses in orbit. This might even lead to a more international SDI or to the realization that SDI may not be needed if such cooperation in joint orbital testing is carried out. But then again, that's the point of the third leg of the new triad for defense.

As a side note on the notion of an international SDI, the only strategy that ever made for peace in the war game simulation called "Guns and Butter" was such an international strategy. In 1970, I played this game to a peaceful stalemate. The simulation has about five teams representing imaginary countries and is played through a series of negotiation rounds for trade, weapons, food, industrial capability, and financial assets. It is rigged to show how war breaks out.

My team's approach was to make as many deals as possible during each round. We also negotiated a percentage of each deal to be given to an international authority in the form of weapons that would be automatically used against any first strike by any team. Within three rounds there was more destructive capability within the international authority than any single player. On the third round, one team did attack and got wiped out.

This left the game in a peaceful stalemate, much to the consternation of the game's designer. Granted, war games do not a reality predict, but they do give us useful ideas. Although we did not have "international SDI" in our vocabulary then, it or some international police force was nevertheless the only winning move ever created in that simulation.

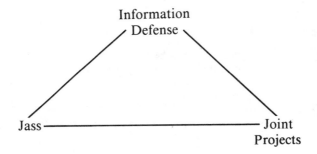

Information
Defense

Jass ———————————— Joint
Projects

New Defense Triad

Military terrestrial and space communications systems could gradually be used for international telecommunications for the development of space as well as to speed up development and trade on earth. The integration of INTELSAT, U.S., and U.S.S.R. military satellites would make an international nervous system that could send signals anywhere at a reduced cost. Communications systems are to future development what canals and roads were to previous development. Just as there is one global interconnected system of airlines, airports, and control towers with procedural agreements, humanity needs a global interconnected system of satellites, earth stations, and software with procedural agreements.

The World Meteorological Organization (WMO) is a good step in this direction. It currently links satellites of the United States, Soviet Union, India, Japan, and Europe for global weather intelligence.

Joint projects could also be created to utilize the great logistic skills of the military to assist relief and economic development work in the Third World. Few civilians are aware of the extent and skills in education, training, and medicine that the military possesses. These too could be used in joint projects.

Instead of Soviet ships blocking the harbor in Ethiopia to Western ships filled with food aid, the Soviets could join hands with the Americans to deliver the relief supplies. Joint projects could be created to develop the irrigation systems, seed banks, improved farming practices, and reforestration needed to prevent such starvation in the future.

Similarly, a regional joint economic development project could be created for Central America. This could be the second step to the

Contadora process that would guarantee a peaceful transition in the region. The Soviets are spending $500 million a year in Nicaragua. If that was converted to regional economic development and matched by America, then a $1 billion annual regional development program could produce quite an impact.

Such joint projects can serve as incentives to enforce treaties. If arms are not reduced on schedule or infractions occur, then certain joint projects are off. A joint mission to Mars might be the last one to be called off; the Central American regional development project would be the first.

Along with such high-profile government joint projects, joint manufacturing projects with the private sector will increase. This is risky for American business, because the Soviet joint venture partner is state enterprise, which is more subject to political manipulation. However, American firms would be able to get political insurance for such joint ventures from the Overseas Private Investment Corporation as they add the U.S.S.R. to their list to protect losses due to politics. Sweden has already begun charting this new territory. According to Hans Stahle, the Chairman of the Swedish Committee for the Promotion of Trade with the U.S.S.R., "Today we understand cooperation as going beyond trade. It includes the joint manufacture of products and exchange of technologies."

An additional incentive for keeping to the treaty could be the threat of SDI deployment. The United States should announce that if there is an infraction, it will begin to deploy SDI and only stop when the infraction is corrected. It should further announce that those elements deployed during the time of infraction will be kept even after the infraction is corrected. Unfortunately, America is rarely able to stick to such subtle and long-range policy balancing with a Congress that changes its mind over time.

We will soon find out if the joint project leg of the future defense triad is at all viable. Secretary Gorbachev stated his interest in a joint mission to Mars at a press conference at the Soviet Embassy during the Washington Summit in 1987. If the U.S.S.R. surprisingly replaces robots with humans in the announced 1994 mission to Phobos and drops a shuttle to the Martian surface, then it is back to cold war and nuclear deterrence all over again.

Meanwhile, the Center for Soviet-American Dialog in the United States and the Soviet Peace Committee in the U.S.S.R. have sponsored annual conferences to identify joint projects to be carried out by citizens. In February, 1988, they brought together 100 Soviets selected by the Soviet Peace Committee and 600 Americans in Alexandria, Virginia. The caliber of the Soviet delegates was superior to that of the American delegates showing that the Soviets have taken this venture more seriously than the Americans. This "Citizens Summit" identified 120 joint projects, such as computer network classrooms, joint book publishing, and conferences on business joint ventures. They are not on the scale of government joint projects, but they do serve to simulate the eventual acceptance of the joint project leg of the new defense triad.

Terrorism and Proliferation of Force

According to the RAND corporation, terrorism is growing 10 to 12 percent annually. At this rate we can expect three incidents per day by the year 2000. Fortunately, only about 18 percent involve fatalities. Nevertheless, that would mean that there would be a terrorist murder every other day in the year 2000.

Terrorists might resort to chemical warfare (like stealing laboratory-created diethylnitrosourea or ENU, which causes infertility and mutations in offsprings) and threaten to put certain materials in public water supplies. One pound of deuterium-tritium for fusion-based energy production releases energy the equivalent of 10,000 tons of coal. Unfortunately, this is a cheap way to get neutrons that could become bombs, and hence all the hijacking problems of fission may still be with us even if we move to fusion energy.

The Stinger missile has shown that the individual can be more powerful than armed fighter planes. In the past, people have bought weapons previously available only to the military. Will individuals in the future shoot down civilian aircraft with Stinger missiles purchased on some black market?

The American approach to deterrence of terrorism by not negotiating was set back by the Iran arms deal in the mid-1980s. An alternative approach proposed by Edna Coffin Choo of Ft. Lauderdale, Florida, in an August, 1980, letter to the editor of *World Press Review,* suggests the following:

Pass a law that any organization whose main aim is destruction, arson, bombing, kidnapping, or the like, shall be termed a conspiracy and, if necessary, include stiffer penalties for this kind of conspiracy; and two, the moment such an organization takes public responsibility for any such deed arrest every person known to be a member and charge each one with conspiracy. It should not be necessary to find actual perpetrators to make the charges stick.

This may have some deterrence effect, but it might also get groups to lie about intention or simply keep changing their name. Less ethical governments might also use this approach as an excuse to eliminate political opposition. Nevertheless, it should be given serious consideration.

When Soviet citizens were kidnapped by terrorists in Lebanon, the U.S.S.R. captured and began killing members of the terrorist group until the captured Russians were let go. No Soviets have been captured since that event. Such a response may be repugnant, but it is the most successful deterrence to further terrorism. Unfortunately, the political evolution necessary for governments to act more responsively toward their citizens and other nations that would diminish the root causes of terrorism will not be completed quickly. In the meantime, repugnant measures will be necessary.

Nuclear power is also moving into more hands. Currently the nuclear club includes the U.S., U.S.S.R., U.K., France, China, and some believe Israel and South Africa. Although the International Atomic Energy Agency is supposed to enforce the Non-Proliferation Treaty that states that nations with nuclear weapons are not to give this capability to nonnuclear nations, we may see Pakistan, Brazil, Iraq, and Argentina get the bomb before the year 2000. Treaties have not always prevented problems in the past. So this cannot be the only prevention strategy of nuclear proliferation. Maybe the superpowers will keep others in check; maybe the progress on arms reduction between the U.S. and U.S.S.R. will change the international climate for proliferation; and maybe preemptive attacks like Israel's on Iraq's nuclear facilities will prevent future nuclear proliferation. But we cannot be certain.

A more satisfactory approach will slowly evolve as we integrate consciousness and technology. As mentioned earlier the world is becoming an electronically interconnected system of Conscious Technology. Many functions of embassies could be automated like telebank terminals today to make a telepresence embassy of tomorrow. This could reduce the number of overseas personnel vulnerable to terrorists' actions and hence reduce the scope of the security problem.

Surveillance satellites make it increasingly difficult for surprises, be they from superpower attacks, terrorism, or nuclear proliferation. Information collection about threats opens our consciousness about real threats rather than false threats. Lt. Col. Stan Rosen of the U.S. Space Command has said that SDI may teach us that there is no technological solution to preventing wars; however, "technology can turn on the lights in the fairly dimly lit room that contains the real threats to our security."

Television cameras have become a key weapon for terrorists. It may be time to use television and a whole range of other technologies to expose threats before they become problems. In the next chapter it is argued that privacy and secrecy will increasingly be an illusion. But this need not mean a centralized government spying on the masses. Instead it can be an interactive and decentralized set of conscious technologies that convinces potential aggressors that something and someone will always be aware of their plans and will be exposed long before they could succeed. Hence, friendlier relations with positive information flows would become the only logical and reliable way for national security.

Improved consciousness improves technology, which again improves consciousness. R&D will be vital to the more complex products of the 21st century. Unique to the information economy: the producer can still own the product after its sale. Information does not have to travel to a market center; through T.O.K., the entire world market revolves around the individual, who is therefore more selective in dealings with others. Proliferation of ways to penetrate electronic data storage and monitor communications will force us to become honest, and honesty is the key to information reliability and quality control. Management by understanding. Network and flextime work systems tied to corporate goals. Quality-oriented performance and sensible time management. In occupations most vulnerable to obsolence, labor unions could work with government and management to train employees for newer jobs to guarantee and perhaps increase income and dues. Employee stock ownership, and sales and supply cooperatives. Savings rates will increase as baby-boomers age. Smart investments for 2000 C.E. include genetic engineering, education, and financial conglomorates. Some sources for keeping up with the staggering new commercial possibilities in space.

Chapter Ten
Business and Economics

Products and services that tend to merge consciousness and technology will be the focus of post-Information Age economic growth. We are already seeing the success of enterprises that make houses, assembly lines, and machines appear more conscious as they add computer chips and voice recognition and synthesizers to their design. Similarly, the sales of artificial biology jumped to over $1 billion with 3 million implants in 1983 and 3.6 million implants, according to the most recent data, in 1985. Those that merge these two growth areas will be the corporate giants of the 21st century. It is reasonable to expect that some multinational corporations will grow to incredible size by the year 2000 with over $50 billion in annual sales and a million employees.

New Origins of Wealth

Mystics teach that wealth is created in the human mind. Technocrats teach that technology is the source of wealth. Today we can deliberately speed up the interplay of technology and consciousness through such phenomena as intelligent computer-assisted instruction, expert systems, and many other approaches identified earlier in the technology chapters. Improved consciousness improves technology, which in turn improves consciousness. This feedback loop is accelerating and will become quite profitable.

In the meantime, people still think in terms of a fixed pie economy.

They believe there is just so much to go around, as if it were you or me over the last drop of oil. Some think in terms of an expanding pie economy. Each sector can grow as we get more efficient and compete to develop new markets. But few think in terms of the invention of wholly new pies or new kinds of wealth.

New wealth is created by putting two or more things in unique combinations that people want. One way to find unique combinations is to apply the universal principles found in one system to another system. Space research and development's (R&D's) dual focus of biology and physics gave us some inkling of how new kinds of wealth can be generated as this hybrid R&D spun out thousands of new products creating more wealth than it consumed.

According to the Midwest Research Institute, the $25 billion spent by NASA on R&D from 1959 to 1969 returned $52 billion to the economy by 1970 and $181 billion by 1987. A Chase Econometric Associates' study showed that $1 billion added to NASA's R&D budget each year for 12 years will add $144 billion to the U.S. economy over those 12 years, and will become a net profit to the U.S. Treasury by the ninth year.

Although NASA has been a valuable stimulus to business and economic growth, its scope is narrower than the interplay of all consciousness and technology; hence, it is reasonable to assume that putting these two factors in new combinations will create far more in the 21st century per investment dollar than did the space program in the latter part of the 20th century.

We will have solved the basic economic problem of food, shelter, and clothing for all of humanity in this generation or by the year 2010. The following chapter on economic development in the Third World covers this in more detail. According to the International Monetary Fund, the world economy grew at 2.9 percent in 1985, 3.1 percent in 1986, and 3.3 percent in 1987. The population growth peaked at 2 percent around 1967 and fell to about 1.7 percent by 1986. The late American futurist Herman Kahn predicted that "by the year 2000 perhaps a quarter of mankind will live in emerging post-industrial societies and more than two-thirds will have passed the level of $1,000 per capita . . . and the global population growth rate will drop as low as 1.3%." The world per capita wealth is growing nearly 2 percent per year and that rate should continue to improve for the foreseeable future.

If we accept a U.S. Government forecast of an annual economic growth of 2.4 percent, then the GDP would become $12.9 trillion by 2035. We expect there will be about 320 million Americans by then with a whopping per capita income of $40,000 in 1985 dollars. Continued economic pessimism is not justified and is dangerous, since it tends to make us think short-term and saps the kind of creative energy necessary for truly long-range development.

However, the United States will have to increase its R&D investment to keep this momentum going. At present, it is slipping. In 1986, foreigners registered 45 percent of all U.S. patents. R&D can be thought of as a resource pool from which we draw knowledge for applied research to invent the future. This pool needs to be replenished. About 2.8 percent of the U.S. GNP is spent on R&D, but at least one-third of that is for the military. Japan and Germany spend about the same percentage for R&D, but much less goes to the military. Hence, Japan and Germany spend a higher percentage of their GNPs, on civilian R&D.

But even this is misleading because the U.S. military R&D often spins out into the civilian economy and has the advantage of keeping innovations secret prior to commercialization. Nevertheless, the complexities of the kinds of products and services in the 21st century are more R&D dependent than was the case in the 20th century. This is not a time to be cutting back in this area. There are already signs that Japan may capture America's lead in biotechnology before the end of this century.

In less than a decade, the United States went from the largest creditor nation to the largest debtor nation. What is interesting is that this happened as the U.S. dollar had a high value, meaning that the buying value of the U.S. dollars paid back will be less than borrowed. If this finances a successful adjustment to the U.S. economy, then it will be worth it. There might even be quite a profit since the U.S. currency lost over 40 percent of its value in the mid-1980s.

We must keep in mind the fact that American demographics contributed to the overall indebtednesses. The baby boomers are just buying their first house, adding extra expenses for their new children, and buying that second car. People 30 to 40 years old tend to be in the largest debt for these reasons. The 77 million baby boomers are now in that big debt age range so the nation as a whole is in big debt with little savings. By 1989 America's personal or private debt was about $8 trillion and the U.S. Government debt was about $2.3 trillion. In 10 years or less, we should see substantial gains in savings again and hence investing as well.

The lower dollar during the late 1980s will begin to reverse the trade debt—over half of which could be made up from the $61 billion lost from copyright, patent, and trademark infringements, according to *Chemical Week.*

Intelligence has always been a key factor in creating wealth. In the past, intelligence was in the hands of only the few. But with the advent of expert systems, computer communications, and the TOK, intelligence can be distributed worldwide giving more people the ability to make more wealth.

Unique Characteristics of the Information Economy

According to Michael Marien in *Futures*, October 1977, Arthur J. Penty and Ananda K. Coomaraswamy first used the term "Post Industrial" in their book *Essays in Post Industrialism* in 1914. The American futurist Daniel Bell developed the concept during the 1960s and 1970s at Harvard University and brought it to a larger audience in his book *The Coming Post-Industrial Society,* published in 1973.

International telecommunications revenues were $95 billion by 1987, according to the American research firm Fost & Sullivan, and they expect it to grow 5 percent a year or to $155 billion by 1996. Nearly 80 percent of the U.S. work force is in services and over half are information and knowledge workers. The information economy has some unique characteristics. The producer can still own the product after sale. Even if I were to do a proprietary study or classified research, my knowledge and wisdom generated during the study will be applied to future work. If you give a speech and receive money for it, you can still give the same speech for another client. The more you circulate information and the more you get feedback, the more your information will achieve value.

If you took a Bell System telephone made by Western Electric and any TV set and threw them against the wall, only the telephone would be working. Why? You own the TV set and until recently Bell continued to own the telephone. It was in Bell's self-interest to make it nearly indestructible so that repair costs would be kept down.

It was also in Bell's interest to reverse planned obsolescence, by programming future capabilities into the phone with the asterisk and pound sign on either side of the "0" for future use of the telephone as a computer terminal. Because it would cost Bell money to replace telephones, the future was programmed into them. TV manufacturers no longer own the TV set after you buy it, and they make more money by selling more and more sets. Now we see that the quality of telephones is becoming like the quality of TV sets as people are buying them rather than paying for communications access.

In the agricultural and industrial economies, once you sold your product, you no longer owned it. There is not the same cumulative economic value as in the information economy. Information expands as it is used, unlike agricultural or industrial products.

Another interesting characteristic of the information economy in the telecommunications age is that you are the center of a world market. In the agricultural and industrial economies, you had to travel to the market. The market was the center around which people revolved. The information revolution means that you are the center and world markets electronically revolve around you. You can communicate with the world via the TOK, which means that the whole world could be in your potential market.

In the agricultural and industrial ages you couldn't travel very far to the market and hence, the number of people in your potential market was severely limited. You were forced to produce what your neighbors wanted to buy, whether or not you wanted to make it. But with worldwide telecommunications access, the total population is potentially within your reach. You will have a greater chance to engage in economic activity that you honestly want to pursue.

As a result, people will not be forced to migrate to new jobs as much as they used to. Also, an aging workforce is less inclined to move. And in fact, people are beginning to slow their rate of moving. In the 1960s, 20 percent of America moved every year. Now it is below 16 percent and may continue to slow. Nearly 10 million Americans were telecommuting to work by 1988, and that number will continue to grow.

Organizational structures are moving from mechanistic hierarchies to market networks. Teleconferencing and electronic offices may not cut down on as much work and travel as expected, but they will make the travel and work more effective, since preparation and follow-through will be improved.

As we have shifted into a service and information economy, it appeared that the productivity of this sector of the economy actually went down. It fell 1.2 percent from 1955 to 1970 and fell 0.7 percent from 1970 to 1985. Although service productivity is now showing gains in the late 1980s, these statistics should not be taken too seriously since we do not know how to measure service producitivity. Should it be more people served per work hour? If so, then educational productivity would go down as the teacher–student ratio goes down. Should it be profit per employee? If so, then how can public employees' work be measured?

However such measurements are finally made, the maturing of computer networks and intelligent expert software integrated into the TOK will result in productivity gains as we move into the 21st century. In addition, competition will become stronger in trade, financial, health, and educational industries forcing productivity gains. Productivity gains in these areas will be key to overall economic growth, since this industry accounts for the majority of human activity.

Why Honesty and Friendship Will Count

Economic relationships will become increasingly based on friendships and personal associations. Because the world market electronically revolves around you, you can be choosier about whom you trade with. It might as well be with the people you like and can count on. You can follow your curiosity through the global communications systems of your TOK and leave a trail that you can analyze to find what you are naturally drawn towards. You can then cross-reference this analysis with feelysis, as explained earlier in this book, to narrow the scope and promote to that market.

How many people do you think will buy your products, services, or conversations? Find out. If only 1,000 people out of a population of 6 billion in the year 2000 or 0.0001 percent of the world would buy, they each would have to buy $100 worth over the course of a year to give you a $100,000 gross income. Are there 1,000 people in the world that would value your services or products over the course of a year at $100? If so, you could make a living doing what you really enjoy for those you really like.

It is true that megacorporations will continue developing global mass markets and that we will experience rapid shifts of opinion and buying behavior within days and hours because of instantaneous worldwide communications. The 1987 stock market crash occurred nearly simultaneously in Europe, Asia, and North America. The tainted Tylenol episode shows how within a day sales ceased and then eventually returned to normal. Such shifts will continue and increase.

But this does not contradict another trend of increasing fragmentation and specialization of markets. The world is growing big enough for both trends to continue. People react to mass marketing with a demand for uniqueness in products, such as clothing and art, and in services, such as newsletters and clubs. As we were both nationally and locally conscious before, we will become more internationally conscious and individually dedicated to uniqueness to show individuality. Our desire to express ourselves uniquely with friends regardless of location will increasingly become more fulfilled.

Honesty could similarly become more common. It may have to become more common because privacy and information security may be impossible to guarantee in the future. With metal detectors in airports, voice stress analysis on telephones, infrared photography, shotgun microphones, and spy dust, privacy is a maybe proposition. If we can get the private notes of President Reagan on the Iranian arms deal, why do we think we can keep our notes safe?

As more private and secret information is computer stored, analyzed, and electronically communicated, more and more ways will be created to penetrate it, until the day may come when we have to surrender and become honest. If you can't do that, then good luck keeping ahead of the clever analysts and code breakers. According to *Omni* magazine, you could tap anyone's phone for $50,000 if you get a spectrum analyzer, a multichannel analog tape recorder, a van with an antenna, a translator from microwave frequency to a standard frequency, a microcomputer, and a dial pulse decoder.

Industrial Age pollution has cost nearly $1 trillion dollars to clean up. Had we known ahead of time, we might have cut this inflationary factor through improved design. Pollution in the information economy is dishonesty, sloppy thinking, and data pollution (too much is disorganized, unreliable, and unwanted). Good old-fashioned honesty with clarity of thought and expression in a understandable framework is the key solution. Pollution in the Conscious Technology economy will consist of imbalances in the effectiveness of feedback loops between consciousness and technology. The solutions to this are the many suggestions throughout this book.

As mechanical standardization was necessary for efficiency in the industrial economies, so too honesty is necessary for efficiency in the information economies. If people made up their own measurements for them, screws and bolts would not fit other machines and hence would not sell. The adherence to data, information, and intelligence standards of honesty will also be necessary to fit into other information systems. One unreliable data base in a data bank will lose clients.

Another reason honesty may become more in vogue is that increasingly information is the product. Honesty is the key to information product reliability and quality control. In the industrial economy you could lie like crazy as long as your physical product was good. But if you lie in the information economy, your clients have reason to distrust your information product.

Because we are more likely to continue to own our information product and sell access to it, it would make no sense to put lies into our own information property. Honesty is an important characteristic in the information product as freshness is to the agricultural product. We have to continue to be honest about that product so that more people will buy access. We also will improve our product by honestly listening and responding to market feedback to keep improving the information product and thereby keep and acquire clients.

Since our consciousness will increasingly become the technology that produces future wealth, we may come to agree with the Egyptian mystic Hamid Bey: "When we find inner, causal reality which produces external conditions and situations, we will see that it is inevitable that we love our neighbors as ourselves and do unto others as we would have others do unto us, and that this law of righteousness is really the law of self-preservation." Such mystic attitudes will become increasingly pragmatic and prudent.

With the advent of two-income families, time has become a more precious commodity. Videotape recorders, electronic financial services, and flextime have allowed the individual to have better control over when and where activities are done. This forces us to be more honest with ourselves and should have a spill-over effect in our other economic transactions.

Management by Understanding

Organizational structures are moving from mechanistic hierarchies to market networks, as documented in *Mastering Change* by Leon Martel and *The New Capitalism* by William Halal. This shift requires a new kind of management. If everyone in the world eventually gets the same advanced technology access, then human resources and the management behind the high-tech will be the key to future success.

Management by understanding integrates a variety of management approaches. The essence of management by understanding is to shift to the optimal management style for each situation. Management by understanding is sometimes by strategic forecasting, sometimes by objectives, sometimes by exception, sometimes by budget, sometimes by opportunities, sometimes by intuition and leadership, sometimes by procedure and policy, but it always makes sure that everyone understands the whole, so that each person is motivated to do his or her part and knows which management style is optimal for a given situation.

New branch managers would be managed by procedure and policy. Those with consistently excellent performance would be managed by exception. Those with mixed performances would be managed by a combination of budget and objectives. Senior management should employ strategic management of the overall enterprise, by allocating resources to take advantage of both the cyclical and structural changes forecasted for their business environment. As much as possible, management should pay employees on the basis of a combination of individual performance measures and corporate sales.

Futurist Robert Theobald has identified four necessities for a system to survive. These can be applied to any management-by-understanding approach:

1. Accurate movement of information (honesty)
2. Some parts of the system willing to bring about change when needed (responsibility)
3. No part of the system trying to take over the rest of the system (humility)
4. No part of the system trying to preserve its exact place in the system, but each willing to be flexible as conditions change (love)

According to Dr. Martin Weitzman of MIT, paying by performance or bonus at the end of the year could reduce unemployment. If sales go down, the company could lower prices to increase sales and recapture the market, but if wages are fixed, this is impossible. Because unions don't want flexible salaries, companies have to lay off people when times are difficult. If pay was based on corporate income, then people would not have to be laid off as a result of cycles in the market and recessions. (There have been 43 American recessions and recoveries since the signing of the U.S. Constitution.) About 25 percent of Japanese industrial workers' income is based on such a system, helping to guarantee jobs rather than fixed income.

Just as income should be based on individual performance and corporate sales, time at work should be based on job requirements and the personal preferences of the employee. We all don't have the same peak hours during the 24-hour day. As much as 15 percent of the American workforce is on flextime. Why not go all the way to a 24-hour society? The 9 a.m. to 5 p.m. work schedule is incompatible with a 24-hour earth in an increasing global economy. And why crowd all together into traffic jams each day at 9 a.m. and 5 p.m.?

Worker loyalty might appear to be difficult, if not impossible, to maintain in such network and flextime systems. However, work will be tied to corporate goals, if performance toward those goals determines income.

Qualitivity

It is commonly believed that the key problem in the US economy is productivity. Economists argue that when Americans focus on recapturing the lead in engineering and manufacturing skills necessary to produce a product economically, all will be well again. It is correct that manufacturing productivity needs drastic improvement, but the future global market will demand more than low-cost mousetraps.

The Conscious Technology view is critically important here for problem-and-solution analysis and the notion of "qualitivity" or the increase in quality per worker hour of production. Conscious Technology is a world view that breaks through sloppy perception and thinking by balancing utilitarian and aesthetic considerations. Japan has recognized this for centuries and uses mystical exercises and attunement prior to work. Findhorn is an experimental community in Northern Scotland that regularly has its members "attune" in small groups prior to beginning work. They hold hands and silently reflect on the work to be done, the people with whom they will be doing the work, and the tools at hand. As those three become one in their awareness, they squeeze hands and begin the job. Their working relationships and qualitivity is such to attract people from around the world.

It has been fashionable to think that if a nation lowered its currency value, it would not need to improve its productivity. It seemed easier to the IMF to recommend devaluations to improve trade rather than to improve productivity, which would take longer. But that is a shortsighted view. If a country improved its qualitivity, it would be able to keep its currency steady without the need to resort to lowered prices, since its products would improve in value and would reduce in cost of production. Complacency is the economic enemy, not the value of currency.

According to the American Productivity Center, American business churns out 190 billion pages every day. That's over 800 pages for every man, woman, and child in the United States every day. Productivity? Yes, but it is also information overload and poor qualitivity. A study by the University of Pittsburgh found that 40 percent of all library acquisitions are never used.

Until qualitivity becomes successful, here are some suggestions on self-defense against information overload:

1. Try to touch incoming paper or see electronic mail only once.

2. Have categories in which to put good ideas you will want later.

3. Continually ask yourself time management expert Allan Leiken's question: "What is the best use of my time, right now?"

4. Separate the noise from the signal; that is, if you are not sure you will need it, throw it out or delete it from your computer.

5. Bargain. If someone wants you to give your opinion on a paper, have that person do some other information synthesis that you need.

6. What is constant, what changes, what constantly changes? Just keep track of the trends and cutting edge. If information simply reinforces trends that you already know, stop reading, throw it out. Read what you don't know relative to your goals.

7. Don't tell people what they already know and insist others do the same.

8. Ask whether knowing this will be of lasting value or temporary value? Follow the wisdom trail, and leave trivial information fads for people who like information overload and indigestion. Constantly try to move data to information, information to intelligence, and intelligence to wisdom.

9. Meditate to allow the mind to synthesize the leaning and meaning of the day.

10. Is information from a primary or secondary source? Misinformation or false information will slow you down. Call the author on the telephone. Stick to the source. Cross-reference everything until you know who is reliable for what.

11. Both reason and feelings can deceive you when used alone. Use each to check the other. When both modes agree, great; when they do not, hold the information in abeyance.

12. Stay away from people who waste your time, are not accurate, and are too verbose.

13. Control when you give and receive information.

14. Attempt to make your responses brief and to the point. Avoid

the temptation of putting in extra fluff to make things impressive.

15. Find key people and have them do your reading for you. Note their subjectivity and correct accordingly.

16. Use situation/management display boards.

17. Look at your situation from the point of view that you have already died. What is important?

18. Do it on one sheet of paper (unless writing a book).

Expert systems will improve qualitivity by simulating the best of our consciousness into our computer technology and making it available to those with less experience. Hence, we will have distributed the best of our engineering to a larger public and shared the ability to easily update design breakthroughs and make unique modifications faster. By 1990 the sale of such artificial intelligence software may reach $1.2 billion and grow to $5 billion in the foreseeable future.

Linking such computer expert programs with robot manufacturing and remote computer communications will allow the customer's very specific requirements to be met. This has the advantages of the economies of scale reached in automation and individual quality control reached by individual attention.

New Life for Labor Unions

Labor unions are losing membership and respect because they have no vision. They cling desperately to the strike as their only lever of power even when membership may not be interested in a strike. The NABET (National Association of Broadcasting Employees and Technicians) strike against NBC television in 1987 that lasted 17 weeks is a case in point.

According to NABET member Max Gratzl, all of the members he knew were quite pleased with the new contract offered by management and were never directly asked if they were in favor of the strike. Even though members were not given money from a strike fund, they were subject to fines if they didn't picket. Prior to contract negations with NBC, NABET members were polled to authorize the union negotiating committee to negotiate. This included the pro forma unilateral power to call a strike, but issues for negotiation were never mentioned. According to Gratzl, "This meant that the union was legally able to strike even though the membership may not have wanted to. The strike was over union prestige, because there was a clause in the contract that said that this contract would not be binding on any future owner." The strike was called just after CBS and ABC had laid off many people, who could and did easily fill the positions along with management personnel. As a result, NABET is weaker after the strike, since NBC got along quite well without the union labor. As the strike wore on, the union finally polled the membership on the issues and asked whether they wanted the strike to continue. The membership voted to end the strike and shortly thereafter NABET and NBC reached a settlement.

In the past, it was valuable to organize power to force management to improve working conditions and wages. These efforts have been successful. Now it is time for a new purpose: guaranteed income rather than continuity of a job. Labor unions should forecast job requirements in each local area and the nation as a whole. Jobs should be listed from most secure to most likely to become obsolete. Those union members that are on the most endangered list would get first priority to receive union training funds for the new jobs coming up.

In this way labor unions could become the engines to recycle their members into new jobs. They would be in a better position to guarantee income if not maintaining the same jobs for their members.

Let's say Joe is a union member on an assembly line. The union has estimated that Joe's job has a life expectancy of three years. Joe goes to his local union and is given a list of the most likely growth jobs and their skill requirements. Joe picks out a job category and is told what the training requirements are, where he can get the training, what the costs will be, and what companies are most likely to do the hiring. Joe calls the personnel offices of each of the companies to confirm that the job requirement is likely to come up, what percentage of the training they will pay if he agrees to work for them, and which training programs they prefer he take.

The union ends up paying one-third of the training cost, the state pays one-sixth, the company pays one-sixth, and Joe pays one-third. The training program starts six months later, meets once a week in the evening, and has three phases that take one and a half years to complete. Joe gets his job with the new company one year before the three-year union estimate that he would be laid off. He does not lose a week of salary. The new job pays him sufficiently more than his training cost, which is made up in six months, and the union keeps a paying member, now paying dues at a higher amount than before.

Joe's new job has a four-year life expectancy, but he now knows that in two or three years his job will show up on the endangered list and that he can again go through a training program to get his next job.

This imaginary scenario is possible. Labor unions can strike a new deal with management and government to get commitments on training funds and the best available information on the changing labor market. They should not give up their role of improving the environment of the work place or of getting reasonable wages for their members. But these old roles are not enough to ensure a future for the labor movement.

The United States was spending $300 billion a year in the mid-1980s for adult education and training. Of this $80 billion is paid by employers and is expected to increase 25 to 30 percent by 1990. One of the reasons for this is the relatively smaller number of people entering the labor market, which forces management to hire substandard employees, which in turn increases training costs.

Management could see labor unions as a partner to make the structural adjustments necessary in the labor force to remain competitive. It is in the government's interest to cooperate both with information and a percentage of training costs to cut the unemployment benefit costs. Each 1 percent of unemployment costs the government $25 billion in payments and lost revenue. This new life for labor unions is in the interests of everyone, since by 1987, as much as 22 percent of all children in America were in families below the poverty level. Such poverty children of the unemployed mean more taxes for remedial education, criminal procedures, and welfare.

An additional role for the unions should be to include employee stock ownership plans for their membership's benefit packages. This approach to involve labor more directly in the ownership of the companies for whom they work, as proposed by Mortimer Adler and Louis Kelso, now covers 10 million Americans. Labor would be able to keep its ownership of the stock, even though workers might move on to new companies with new skills. In this way labor unions would be able to help their members build equity while maintaining their mobility in the changing labor market.

Economic restructuring has really just begun. For example, it is reasonable to assume that the majority of all assembly-line workers today will be replaced by computers and robots by the year 2000. Continual restructuring will have to be faced for the foreseeable future. Added to this, the cyclical changes as distinct from structural changes will make this new role for labor unions the key to their future survival.

Taxes

Doing financial transactions via your TOK will let you pay your taxes at the time of each transaction. This will avoid your once-a-year mad rush in April and help cut back the "tax gap" between what should be paid to government and what is paid to government. Such a practice would also help the government's cash flow position. The government might give some incentive like a percent off your tax rate.

Let's say that you are in a restaurant. Instead of paying the bill in cash or by using your credit card, you simply go to the cashier and speak into a TOK giving your social security number. The TOK switches to a data bank that matches your voiceprint and responds with your name, saying "ready for transaction." You would say "Debit my account (the amount of the check) and credit (the tax identification number of) the restaurant's account." The restaurant's TOK would come back with the restaurant's account credited and tax paid to the government. You would receive confirmation that the bill is added to your business deductions for federal and local tax purposes.

Negotiating Points between Capitalism and Communism

Communism as an economic development theory is falling steadily from world credibility. Recognizing this in 1981, Andropov declaimed on Radio Moscow, "From each according to ability, to each according to success." However, there are some points that can be kept that might help its proponents save some face and hence make it more likely for a more peaceful transformation. Pragmatism is becoming the key ideology to resolve the contradictions between free and controlled market ideologies. We are also engaged in an age of closure. We are deliberately working to close the gaps between the haves and have nots, between the mystic and the technocrat, and between chemistry and physics. Why not between the capitalist and communist?

Collective or group activity is advantageous for cutting the costs of supply. Buying collectives or cooperatives can get great discounts that individuals cannot achieve. Collective activity for sales is also advantageous compared with individual efforts. Small farmers acting alone have no chance to get into international trade. By pooling their produce for large shipments, they can command foreign market attention. Similarly, small businesses may not be able to afford national or international market research and advertising. If they act as a collective for these purposes, they can extend their market penetration.

A third area for collective activity is research and development (R&D). Associations of corporations are forming to handle the really extensive R&D projects that no one corporation wishes to tackle alone. Microelectronics and Computer Technology is one such grouping. Possibly IBM might begin putting out bids or form such an association so that it will be able to keep leadership as we move into the fifth generation of computers for artificial intelligence. This development requires a major research effort across many specialties over a number of years and costing a fortune. If IBM doesn't do it, Japan may walk away with this future key element of Conscious Technology.

When it comes to the actual production of a product, however, individual activity far outperforms collectivization. One percent of the farmland in the U.S.S.R. is available for individual rather than collective cultivation. That 1 percent produces 25 percent of the food consumed in the Soviet Union. The failures of producer cooperatives are legendary in the Third World. The only successful so-called "producer" collective I have ever seen, turned out to be a collective effort for supply and sales, but each member did their own production and received their own income from that production.

Private ownership is also a sticking point between communism and capitalism. Capitalism holds that the consumer or individual citizen has

The first bridges between capitalism and communism will be built in our minds.
Drawing courtesy of Champion.

228   BUSINESS AND ECONOMICS

a right to private property; communism says "the people" via the state is the rightful owner. If the producer retains ownership rather than the state or the consumer, then the specific producer, whether private or state enterprise, reaps the fruit of its labor.

Employee stock ownership plans are another significant method to have workers own the means of production and redistribute society's affluence and consumer power. As mentioned above, this could be one of the benefits that labor unions could foster. Instead of having the state control the means of production on behalf of the people, the people could have control directly through stock ownership.

An employee stock ownership plan is a legal device used by a company to form a trust in the names of its employees. The trust applies for a loan and uses the money to issue new stock shares to pay for capital expansion, advanced robots, and the like. The stock shares are apportioned to employees. As the loan is repaid, these stock shares are released into the personal accounts of the employees.

The political sociologist Kathi Friedman points out that there are enough stock ownership plan variations that the people could indeed own the means to production and the technological wealth that machines produce. Along with the Employee Stock Ownership Plan (ESOP), there are at least three other possibilities: (1) retirement plans could be modified to become Individual Stock Ownership Plans (ISOP) for people not covered by ESOPs such as government workers or the self-employed; (2) consumers of electric utilities, mass transit systems, etc., could be eligible for Consumer Stock Ownership Plans (CSOP); and (3) local community residents could become stockholders in development corporations forming a General Stock Ownership Plan (GSOC).

In each case, the method and rationale is the same: as business modernization occurs, credit is extended to new individuals (as opposed to current stockholders) to become owners of stock in the profitable enterprise. As the enterprise increases its wealth, the loan is repaid, and new individuals become holders of income-producing stock. This is a peaceful approach to decentralizing the wealth of a nation without state control. Such approaches would be superior to the collectivization of communist regimes and the income transfers of the welfare state under more democratic regimes.

Adding collectivization of sales and supply, while reinforcing individual production and ownership, to the ideological arguments between communists and capitalists may help to move the currently destructive conversation off dead-center.

Become an Investor

Unemployment should continue to fall in the Industrialized countries because of the falling rate of entries into the labor force. Employment growth in the United States is nearly 2 percent while the growth of new entrants into the labor force is about 1 percent a year. However, the children of the baby boom or "echo boom" will begin to enter the labor force in 1995. So it is likely that we will see unemployment begin to rise again, especially when the advances in automation are taken into consideration. Hence, we should begin to think about how we will make an income after the year 2000.

Increasingly, our individual income will come from two sources: (1) from our unique products and services for which we have found a global niche and (2) from a variety of investments and types of investments.

Currently, there are 3.4 workers in America for every retired person. That ratio will fall to less than 2 by the year 2035. But this understates the problem because the cash requirements for the elderly will rapidly increase. As income requirements and medical costs increase for the retired, a new age prejudice could become severe. To head this off, the elderly could augment the amount of money they will need from the younger work force.

There is a deep and persistent fear that if we automate everything, we will not be able to earn an income. We have seen automation reduce farmers to 2 percent of the American labor force; 94 percent of Japanese union members polled felt robots will lead to unemployment. Yet any industry that slows the pace of its automation will go out of business. So what to do if the new role for labor unions is not adopted or doesn't fit your circumstances?

One reasonable response is to invest into what replaced you. We could become a nation and eventually a world of investors and think tanks, voting economically for the future we want to live in. Unfortunately today, to invest in, say, Rockwell International you would be investing into their whole corporation. You would be economically voting for both the Space Shuttle and the B-1 bomber. People are becoming far more interested in putting their money into corporations that build what they believe to be a better future, even if the return may not be as high. The success of the Calvert Group is an example of attracting such "socially minded" investors. According to the Social Investment Forum, over $300 billion have been invested by such a criterion.

Imaginative investment houses and corporations will team up so that you could just invest into, say, that cost/income center in Rockwell making the Space Shuttle. With the TOK you might put out a bid saying you want to buy or invest $10,000 in a robot to manufacture Interferon or some new product that you are happy to see succeed. A corporation or new enterprise might be computer-matched with you. Its representatives could respond by saying what they want to do.

The potential investor could transfer money to an escrow account before receiving the corporation's business plan, as a test of sincerity. However, great care will have to be taken to avoid giving easy access to competitive corporate spies. When both the investor and the business are satisfied, a deal could be struck as to the numbers of stocks, equity position, or a loan to the corporation.

The key ideas here are to invest just into that part of the corporation you want, and to be able to send out an announcement saying just what you want to invest into, so that the corporation and brokers compete to get your investment tailored just how you want it. This would be qualitivity applied to investment services.

Some will argue that this is impossible considering the extremely low saving rate of 2 to 5 percent in America during the 1980s. In 1987 it was only 3.2 percent of disposable income. People won't have the money to invest. This is a temporary and predictable condition of demographics, which will be followed by a large increase in the savings rate beginning in the mid-1990s, as explained earlier in this chapter.

The stock market has gone up over 300 percent from 1983 to 1987, completed a full correction by the end of 1988, and seems poised to rise even further. The percentage of Americans' income from investment and savings has doubled in the last 20 years. By 1988, a total of 47 million

American individual investors were in the stock market, with an average of $6,200 per investor. And all this before the big savings increase has begun. This bodes very well for the long-range prospects for the U.S. economy and the individual investor. Even the United Kingdom grew from 6 percent of adult Britains investing in their stock market in 1979 to 20 percent just 10 years later.

Ideally, you should invest in those activities that are more likely to bring about the future you want to experience and that will yield a good return. Good long-range investments will be with ventures that more directly merge technology and consciousness such as those listed earlier in the technology section. Some obvious categories include electronic repair, electronic component replacement chains, automated aquaculture, robotics, bioengineering, bionics, fiber optics, and material sciences.

The American Society of Mechanical Engineers is developing a computer model that should help the investor assess the economics of future technology. When it is ready for the public in the early 1990s, it will be used for the investigation of

1. Return on investment for R&D efforts in a particular area
2. Market and profit potentials of planned new products
3. Appropriate timing for investment in new technology
4. Comparative economic effects of alternative materials, designs, and manufacturing processes
5. Ripple effect from the introduction of new products
6. Optimum return from alternative product mixes
7. Short-term and long-term allocation of resources (human, material, and capital)
8. Productivity of human resources and capital investment
9. Needs for labor, energy, material resources, transportation facilities and pollution control equipment for a new product
10. Competitiveness, nationally and internationally, in quantitative measures

Until this model is available, the following discussion offers some information to whet your long-range investment whistle.

Smart Investments around the Year 2000

As the baby boomers age, vast growth will occur in all forms of medical care and retirement services. Special financial packages, home medical electronic monitoring, anti-aging drugs and treatments, special travel services with medical supervision, retirement and nursing homes, hot meal delivery and home care chains will become the 21st century franchise bonanzas.

The first genetically engineered product to go on sale was a vaccine against a diarrheal disease that kills millions of piglets and calves. It came on the market in 1982 and was offered by a Dutch chemical firm. So you need not limit your investment only to American firms.

We can now patent life. In 1980 the United States Supreme Court agreed that patents could be issued for microorganisms. In 1985 plants were added, and in 1988 mammals were added with the Harvard University's genetically engineered mouse for cancer research. One of the earliest patents on life was awarded to Ananda Chakrabarty of General Electric for the product and process of making bacteria capable of degrading crude oil. This is very effective for cleaning out oil tankers rather than flushing them with seawater and it leaves a digested material useful as a fertilizer for farming.

Plant genetics—rather than fertilizers and pesticides—have led to record crops. Food production will have to go up considerably to ensure a world well fed. Hence, investments in agricultural genetic engineering should prove profitable.

Education may well emerge as the single largest industry before the year 2000. Businesses that develop employee training for the electronic workplace, computer-assisted instruction, and a host of support services for both public and adult education should show sustained growth through the turn of the century.

Technology to "know thyself" will find growing markets, especially when people realize that they can make a living by finding their unique market niche in the global economy.

Electronic games will go international and on-line with computer communications. Some could have pretty dramatic value like those envisioned by the American futurist Buckminister Fuller when he proposed the "World Game." Imagine another one called "Intergalactic" with current players like Rockwell International, McDonnell-Douglas, Grumman, and TRW. Could you imagine Isaac Asimov playing the role of TRW, Gerry O'Neill playing Grumman, and the chief executive officer of a competing aerospace company playing Rockwell in a simulation to write or play out a plausible scenario for a successful economy in outer space? Cash prizes could be paid from a percentage of the income derived from fees to play the game. Winning plays and strategies might make interesting reading in international journals.

Look for big mergers and joint ventures like that of Data General and Nippon Telephone and Telegraph, who are joining together to produce equipment for the Japanese market—even American firms joining Japanese car manufacturers to produce Japanese cars in the United States for export back to Japan. Nine of the ten largest banks are Japanese and 9 percent of American banking assets are owned by Japanese banks, according to the Federal Reserve. These banks are matchmaking joint ventures between companies such as steelmakers like Yamato Kogyo of Japan and Nucor of America.

Such large-scale mergers cover many smaller projects that could prove attractive as investments in subcorporate units as explained earlier. Supermergers help guarantee larger market share and hence more security for the smaller elements within the megacorporate structure. In this way the investor gets the advantage of large size and opportunity to vote economically for a specific project.

Increasingly, First World export will consist of entrepreneurial talent to create joint ventures in the developing world. There is a vast untapped potential for all kinds of development from light manufacturing to oil exploration in enormous areas of Africa and China. Such export of entrepreneurs should not be discouraged. First World economic growth will depend on the growth in buying power of the Third World, buying power that comes only from increasing business and that is the job of the entrepreneur. Innovators could list their projects via the TOK to attract investors worldwide.

One key area for such joint-venture development is in the Arab countries. As many as 250 cities have been created from scratch over the past 50 years in the oil-rich Islamic areas, resulting in an instant renaissance of Islamic architecture and business. There has never been a region that built so much, so fast. Granted, the construction is now slowing down and Japan has replaced OPEC as the largest investor, but there are plenty of opportunities to turn these early infrastructural investments into profits.

Another big area that was opened for joint venture in 1988 is the Soviet Union. A consortium of Kodak, RJR Nabisco, Johnson & Johnson, Ford, Archer-Daniels-Midland, Chevron, and Mercator has formed to develop markets in the U.S.S.R. However, special barter arrangements may have to be devised to get profits converted to hard currency in First World bank accounts. This is done simply by using rubles to buy Soviet products that can be sold in the First World.

A basic trend is developing in the globalization and integration of financial tools and mechanisms—more individuals will make investments anywhere in the world from the privacy of their home computers. This could result in the elimination of traditional exchanges, and will mean increases in computer communications and intelligent expert software which allows users to automate much of their investment research. Companies seeking such investors' money will cooperate to get the basic electronic infrastructures set up and then compete for these investors' dollars.

Americans are well conditioned to play into the world financial markets with more than 70 million credit card holders in the United States alone by 1988. The 50 million Visa and 22.5 million American Express members can access financial power from Timbuktu to Paris. Replacing the plastic card by voice recognition devices will be a welcome evolution. The financial institutions are rapidly sewing up multinational corporate relations to form globally integrated one-stop-shop businesses. Credit card companies, banks, stock brokerages, mail-order houses, real estate firms, insurance companies, telecommunications conglomerates, and various retailers are forging marriages and affiliations to form a one-stop worldwide shopping empire.

Walter Wriston the former head of Citibank, said in the early 1980s that "the financial marketplace today is everywhere, anytime. The parties to the transactions could be anyone with the ability to punch in the right numbers anywhere ... In this kind of world, electronics have become money, credit, securities or savings, and are more real than places."

The Discover Card gives access to Sears, Dean Witter, Coldwell Banker, and Allstate Insurance companies. This new capability will have such power that the investors don't mind losing $150 million to $300 million during the first three years of the introduction of the Discover Card. What return on their investment do you think they expect in the tenth year if they can lose that much to get a hold on this new financially integrated market?

Such giant corporate mergers offer a complete consumer package. People will be expected to start and stay "all the way" with one megacorporation. The megacorporations will try to nurture loyalties just as governments promote nationalism. This could lead to megacorporate wars, albeit less violent than their national counterpart. In any case, they will make great investments for the long term.

About 400 new financial instruments and products were created for the investor between 1985 and 1988. Surely, there has to be some mechanism just right for you.

Economics of Space Industrialization

Some people argue that there is never enough real work for the entire public to be occupied; hence, the creation of temples and tombs during the Ancient Egyptian period. Why not useful projects like migrating to space? Some have suggested that's just what some Egyptians had in mind but the pyramids were the best they could do. Now we have the technology to go, and as explained earlier, space R&D has become a net profit to the U.S. Treasury.

The *National Geographic* cites General Vladimir Shatalov, chief of Cosmonaut training, as claiming that the Soviet Union will earn 50 billion rubles annually by 1990 from space business involving semiconductors and pharmaceuticals. Although the Soviet Union is still testing its Space Shuttle, it does have rockets that can carry up to eight communications satellites and drop them one by one into orbit. This is a feat the American Space Shuttle has yet to match. Even the European Space Agency's Ariane Type 3 rocket launched three satellites from Kourou, French Guiana, on March 12, 1988. Meanwhile, Mir (meaning "peace") was launched in February, 1986, as the basic unit of the Soviet permanent space station. The Soviets have space migration and industrialization as part of their national policy and claim that it will become a major factor in the global economy.

236

For example, photovoltaics depend on major cuts in cost before they can become a factor in our earthly economy. Space manufacturing of solar power satellites that are three miles wide and seven miles long will require "mechanical spiders" to spin the webs of photovoltaics that will also serve to get the economies of scale necessary to reduce costs. These mechanical spiders will roll out microthin sheets that can be tightly packaged and "dropped" back to earth in fire-resistant containers that could splash down in the ocean.

Ironically, the fans of terrestrial solar energy have not embraced the cause of solar power satellites or space manufacturing—the very mechanism that will bring the cost of photovoltaics within reach of the larger market down on earth.

Space tourism will become quite the in thing even for those who cannot afford the $1 million ticket. Imagine a space flight lottery. What percentage of 6 billion people in the year 2000 will pay $10 for a chance of a lifetime? If only 0.1 percent or one out of a thousand people would do it, the space lottery agency could buy a shuttle flight and make a gross profit of $45 million per lottery. More efficient space shuttles will be built in the early 21st century making all this even more attractive.

Contracts have already been given to develop parts of the National Aerospace Plane, which will take off and land from a runway. It will go into test flight around 1994 and become operational around the year 2000. The cost per passenger on the space plane will be greatly reduced from that of the Space Shuttle.

The first space product developed for commercial sale was microscopic latex particles for "standard reference material" used to calibrate sensitive scientific instruments as well as in industrial processes. It is available from the National Bureau of Standards. The zero gravity and zero vibration environment makes it possible to make perfect spheres that are extremely small. They also have such medical applications as measuring the size of pores in the wall of the human eye in glaucoma research or pores in the wall of the human intestine in cancer research.

Understanding all this, India, with one of the poorest GNPs per capita in the world, has the eighth largest space program on earth. It has learned what few seem to comprehend—that space is the best investment a nation can make.

If you want to keep abreast of commercial possibilities in space, you can contact the following NASA Centers for Commercial Development of Space. They occasionally hold seminars for investors.

- Batelle Columbus (Ohio) Laboratories for materials process research in metals and alloys, glass and ceramics, polymers, electronic and optical materials
- The Institute for Technology Development, Jackson, Mississippi, for remote sensing technology
- Consortium for Materials Development in Space, University of Alabama-Huntsville, for commercial materials, including experiments in orbit, commercial applications of physical chemistry, and material transport
- Center for Macromolecular Crystallography, University of Alabama-Birmingham, for space-grown crystals for pharmaceutical, biotechnology, and chemical applications
- Center for Space Processing of Engineering Materials, Vanderbilt University, Nashville, Tennessee, for space processing of metals, alloys, and composite materials
- Center for Development of Crystal Growth in Space, Clarkson University, Potsdam, New York, for a broad spectrum of crystal growth techniques
- Center for Space Vacuum Epitaxy, University of Houston, for semiconductor materials and devices, metallic materials and devices
- Center for Space Automation & Robotics, University of Wisconsin-Madison, for robotic systems to replace many astronaut functions, and development of an automated greenhouse for space food and supply
- Center for Real-time Satellite Mapping, Ohio State University, Columbus, for collection, conversion, and distribution of remotely sensed geographic data

Although people are beginning to realize how much money will be made in space, they do not yet comprehend the staggering diversity of products, from tourism to energy, that will be created in our lifetimes. This medium for new wealth will expand our minds so much that our notion of business in the 20th century will seem at least as primitive to the 21st century as we now see the 19th century.

Economic development plans for third world countries ignored the components of small business and agricultural development. These plans are responsible for the countries' debt crises today, since the infrastructure simply could not pay for them. The United Nations, good at collecting and disseminating information, has not been very good at implementation. Countries in the early stages of development can keep their economies going by barter (which preceded cash transactions in our own early development).

Developing countries are taking control of repayments of debt. Private sector development and privatization of state companies are increasing. It will take less time and money to get developing world communications on a par with advanced nations than to do this with their agricultural and industrial capabilities.

The oceans and surface water on land hold vast potential for aquaculture development. Experiments in the Middle East and other desert areas have shown that they can be made to bloom.

Chapter Eleven
Economic Development in the Third World

It has not yet dawned on the industrialized world that next to the prevention of World War III, Third World economic development is the most important issue facing the future of civilization. The future of humanity is very much a Third World phenomenon. Three out of four humans live in the Third World, as do 90 percent of all people under the age of 15.

With the stark realization of the global implications of the Third World debt crisis, regional wars evolving in the developing world, massive migration and famine in Africa, environmental time bombs inherent in rapid industrialization, massive illiteracy, political instability, and the sheer population explosions in these regions, the richer countries will need to take Third World development far more seriously than they have taken it in the past.

The chart on the next page illustrates the breadth and depth of the issues that when combined show the magnitude of the importance of Third World development for the success of humanity.

Poverty in the developing world is not the same thing as poverty in the industrialized world. Many people in the developing world are grouped in abject poverty by First World analysts, because of low cash income as compared with that of the United States, lack of formal education, or poor access to western medicine. Some will say that by the year 2000 one in four will be in this situation in the urban areas and one in two in the rural areas. As many as 1 billion people do not now have predictable or clean running water.

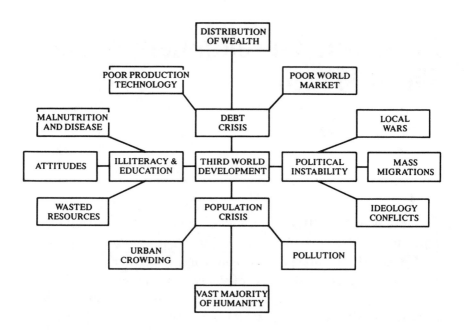

But these people, especially in the rural areas, do not have the poverty consciousness that one might imagine. They have learned how to survive and may well spend the same percentage of time being happy as "rich" people, even though they may spend more time being physically less comfortable. (This, too, will change with the use of the malaria vaccine and other advances in tropical medicine.)

Unlike many in the industrial nations, most in the Third World own their land and house. Their extended family gives them a quality of life that cannot be bought by lonely but richer industrial citizens. The extended family replaces some of the needs for daycare fees, baby sitters, insurance premiums, and other costs of individuals living in purely cash and industrial economies. Financial comparisons are misleading because money is not as necessary for the basics of life as it is in industrial cultures.

Economic Development of the Poor Majority

People who argue that the only salvation for the poorer countries is education and consciousness raising are just as wrong as those who argue that the transfer of technology and money is the only salvation. We need to optimize many tactics into a blended system of consciousness and technology.

The purpose of development is enlightenment. Enlightenment is achieved by the proper balance and merger of the mystic and technocratic views of life. Humans have tended to be more romantic than systematic; and hence, development programs have jumped from one maximizing strategy to the next—rather than striving for an optimum blend of many approaches.

The Marshall Plan worked in Europe and Japan because these cultures already had a business and technological awareness that could absorb and balance the rapid industrial development after World War II. But similar attempts to implement "Third World" Marshall Plans have resulted in the debt crisis today. These poorer countries never had the business and technological awareness necessary to set the proper policies and priorities in order to get the same results as Japan and Germany.

Many believed that simply duplicating the "things of development" like factories, schools, hospitals, and highways would make for success. But how were these countries going to pay for all this? Salaries for doctors and teachers, machine repairs, road maintenance? Where did people think the money was going to come from?

Normally, nations tax business, but there was little business to tax. The majority of taxes in richer countries is paid by small business and people who work for small business. Without a major effort to strengthen and expand the smaller economic activities and the consciousness to manage the technological change, the policy of duplicating the "things of development" was doomed to failure.

If we had done our futures research then, we would have forecast the resulting debt and recommended instead a major effort that would have included small agricultural and industrial development. This would have created the wealth over time that could have afforded these schools and hospitals.

If you consider the amount of money spent on development by the

United Nations and compare that with added real economic growth, you would have to conclude that the U.N. has proven itself to be a poor developer per dollar invested. This was painfully recognized in Sir Robert Jackson's *UN Capacity Study* for the United Nations Development Program in 1970. Solid recommendations were proposed in this study to improve the functioning of the U.N. Development Program, but they were never acted upon. Instead, countless and expensive conferences are held to talk about the problems. U.N. agencies have proven quite valuable for information, but not very effective when it comes to implementation.

Most people in the Third World are subsistence and semi-monetized farmers. Recognizing this fact 20 years ago, President Banda of Malawi preached repeatedly that people should not look to others for wealth, but under their feet. He made heroes of the small farmers and created a national system of buying their production. Today, Malawi is a net exporter of food and has its own foreign food relief program for neighboring Mosambique. One can argue that Malawi gets income and avoids some unemployment problems by exporting labor to South Africa, and that the absence of television prevented false expectations, but the fact remains that the urbanization catastrophe that is apparent in the rest of the developing world didn't occur in Malawi, which focused on village agricultural development.

Leaders that glorified urban workers or by ignoring their village counterparts denigrated the farmer have created a generation that will not dirty their hands in farming and prefer to loiter in overcrowded cities looking for nonexistent jobs.

Kenya's 17 million inhabitants get a half million new "school leavers" a year, which is likely to grow to three-quarters of a million by 1991, who leave with a useless education only suitable for low-level nonexistent civil service jobs. Instead, the education should be geared for survival in their own environment, that is, small-scale agriculture and industrial production.

When children learn arithmetic, they should be taught it in the form of a cash book, so that they can understand how to distinguish between the family and business money. When they are taught to read, they should read stories of how successful people in their country moved from subsistence to surplus. Lesotho is currently making this transition throughout its entire system in the most extensive USAID education project in history.

Hut in Africa

Development projects should build on what is working by finding the "winners" and building around them their way. For example, Dominica, essentially a one-crop country, had its bananas wiped out two years in a row by hurricanes. The obvious answer was to get small farmers to diversify. Instead of bringing in some First World agricultural expert, a one-acre farmer was found who produced 40 different crops on that acre, netting US $4,000 a year. He was helped to create a program that changed farming practice to some degree among half of the small farmers in two years and received the Silver Medal from the U.N. Food and Agricultural Organization. His success proved that he had the right consciousness and technology for the situation.

People are "underdeveloped" because of both wrong consciousness and technology, whether they are in Haiti or America. Such people tend to be fatalistic and act as if they are just so many ants floating down the evolutionary river, as described earlier. Development will not happen until the grip of fatalism and dependency is broken in the mind of the Third World. As long as people define the solution to their problems as outside their control, they are dependent and will remain underdeveloped. They define the solution to their problem beyond their ability to solve it. More developed persons define a problem in such a way that it is within their ability to solve it or to at least take the first step on the road to solution.

Much of the developing world has bad attitudes toward business and foreign investment. Granted, there are many reasons why these attitudes exist. But countless good investments and investors have been driven from Third World shores that could have helped. There are some notable exceptions. For example, about 700 American corporations have invested $4 billion in Singapore. It has a free economy and enthusiastic people.

But consider the rest of these countries. Most business people from the industrial world who have tried to invest in poorer countries have met a labyrinth of insults, indecision, confused signals, lack of commitment, and politically motivated labor unions who jack up the labor price after agreements have been signed. Many developing countries have some attitudinal house cleaning to do before large-scale foreign investment will really make a difference.

In the meantime, individuals from the more successful Third World countries should be sent more often to the poorer countries. They share a more similar consciousness and a sensitivity to technology transfer that First World nationals often do not. There would be more trust of such professionals and they would come at less cost than the First World professional.

If the technology of automation is fully transferred to the Third World by 2025 to 2035, then how will average people get an income? By finding unique personal international market niches and investing just like the First World via the TOK, as explained in the preceding chapter. But that may take 35 to 45 years. In the meantime, there are some major revolutions pending, much like the Green Revolution fathered by Dr. Norman Borlaug, who received the Nobel Prize for Peace for his work in plant genetics in 1970.

The Barter Revolution

The Barter revolution will stimulate the economic development of poorer countries that do not have the foreign exchange to get very much involved in international trade. Lender institutions and nations are against barter as an economic development tactic for poor countries, arguing that barter would diminish further foreign exchange earnings. Barter does not help lenders get their money back. But this is shortsighted. Cash transactions can evolve from trade experiences that originated as barter.

The current financial balance of trade is always a zero sum game—improving your balance of trade at another's loss. Barter need not be this one-sided. In the early stages of economic development, barter preceded cash economies. Since much of the Third World is in the relatively early stages of international economic development, its members may have prematurely skipped a step by plunging into cash transactions in international trade instead of enhancing barter arrangements.

Let's say Guyana has rice but no foreign exchange to buy oil. Without barter, its economy, which is dependent on oil, is dead. With barter, it can exchange its rice for oil from Trinidad and Tobago. This creates a ripple effect in other parts of the economy that earns cash. For example, oil is necessary to run systems that produce lumber for export. The exported lumber can earn foreign exchange, some of which can go to creditors.

In this example Guyana is able to keep its economy going with foreign oil without loss of currency. Barter can be thought of as pump priming an economy that lacks cash for international trade. A slightly more complex arrangement can involve cash. For example, Jamaica might want buses but lacks the U.S. currency to buy from General Motors, which insists on cash. So Jamaica could ship bauxite (or, more likely, alumina) to a European company, which pays General Motors in America for the buses. Barter arrangements can be far more complex than these examples involving more countries and products.

Another version gets around a classic problem for foreign investors in developing countries. Let's say an American firm agrees to a joint venture in a developing country to build a factory. The American firm expects to sell products from the factory in that country, but wants to take its profit out in U.S. currency. But the government doesn't have enough to give to the investor. So, instead of receiving profit in cash, the firm takes some of the products as barter, sells them overseas, and deposits the hard currency in its U.S. account. This is exactly how Armand Hammer and Occidental Petroleum will get profits out of the Soviet Union from a joint venture to build plastic factories in the Ukraine.

As international business continues to explore the many ways to operate without hard currency, we will see a rapid growth of trade with poorer countries. The city of Miami has opened the first international exchange specifically for barter transactions. Currently, the international barter market is worth about $500 billion and some have estimated that it could reach as high as 50 percent of all international trade by the year 2000.

As stated earlier, barter is a stimulant for a stagnant economy with little foreign exchange—which characterizes nearly half of humanity. Hence, it has the potential of being a revolution for economic development, even if only for the next 10 to 20 years. But it is not the wave of the future for the Post-Information Age global economy.

The Debt Revolution

Originally, the First World financial institutions were in command of developing countries' financial situations. That command has now switched to the developing countries. It is said "When you have a small debt, it is your problem. When you have a big debt, it is the bank's problem."

Third World debt repayments are likely to be rewritten along the lines that Peru has set. Peru has fixed its repayment at 10 percent of its export earnings. This is low enough that it will not cripple a nation and at the same time it gives the First World a real incentive to make sure trade with the developing countries will improve.

Another proposal keeps money in poor countries by allowing lending banks to buy shares in local investment authorities as some percentage of what might have been the repayment of the original loan. This further increases the First World's incentive to see to it that those enterprises succeed. So far, this exchange of debt for equity in Third World businesses makes up a very small fraction of the cash value of late payments, but it will grow and can ease the sense of crisis for both the creditor and debtor.

The Private Business Revolution

Keep in mind that the developing world will increasingly inherit cleaner, more efficient, and less costly technology as we move into the future. For example, Brazil is already planning a "Third World Car" to be sold at $2,000 a copy during the 1990s. Peru is manufacturing and selling IBM-compatible computers to Czechoslovakia and Germany. You may have paid $500 for a hand-crank calculator in 1960, but the first calculator bought by some today in the poorer counties may cost only $20.

The basic trend in Third World development is toward private sector development and away from bilateral aid for large-scale public sector projects. Even traditional relief agencies such as CARE, Catholic Relief Services, Save the Children, and Foster Parents Plan have begun small business development programs directly within the private sector. There will always be a need for relief work, be it with the public or private sector. But private relief agencies are coming to grips with the notion of "teaching a man to fish" more often than in their past.

U.N. agencies such as UNDP are looking at how to skip government aid and go through private voluntary agencies (PVOs) that work directly with the grass roots private sector. Unfortunately, most of the "development" programs today are still relief-oriented instead of developmentally oriented.

Development programs will themselves have to get off the dole, not only because of tightening budgets, but because it is bad policy to ask people to become independent when those programs and employees are government subsidized.

Development programs cannot become self-sustaining until the development professionals change their attitude from doing things *for* people to doing things *with* people. Every program should be designed with the beneficiary and with an eye toward how the program can earn its way.

Development programs can both expand the economic participation of the poor and at the same time make money to financially support themselves. They can charge interest rates and take equity positions in small businesses that they help start and expand. In this way, the program gets rewarded in proportion to the economic growth stimulated. This seems fair. It also tells clients that development programs have to play by the same private sector rules that clients have to accept.

In 1985 only 85 of the 2,300 American-sponsored projects in Africa were for small enterprise development. Methods are being invented to convert relief programs into economically sustainable development programs. For example, Ethiopian food aid could be used as barter to save locally adapted seed and create a business for a national seed bank. During the recent droughts, farmers in partly rain-fed areas woke up one morning to find that their village of 40 had grown to 4,000. These farmers had saved enough grain to use as seed for next year's planting. With the enormous migrations of starving people into their villages, the farmers were not able to keep this seed. Once all seed is used for food, the genetically adapted grain is lost forever from the gene pool. Foreign-aid seed takes years to adapt to local conditions. As a result, famine returns again, even if the rains return.

An alternative is to use the foreign-relief grain as barter to buy locally adapted seed from the farmers. The local seed is then treated so that it cannot be eaten and is stored in local shops for the farmers to borrow next year. The local shopkeepers are initially paid for this service in grain from the relief program. When the farmers are ready to plant next year, they borrow the locally adapted seed from the shopkeepers and pay back the shopkeepers twice the amount in grain from their harvest.

This converts the grain and personnel originally allocated for food relief into a business for seed multiplication while saving the endangered genetic stocks of Ethiopia. Such a program was partly put into practice by an

American private voluntary organization before the Ethiopian government stopped it for political reasons that had nothing to do with the principle of converting relief programs into economic development programs. Nevertheless, some seed was saved and the principle I have described was demonstrated sufficiently to stimulate other efforts.

Relief-oriented refugee programs can also be converted into development programs. Instead of simply maintaining thousands in tent cities, small business development programs are now putting people to work in such countries as Pakistan, Somalia, and Honduras.

Privatization is another trend sweeping the Third World. State-owned telephone companies are being sold off to private entities in Mexico, Sri Lanka, Malaysia, Korea, Thailand, and Bangladesh. Public housing is gradually being sold off in Cuba and the People's Republic of China. Airlines are being sold to the private sector in Thailand, Singapore, Korea, Turkey, Bangladesh, and Malaysia.

Government sewer systems could develop waste treatment plants that make a profit. Such plants would produce methane gas and algae that can be used as feed for cultivated shrimp, and the remaining material can also be sold as fertilizer. The Bioshere II project in Arizona developed over the last 10 years is showing how to live in space and answer the question What technology and biology is required to create an independent biosphere? In the process of conducting more advanced research, the project is also proving some down-to-earth matters such as showing that green plants can grow in dirty water and that these plants can then be used for food, energy, and fertilizers. These and other approaches to waste systems should give a net profit sufficient to attract private business to buy government sewer systems.

In 1977 His Excellency Ambassador Asal B. Idzumbuir of the Republic of Zaire proposed that Third World countries should be able to financially invest in the development of space so that they would be able to share in the future profits proportional to their investments. He realized that great wealth will be created as space industrialization expands in the future and that poorer countries had no chance of getting involved on their own. So the only way to avoid being left out of the next major step in human evolution would be for developing nations to invest in some international system such as INSPACECO explained earlier. This could be an element in a strategy for Third World long-range financial security.

But it must be stressed that policy reforms within developing countries that create a healthy private business environment are not enough. Letting prices be set in a free market, selling off government enterprises, and creating incentives for foreign investment should not be seen as the solution to poverty. Otherwise, policy reform will be just one more maximizing strategy that everyone romantically rallied around to be disappointed one more time.

There is absolutely no chance to solve the debt crisis until the basic economic development of the poor majority is tackled head on. This means wading into a complex mess of problems that do not lend themselves to sweeping generalizations like import substitution, export promotion, massive growth in tourism, or rewriting loans.

Import substitution looked fine on paper: instead of the developing countries shipping out raw material and importing finished products, they could finish them locally and buy them locally. The reality is that they had to import capital, technology, and advisors at a very high cost in order to produce these substitutions. The hidden costs were even greater. Rural workers left agricultural production for urban work thereby necessitating a bigger food import bill, and new roads, schools, sewers, police, and housing had to be provided with still more imported capital.

The Third World did not have a chance to get the foreign capital back to pay the loans. So, a new sweeping generalization came in: export promotion to pay for the failed import substitution policy. To get into the world export market, large production runs are necessary to command the attention of importers. Because poorer countries were not organized for such massive production, more capital, technology, advisors, and in many cases, raw materials had to be imported. This put many of these countries further into debt. Thus, the policy of import substution is also not working.

Tourism was another failed policy. Big hotels and infrastructures were built, running up the debt once again. Very little came from the local countries. Local systems were not brought into the planning process and were not prepared to supply the tourist industry on a regular basis. As a result, the building materials and supplies were more predictable if imported rather than bought locally. The tourist managers have calculated the total import cost of their system, added their profit, set their prices, and act as if the tourist areas were independent zones within these developing countries. Hence, little development is experienced among the poor majority.

We will still need to rewrite many loans, but we should do so with a much sharper focus on the end user of the loan. For example, the World Bank and other institutions give loans to local development banks. These institutions often teach the local bank officials various forms of financial and market analysis. The loan application form that the local bank uses with its clients—the local entrepreneurs—reflects such market and financial training. So far so good. But what about the entrepreneurs themselves? Do they get along with people? Do they know the business? What are their reputations? Are they well linked into suppliers and buyers? Do they know how to keep financial records and use them for decisions?

Naturally, the World Bank deals with systems that are very large-scale and cannot get involved in the details of small business entrepreneurial personality. Because the large financial systems don't do this, smaller local development banks too often follow the lead of the "big boys" and forget that it is a human being that is getting the loan. As a result, the loan application for one chicken farmer will look the same as another, since the market and financial analysis is the same. Yet two chicken farmers could be quite different in their ability to repay the loan.

This situation can be changed. A condition for rewriting loans to such local development banks could include a provision that equal attention must be given to the analysis of the entrepreneur during the loan application and approval process. Focusing on the consciousness of the entrepreneur as well as the technology of the business will give a more balanced view of the future success of the loan.

Agricultural development programs and policies must treat the farmer as an entrepreneur. The smallest farm is still a private business. And there are more such small businesses in the poorer parts of the Third World than any other activity. So, if we are to influence the destiny of the poor majority, then we need to aim a greater percentage of development forces at the subsistence farmer. As much as 80 percent of the farms in developing countries are 12 acres or fewer, and half of these farms are under

2.5 acres. This is the reality of much of the Third World. This is the rock on which to build the house of development. America never left its agricultural base. Why should the developing world?

Naturally, there are some exceptions, like Singapore. And granted, great agroindustrial complexes will eventually produce much of the food now produced by subsistence farmers. But the gradual process of consciousness growth and technology transfer with today's subsistence farmers will lead to such innovations as multicropping among solar panels and wind energy machines. In the meantime, our attention must turn more to the subsistence farmer.

This is not to say that now we should move to a sweeping generalization and forget about everything else. It does mean that small farmers in the poorer parts of the world should get central attention in a holistic approach to development. Barter, swapping Third World debt for First World equity, policy reform, import substitution, export promotion, tourism, and rewriting loans all have their place in a complex set of strategies. None are panaceas. But together in an optimum balance, the private business revolution can succeed.

This holistic approach is complex. How can you reach an optimum balance? Even if you could, how could you implement it? The world is in constant flux. And there are so many decision makers or actors in the development process.

New kinds of large-scale management techniques are required to connect the individual villager with people and information sources worldwide. Also required are situation rooms that let key decision makers get the big picture clearly enough to make useful policy. Such international information management and communications systems have been used for years by defense and space agencies to manage their large-scale and complex projects. Images of situation rooms and satellite communications come easily to mind, but in Burkina Faso? Haiti? Burma? Or the offices of USAID, UNDP, and Japanese development authorities? Those involved in economic development with the poor majority tend to be ignorant of the cost/effect of such management approaches. Both developing countries and donor nations have resisted such high technology approaches. But this too is changing.

Typical classroom in rural Africa.

The Communications Revolution

The communicaitons revolution will be the central factor in making the holistic approach work and in bridging the development gap. In the agricultural and industrial economies, the marketplace was the center around which all the people revolved. In the communications economies the center trades places with the orbit: each person is the center and the world market electronically revolves around each of them. It is possible for this dreamlike communications age to be achieved nearly simultaneously in the First, Second, and Third Worlds, unlike the agricultural and industrial ages. This reduces the disadvantages of geography and the smallness of local markets. It is not possible for most developing nations to pay for the training and salaries of enough doctors, teachers, and other professionals. But it is possible for developing countries to communicate to that knowledge via local TOKs.

We could have INMEDSAT to connect the world to the best of medical diagnosis and treatment and INEDSAT to connect the world to the best of instruction in all fields. These would be accessed via the TOK. It will take a great deal of time and money to get the developing world on par with the agricultural and industrial capabilities of the advanced nations, but it will take far less money and time to get the developing world on par with the communications capabilities of the advanced nations. Once communications parity is reached, agricultural and industrial parity will be easier to achieve later than if the communications were not in place.

A key factor in the integration of the developing world into the global economy will be Third World trade with the Third World, not just to or with the First World. The highways that will open this inter Third World trade will be electronic. Computer networks will make possible easier connections to find markets and close deals.

The African Strategy Conference sponsored by PfP International, IBM, USAID, Rockefeller Brothers Fund, and PACT held in Lome December, 1986, discovered that no one had a map of development actors and hence, there was no way to connect the development system to create and carry out a coherent strategy. The chart below is one crude beginning for such a map.

DEVELOPMENT COMMUNICATIONS MAP

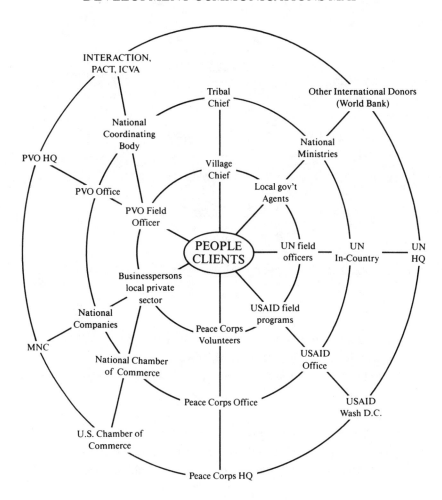

The next chart is designed to help each of the actors in the development process create his or her own checklist of who they should be in contact with and about what during the development process.

Each step in the development process involves a number of actors
with whom you should communicate. This chart provides a checklist of
actors that one should communicate with at various points during the development process, and also identifies a variety of communications medi-
ums that can be utilized.

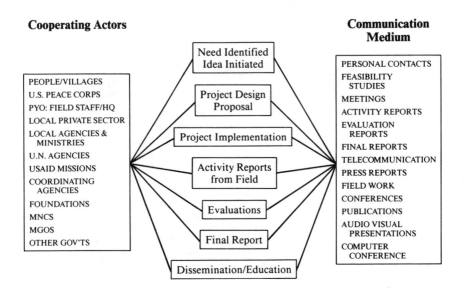

Cooperating Actors

Communication Medium

Cooperating Actors		Communication Medium
PEOPLE/VILLAGES	Need Identified Idea Initiated	PERSONAL CONTACTS
U.S. PEACE CORPS		FEASIBILITY STUDIES
PYO: FIELD STAFF/HQ	Project Design Proposal	MEETINGS
LOCAL PRIVATE SECTOR		ACTIVITY REPORTS
LOCAL AGENCIES & MINISTRIES	Project Implementation	EVALUATION REPORTS
U.N. AGENCIES		FINAL REPORTS
USAID MISSIONS	Activity Reports from Field	TELECOMMUNICATION
COORDINATING AGENCIES		PRESS REPORTS
FOUNDATIONS	Evaluations	FIELD WORK
MNCS		CONFERENCES
MGOS	Final Report	PUBLICATIONS
OTHER GOV'TS		AUDIO VISUAL PRESENTATIONS
	Dissemination/Education	COMPUTER CONFERENCE

These may seem like obvious and easy things to do, but The African Strategy Conference found none of this in existence.

As we look around the developing world, we find a landscape littered with development projects milling around like so many uncoordinated cows. Why? Because there is no brain to the development process and no nervous system to connect development muscle to that brain. This fragmentation loses the synergies that come from strategic coordination and squanders precious development dollars on duplicative and mindless activities.

Situation rooms similar to the old war rooms should be created to track development in each country so that one could see the possibilities for strategic coordination. These rooms could be owned by a board of directors composed of members of the most influential private and public institutions that directly affect economic development of the poor majority. Information from these institutions could be used as a basis for in-camera meetings to help the board become a neutral center and prioritize issues to be discussed with the government. Each board member would create his or her own approach to government so that the situation room would not be politicized and the board would never need to agree on strategy or tell its members how to lobby. Instead, they would just need to agree on what issue they will all be working on that particular month. This could connect the national policy dialogue with the grass-roots development process.

Metapraxix Integrated Boardroom.

The leader can have access to any number of audiovisual information facilities, including TV, radio, video, slides, external databases, video conferencing, and output from a microcomputer. All these facilities are then controlled with a simple 12-digit infrared keypad like that used for remote control of television.

Such situation rooms would be in an excellent position to carry out market research, identify what training is needed, expedite problems, take equity positions in business, broker foreign investment, and act as an employment agency to earn economic support for programs rather than their being continually dependent on donors.

Although it is true that many executives don't like to use computers and that computers for languages such as Arabic do not have standard keyboards, there is a simple solution. With $1,000 a 200-word voice recognition addition can be placed in a computer. For those who do not or will not type, this lets them speak to their computer and makes many of the problems with keyboards irrelevant.

The situation rooms in Third World countries could be electronically connected to make international efforts more successful. The data and information for these situation rooms can come from the many field officers in each country. And these field officers can draw on the entire world network for assistance. Such an approach would make it possible to find and network the winners in small-scale agricultural and industrial development to speed up the process. They would be internally as well as internationally linked.

InterAction is composed of 110 nonprofit Third World development organizations whose policy it is to foster coordinating bodies in each country in Africa. These coordinating bodies of private voluntary organizations (PVOs) are intended to coordinate the implementation of development projects. They should hold their monthly meetings in such situation rooms to feed information to the board as well as learn the latest priorities in the national policy dialogue.

Ideally, such coordination could provide a coherent map of development activity. This map would make it easier to identify the gaps in the process and would contribute to the formulation of national economic development plans and budgets. It would be made available to foreign donors so that foreign financial assistance would have a more coherent impact.

Airlines have been using such large-scale systems as international electronic situation boards for years. You can buy a ticket to go anywhere from anywhere and their electronic bulletin boards will be updated the moment you purchase your ticket. All airlines' reservations are kept up-to-date via computer communications. Yet development professionals who have a far more complex international management problem think you are crazy to suggest the same kind of system for coordination of development assistance. They often act as if it can't or shouldn't be done.

Imagine the airline situation without computer communication. A mess? This is similar to our current situation in development coordination. The development community as a whole does not understand the information/communications economy and the implications for development.

Low-cost and worldwide computer communications is rapidly becoming a key link that involves more people in world trade as well as the free flow of information. The strategic technology that brings down this cost and opens more of the world market is the installation of Data Packet Switching (DPS) equipment in every nation. Currently over 60 countries are so connected for low-cost computer communications, 40 of which are in the Third World.

DPS allows anyone to make a local public telephone call to connect his or her computer to worldwide information systems at an average of $10 per *hour.* Without DPS added to the local telephone authority, computer communications would be too difficult and expensive for development programs to use.

Just as land, seed, and tractors are the things that make money in the agricultural economy and machines, raw materials, and energy are ingredients for the industrial economy, so too satellites, computers, telephones, and data packet switching are the things that make money in the information and communications economy. This is not well understood in the First World, let alone the Third World, since this is the economy being invented today. It is much like trying to explain the things of the Industrial Age to a serf during the feudal period in England.

International telecommunications access is a comparative advantage that foreign investors look for when considering larger investments. A country that has DPS shows that it is serious about development and wants to offer a state-of-the-art infrastructure to attract investors. The cost of a DPS should be recovered from added personal income taxes, import duties, and corporate taxes within the first year.

Such public dial-up access expands international trade by making it possible to access various international data banks that have market information updated regularly. It puts the Third World citizen in easy touch with major trading, investment, brokerage, and market research firms. International advertising becomes cost effective for the smallest of businesses. One can even buy and sell stocks via such systems.

It is not possible to import or train the necessary teachers to give the kind of education needed to bring many countries into the modern world in this generation, *But it is possible to communicate to that capability.* Consider the cost of training and paying enough teachers to get a 1:30 ratio of teacher to student in the Third World. Then consider the cost of installing public dial-up data packet switching, which allows any computer to tie into the best curriculum the world has available. This is the only way to have the best educators available to all people. It is a savings to the national treasury and a benefit to the educational system of the country.

The same case can be made for health services and medical information access. We know there is not enough money to buy sufficient medical training and equipment to give universal First World diagnostic quality to all of the Third World. There simply is not enough money to train, pay, and generally support enough doctors in the developing countries. But there is enough money to extend proven telemedicine to the entire world at the diagnostic standards of the First World. It is possible to have medical assistants supported by access to the Library of Medicine data banks, the best doctors within their country, and medical referrals worldwide as this medical expert computer program evolves.

Medical assistants could take on-line courses to improve their capability at far less cost than the current practice of sending them to England. Granted, it is better to be there in person, but it is better to communicate to the education than to hear "Sorry no funds this year for your training in the UK."

India has the largest pool of scientists and engineers next to America and the Soviet Union. With international computer communications, these professionals in the Third World could work on First World projects. For example, unanalyzed data is building up at an incredible rate because First World professionals' time costs are so high. Less than half of NASA's data has ever been looked at and less than 10 percent has been fully analyzed. So much could be farmed out to Third World professionals who would have mainframe access via computer networks at far less cost. This is not to be viewed as exporting jobs because these jobs are not being done in the First World.

In the past, the First World imported raw material from the Third World and sold finished products. With the communications revolution, it will be possible for the Third World to import raw material (data) and export finished products (information and intelligence).

USAID should be directed to pay for the DPS equipment to assist development objects. If the remaining 140 countries and territories all bought at the same time, the installation costs per country could drop to an average of $25,000 for public dial-up computer communications. Individually, a country could buy at costs from $40,000 to $100,000 from vendors like GTE and Siemans running $5.6 to $14 million instead of the suggested all-at-once program costing $3.5 million for 140 countries and territories.

It is also in the First World's interest to complete the international data packet switching system since it (1) speeds, makes more accurate, and cuts costs of international communications; (2) allows the Third World to access First World markets at the cost of international mail; (3) improves international management and increases free flow of information; and (4) makes access to First World medical, agricultural, educational, and economic data bases cost effective for the first time in the developing world.

It is a disgrace when you consider that such computer communications technology has been around for over 15 years and that the First World has not moved on this issue! The satellites are up, the earth stations are in place, the computers have come down in price, the most unsophisticated of telephones will work (I have personally tested them in Latin America, Africa, and the Middle East), but there is no data packet switching to make it all useful and cost effective.

The Blue Revolution

The Blue Revolution could be as significant as the Green Revolution. According to FAO statistics, the falling world fish harvest has finally begun to grow again and is now at an all-time high. This is primarily due to big gains in anchovetta from Peru and general efficiencies in Asia. Unfortunately, African catches are still falling.

TOTAL GLOBAL CATCH IN MILLIONS OF METRIC TONS

1971	70.8
1975	69.7
1980	60.0
1985	85.2
1986	89.2

There seems to be no reason why we could not move to 100 million or even 150 million tons in the future. Granted, there are biological limits. Big fish eat little fish, which in turn eat plankton. But all species have not been fished and there are no adequate stock estimates to determine how much of each species can be taken without depleting the species. And aquaculture is still a relatively undeveloped industry.

According to the most conservative estimates, net farming in lakes, lagoons, and oceans can increase world harvest by 50 percent in several years in both fin and shell fish. Entrepreneurial and management talent must be found and stock must be replaced at a proper rate.

The Gulf of Thailand was one of the Pacific's richest fishing grounds over 10 years ago, but today it is nearly depleted. Large-scale artificial reefs and cylinder nets for fish farming could bring this area back in several years. One growth possibility is Atlantic krill, planktonic crustraceans and larvae, which could add 50 million tons alone per year; however, we do not yet know how they will respond to heavy exploitation. But they represent a very rich source of protein to add to foods.

As recently as 1978-79 the U.S. annual per capita consumption of beef was 200 pounds, 40 for chicken, and just 8 for fish. Americans now eat more chicken than beef. Even though a good portion of Americans tuna consumption has been replaced by chicken, we will see increasing fish consumption by Americans. Why? People will get bored with chicken. Health food promoters are beginning to talk more about fish than they used to. The Japanese 10-point IQ average higher than the U.S. will become increasingly annoying. People think fish is the IQ or brain food. Ads will push this theme: "Fish! The intelligent choice!" or "Don't be chicken! Be smart! and Eat smart!"

Americans are beginning to imitate Japanese ways, which includes a lot of fish. Fish will become an "in thing." As a result, people might be willing to pay more for fish than chicken and beef. The U.S. economy will start another long growth period in the 1990s, meaning that price may not be as big an issue as in the past. As the demand goes up, more development will occur. Increased supply will lead to a lower price. This will bring into the market those who are more price conscious. The day could come when more fish will be consumed in America than chicken.

If these trends are correct, there will be good financial incentives for rapidly developing fish farming industries in the Third World. Surface waters in Africa and the oceans surrounding that enormous continent hold vast untapped potential for development.

Innovations in aquaculture are bound to occur in such areas as additions to waste treatment plants, genetic technology, ocean farming, robot boats and fishermen, and closed environment aquaculture for high-priced items like lobster, shrimp, and oysters.

The Brown Revolution

The coming Brown Revolution is another hopeful area for the Third World. Deserts cover one-sixth of the world's surface. According to the U.N. Environmental Program, 6 million hectares of Africa becomes desert each year and 20 million hectares fall out of economic use. We have known for many years that metal "snow fences" can stop this desert drift, but no large-scale effort has been made to put these in place.

Preliminary experiments in closed environmental agriculture in the deserts of Saudi Arabia, Abu Dhabi, and Arizona indicate that the deserts can bloom. By 1987 Saudia Arabia produced three times the grain necessary for local consumption because of new applications of enclosed environmental systems.

Giant agricultural systems enclosed within tubing 50 feet wide, 15 feet high, and hundreds of miles long with railroad tracks running down the middle could make agricultural export a possibility in the Sahel. Rows of such tubing alternating with solar photovoltaic sheeting could make the

Artist's concept of undersea aquaculture
Courtesy of Champion

ECONOMIC DEVELOPMENT IN THE THIRD WORLD

deserts energy exporters as well. When solar power satellites are constructed in space in the next 15 to 20 years, the price of photovoltaics imported from space will be low enough to make this a possibility. The energy generated on these space-constructed photovoltaic sheets in the deserts could be microwaved via satellites to other earth stations.

Preventing forests from turning into deserts is important for dealing with the greenhouse effect of carbon dioxide's build-up heating the atmosphere, since green plants are essential for converting carbon dioxide to oxygen. We also must insist on preserving wilderness from an economic point of view. For example, according to the International Institute for Environment and Development in London, "A wild wheat from Turkey saved the U.S. prairies from an epidemic of stripe rust in the 1960s. An Ethiopian strain protects California barley from the disease 'Yellow Dwarf.'" The same institute also points out that there are about 80,000 edible plants on earth, but only 3,000 have ever been used, 150 cultivated, and fewer than 20 make up 90 percent of the world's food supply.

Of the world's 1.1 to 1.4 billion hectares of arable land, only 700 million are farmed. The FAO estimates 3.19 billion could be arable. It is also estimated that one-third of all agricultural production spoils because of pests, micro-organisms, and loss during transportation. Food can be radiated to prevent such spoilage; covered trucks and improved storage can also prevent loss. Solving these problems would have the same effect as increasing world food supplies by 33 percent.

In 1960 an average of 1.3 metric tons of grain per hectare was produced. By the most recent data, that had grown to 2.2 tons. According the the U.N. Environmental Program's Annual Report in 1977: "The total calorie and protein content of today's food production is more than twice the minimum requirement of the world population," even though one-eighth of the world is living below minimum consumption. There is no question that there is enough land to produce more than enough food for the largest population forecasts of the future.

According to the late Merritt L. Kastens, editor of *Food Industry Futures,* "In the Soviet Union, one-quarter of the total agricultural product, three-fifths of all the potatoes, and one-third of the meat are raised on *private plots* that account for less than 1 percent of the arable land. Why? Because a 'peasant' can make as much in a day on the legal private market as a schoolmaster makes in a month." If the Soviet's would give up collectivization and allow private production on more than 1 percent of the arable land, they could feed themselves, export, and help feed the world. Those wanting to stop world hunger should turn their attention to changing collectivization approaches in the Soviet Union and in the developing countries following the Soviet example. It seems that some of the new directions of Parastroyka and Glasnost are moving in this direction.

Petrochemical fertilizers are a major expense to Third World agriculture and will add future costs resulting from the environmental clean-ups necessary to deal with polluted ground and surface water. We can expect the elimination of chemical fertilizers by biotechnology. In the meantime, we can grow fertilizer. According to Batelle's North West Laboratories, tomatoes fertilized with algae had 45 percent more growth than those treated wtih petrochemical fertilizers. Algae can be rapidly and locally produced. This would help make small farming profitable.

Other more naturally occurring and cost-effective approaches are being developed in the Biosphere II project in Arizona mentioned earlier to determine what is necessary from technology and what is necessary from nature to make an independent environment in space. A venture capital corporation backing this experiment to put eight humans in a several-acre sealed environment for two years will have the evidence necessary to market naturally occurring systems that will be useful for Third World agriculture.

In conclusion, the Third World can economically succeed even with moderate successes in the coming revolutions in barter, debt, business development, communications, aquaculture, and agriculture. And it is in the economic and security interests of the First World to work with the Third World as a top policy objective.

We get what we pay for: wonderful school input but terrible performance. We should pay teachers and principals according to student performance. Topics include the following: twenty areas to explore improved brain functioning; ways schools can produce a profit; modification of curriculums to a futuristic approach for better learning; and the spherical curriculum, which is a holistic approach, showing a student's strong and weak areas. Immediate application and feedback worldwide will motivate students to learn to "read" people and institutions as well as to read and write words. With computer-assisted education, apprenticeship in the workplace, and humanistic education of the whole person, and instruction via remote access to the computer, giving students more individual attention than most classroom instruction, higher grades should result. (The weak link is the overworked teacher.).

Chapter Twelve
Education

With the arrival of the Tree of Knowledge (TOK), almost anyone can learn almost anything, almost anywhere. With the breakthroughs in brain research and their coming applications almost anyone will be able to increase his or her intelligence to what we call genius today. Unfortunately, all this is a generation away and the status of education today is terrible. Granted, over half of all of humanity between 6 and 23 are in school for the first time in history, but are they getting an education that even begins to approach the sophistication necessary for the 21st century?

You would think that the United States, with a Gross National Product approaching $5 trillion a year, would be producing the most intelligent people on the earth and would have wiped out illiteracy. But no. As much as 40 percent of American adults do not have full literacy: 20 percent are functionally illiterate and the other 20 percent are marginally literate. Only 70 percent of American youth are graduating from high school. In some urban centers, the high school dropout rate is nearly 50 percent. Why? We have no positive, compelling, multifaceted vision of the future to motivate people to become intelligent.

The space program's mission to land a man on the moon stimulated the greatest concentrated educational effort in history. The American space industry spun forth the greatest advances in medical science and electronic technology ever seen. The goal was tangible and the Soviet public relations threat and potential military advantage was real.

Today Japanese IQ averages 10 points higher than America's and the

Soviet Union has placed eight space stations in orbit to America's one. It is likely that the Soviet Union will land a man on Mars before the year 2000, which will be five to ten years ahead of the United States. Richard Hoagland, in *The Monuments of Mars,* suggests that the Soviets might even take off by 1992 to coincide with the 500th anniversary of the discovery of the Americas by Christopher Columbus and the 75th anniversary of the Russian Revolution. This would leave the United States as a second-class power in the eyes of the world even longer, unless the proposed joint mission to Mars occurs.

In 1986 there were 311 Japanese studying at the U.S. National Institutes of Health to take back the state-of-the-art in biology to Tokyo. Three-quarters of them were on U.S.-paid NIH fellowships. More foreign students got their Ph.Ds at American universities in physics, mathematics, and engineering than Americans.

American children spend more time in front of a television set than inside a classroom by their 18th birthday. And more frighteningly, they spend more time watching TV commercials than doing their homework. We need a bold new challenge and strategy to electrify education. Otherwise, all the educational technology in the world will not prepare us for the potentials of the 21st century.

The 10-10 Program to Increase Intelligence

People are now ready to throw more money at the problem, forgetting that the rate of decline of American student performance was matched by the rate of increase in educational funding. If we don't change the nature of what we are *paying for* in education, then we will just be throwing good money after bad.

We have made the fundamental mistake of paying for educational inputs, rather than educational outputs! We pay teachers on the basis of their years of experience and education, *not the results they achieve with their students.* We evaluate education on the basis of inputs like teacher-student ratio (Japan's is 1 to 49, which many Americans would say makes education impossible), not dollar per achievement test scores. We pay for numbers of books in the library per student, not for books read per student.

We get what we pay for. America has wonderful school inputs, but terrible student performance. The average American expenditure per student as of 1988 was $3,867 (twice that of Japan), which is up 13 percent since 1982, adjusted for inflation.

We should pay teachers on the basis of the performance of their students. Every school district can choose whatever standard testing it wants. If the students' results over the year go up the standard amount, the teacher would receive the standard salary incease. If the results go up beyond the standard, the teacher would receive the normal pay increment plus a bonus. But if the test scores don't go up the standard amount, then neither should the teacher's salary. And if there isn't improvement over the next year or two, then the teacher should go elsewhere to make room for those who can improve students' intelligence.

What about the teachers of slower students? They would still be evaluated on the net change from the beginning to the end of the year. If students averaged 30 percent below standards at the beginning of the year and 25 percent below standards at the end of the year, the teacher would still receive a raise based on the 5 percent growth. In many cases it is easier to get substandard students to show a dramatic gain than average students. However, there are also some students for whom even preventing a decline in performance is a miracle. Under these circumstances exceptions should be made, as long as the principle of paying by output rather than input is not violated.

What is being proposed should not be threatening to any teacher who is either making the normal improvements or exceeding them, but it will be threatening for those who aren't. Hence, there is likely to be strong resistance to this idea. The teachers unions will also resist, because it appears to threaten their power over wage negotiations. But that need not be the case. The standard pay increments would still be negotiable as they have been in the past.

Educational performance is a joint effort of family, community, media, and the school. As a result, the teacher is not the sole determining factor, but the teacher is the one element school budgets can directly affect. Presidential leadership will be required for the other factors.

Along with teacher financial incentives based on performance, school districts should also index principals' salaries to the overall performance of the student body. The same should go for state officials as well. Business pays for performance, why not education?

We should have an education system to make us intelligent. Intelligence—that's the product. And *that is what we should pay for!* Results! Not inputs!

By intelligence, I mean the ability to learn and reason abstractly with knowledge to solve problems. Regardless of what proportion of this ability is determined by DNA and what proportion is determined by environment, the overall expression of intelligence can be increased. The increase or decrease of this capacity can be inferred from changes in achievement on various forms of testing.

If only 20 percent of intelligence is environmentally determined, then education can certainly intervene to develop this proportion. And education can also affect the process of bringing the DNA-determined proportion to fuller expression. With advances in genetic research, we may even be able to alter inheritance.

Our knowledge of brain functioning is exploding, but what applications are reaching the classroom? We know that clusters of ribosomes in brain cells manufacture new proteins for learning, but can a teacher tell you the link between teaching and the stimulation of these ribosomes? The very fact that this sounds like a silly question tells you how far apart brain research and classroom education is today.

Just as the American White House stimulated a whole series of activities through its test for physical fitness, it should announce the goal of increasing the general intelligence or some measure of performance by 10 points in 10 years and encourage school districts to pay teachers on the basis of student performance. This should not be confused with the Presidential Academic Fitness Award for high grades and test scores. The Department of Education was at a loss to identify any differences this program made after five years.

The President should work with our educational leadership and the scientific community to create the proper set of stimuli to improve intelligence and performance.

One step in this process has been taken by the Council of Chief State School Officers. In 1987 they formed a 17-member consortium to make recommendations to the U.S. Department of Education's Center for Educational Statistics on the knowledge and skills in mathematics to be included in the National Assessment of Education Process tests for 1990, which may be conducted on a state-by-state basis. The National Science Foundation is especially interested in the consortium's recommendations for student reasoning and analysis abilities. Possibly these test scores could be a basis for paying mathematics teachers.

We are wrong to think the bright do not need help and that the less bright cannot be helped. The objective is to improve all performance. If teachers' salaries were indexed to the rise and fall of students' performance on IQ or other tests over the year, then the lag time from scientific research to educational application would be shortened. As the United States averages 10 points below the Japanese in IQ, there does seem to be room for us to grow.

We could argue that IQ tests are not the best measure and that they can't change much since intelligence is genetically determined, but they do measure something that needs improvement and that can vary somewhat according to environmental factors. It should be one of the jobs of the teacher to influence and increase such changes.

IQ testing is such a controversial issue that it could prevent the public acceptance of the overall goal of improving student performance. I would recommend that each school district make up its own mind whether it wants to focus on IQ, brain functioning, critical thinking, or content mastery. I believe that a focus on IQ would produce the best results, but if agreement is not possible, then it is better to find a consensus on another standard rather than mire the public in an endless no-win argument. Certainly, all will agree that most children are not acheiving up to potential and some will agree that even potential can be increased. What remains is to agree on how to measure change in intelligent behavior and how to pay for such change.

According to the U.S. Office of Education, as of 1987, 31 states have have begun some version of performance-based teacher incentives. However, the suggestion made here should not be confused with the current trends in "merit pay," because that often boils down to the principal and or other teachers deciding which teachers are performing well and which are not. Merit pay changes may also say more about the ability of a teacher to negotiate with the principal than the teacher's effect on student intelligence. Merit pay can lead to cliques or cronyism and is not necessarily based on objective standards as might appear from a distance.

Once the local school district chooses whether it is focusing on IQ, brain functioning, critical thinking, or content mastery, each school district would pick whatever standard test it wants to measure that focus. It could be the Stanford-Binet intelligence test, the California Achievement Tests, the math test recommendations to be put forward by the Council of Chief State School Officers, etc., or a combination of them. But all students should be tested. The current National Assessment of Educational Progress is no substitute, because it tests only a random sample of 25,000 students at 9, 13, and 17 years old.

If it were clear that salary was geared to enhanced IQ, all of a sudden we would see curriculum workshops that would integrate the current state of brain research into the classroom environment. Methods for increasing brain performance and improving thinking are still in their infancy, but there is sufficient research out there to be integrated into the classroom. We know that perceptual exercises as well as physical exercises, motivation, and nutrition improve intelligence. We are also finding that brain chemistry can be improved. We don't have the "smart pill" yet, but we can medically treat some forms of low brain performance. We also know that if parents give consistent love to their children and diversity of environmental stimulation, their children's intelligence will be developed more rapidly. Why don't we engage the world in a major effort to find out how to increase intelligence?

I agree with those who say that education has swung too far away from teaching content in favor of thinking skills. But this does not mean that we should downplay analytic skills while we improve content mastery. The way thinking skills have been taught integrates little of what we know about brain functioning. We need to beef up our content and refine our approach to improving brain functioning.

Some forms of thinking are a set of teachable skills, such as reasoning from principles to specifics as in physics, math, and logic. Some forms are not separable from content, as in philosophical analysis that compares epistemological statements with metaphysical ones. We need not waste time arguing about content-centered skills versus abstract skills. Instead, we need to distinguish which are which and teach both appropriately. In addition, character traits are also important such as honesty and thoroughness in order to succeed in reasoning skills. Character traits and skills should be approached as mutually reinforcing.

Environmental factors such as nutrition in the cafeteria would become an issue, along with lighting, color, and texture in the classroom. We know from studies of Albert Einstein's brain that increased number of glial cells and capillary complexity in the brain is correlated with higher IQ. Since increased carbon dioxide in the bloodstream stimulates capillary growth, maybe we should argue about whether children should hold their breath more often?

The President should direct his Science Advisor to bring together all of the research that documents ways to improve intelligence and share that with the educational leadership to develop a mental fitness program similar to the successful White House physical fitness program in the 70s.

In addition, the President will have to lead campaigns through the media to get parents to read with their children, urge TV shows to positively reinforce learning, and in general set a new public attitude toward educational support. Otherwise, the teacher incentives will hit less fertile ground.

Body building has become a major trend in North America and Europe. Isn't it about time that we made "mind building" a major trend? The American futurist Gregg Edwards coined the term "mind building" to refer to the deliberate restructuring of one's memory system based on how one uniquely remembers, as distinct from popular and linear categories that tend to fragment the mind. "Memories are messages to the future," he says. How one structures those memories determines the intelligence of tomorrow. Just as the quality of each item that composes a house determines its overall excellence, so too the quality of what we put into our mind determines our intelligence. We've got manuals for everything from building a house to running a computer, but where is the manual to increase intelligence?

Teaching logic will certainly help, but that is not enough. Correct logic using faulty assumptions increases stupidity, not intelligence.

We know that certain mental states are better for the passive retention of information as distinct from active participation. Should we teach meditation and biofeedback in the classroom to achieve these states? Subliminal learning through taped suggestions below the normal threshold of hearing has produced good results in improving self-image, reduction of smoking, weight loss, and language acquisition. Should we play tapes of the multiplication table on schools' public address systems?

Brain functioning is enhanced by increased circuitry between the right and left hemispheres of the brain. Should we teach all children how to juggle and balance on a rope to stimulate these neural pathways?

In a recent study, Drs. Bernard Brown and Lilian Rosenbaum of Georgetown University found that IQ scores dropped with increasing stress, particularly on the information, digit spans, block design, and vocabulary tests. The scores declined from 105 to 91 as stress increased from zero problems to more than 15 problems. "We found that the scores for children with poor vision declines more than 60% under high stress on the block design and information tests, a level so low that they could not be expected to succeed in school." Their research further discovered that children who were held back a grade or were assigned to special education classes showed a decline of 15.5 percent in IQ and 33 percent on the information subtest.

It seems that we can worry ourselves stupid. Mystics have always taught that a calm and focused mind is more intelligent. Biofeedback, meditation, and other ways to reduce stress should be considered as important as the teaching of analytic skills to improve brain performance. Organizations as diverse as the New York Telephone Company and the U.S. Mint in Philadelphia who carried out meditation programs for their employees reported that employees had fewer sick days, reduced hostility, improved clarity of thought, and better control over events in general.

According to Eye Kraft Optical, Inc., "Full spectrum light has been proven to produce marked emotional and behavioral changes in emotionally disturbed people causing . . . improvement . . . heightened sense of well-being and increased activity at work and play." The Green Street Elementary School in Brattleboro, Vermont, reports that sick days fell 24 percent after the installation of full-spectrum lighting in the school. Should we throw out the fluorescent lighting in our schools and replace it with full-spectrum lighting? And replace our children's glasses with full-spectrum plastic lenses?

Authors Francine and Harold Prince in their book *Feed Your Kids*

Bright document research conducted in a school system in Alabama showing that a change in diet improved IQ and reading scores, as well as grades. The "smart" foods included milk, yogurt, cheese, whole grains, papaya, mango, broccoli, fish, dry beans, peas, and a variety of fruits and berries. Lead in drinking water may lower IQ. Should water filtration systems be added to schools' plumbing?

According to Alexander Schauss at the American Institute for Biosocial Research in Tacoma, Washington, about 90 percent of hyperactive children studied had copper poisoning, food allergies, or an imbalance of magnesium and phosphorus. Although this particular research is under dispute, there is no question that chemical imbalances in the body alter behavior. Should we give blood tests to all children to see what may be needed to chemically improve their brain functioning?

Electromagnetic fields in the radio frequency focused on monkey brains have increased brain performance. Should we radiate our classrooms with radio waves?

A neurotransmitter called norepinephrine stimulates mental alertness by improving your ability to carry messages from one nerve cell to the next. It is secreted by the brain when stimulated by tyrosine, an amino acid. Vasopressin is available by prescription to aid memory. Why not include such pharmaceutical additions to our education programs? We would be arguing about the right things: what makes a difference in brain functioning and how do we integrate such findings into our education.

Increasing intelligence as an educational objective got national attention in Venezuela, which opened the Ministry of State for Human Intelligence in the early 1980s. With a change in administration, the ministry got folded into the Ministry of Education. Some in Venezuela did not hold this new effort in high regard, saying that it was nothing more than a nutrition and teacher training program. But nutrition is a key factor in brain functioning. Consider Africa, where approximately 50 percent of the population experienced protein malnutrition during their childhood. Protein malnutrition can lead to mental retardation. The Venezuelan Ministry of Human Intelligence was able to train over 50,000 teachers in methods to increase innovative thinking as developed by Dr. Edward De Bono of Cambridge University.

We should look at new approaches such as the Venezuelan efforts and add to them programs to teach parents with newborns how to stimulate intelligence and learning. Getting parents into the educational force for excellence will be the most difficult task. It will require nothing less than a fully committed political leadership to continually speak to the parents of the nation and for the President to bring in the cultural leaders of the age to dramatize through popular movies and music how parents can improve their children's intelligence.

Political leadership will also have to sit down with the entertainment industry and point out how it has often negatively reinforced learning and schooling in general. Possibly the White House could periodically list the top 10 entertainment shows that foster healthy attitudes toward learning and the bottom 10 that are keeping us stupid. No freedom of artistic expression need be abridged in this effort to call attention to the attitudes being foisted on the public.

Meanwhile, methods for increasing brain performance and improving thinking are still very much in their infancy, but here is a summary list of areas for exploration:

1. Nutrition
2. Exercises—juggling, balancing, integrating right/left brain activity
3. Mild electric shocks
4. Electromagnetic radiation
5. Diversity of environment/consistency of love
6. Zinc for memory
7. Increasing capillary complexity by holding the breath
8. Think tricks
9. The study of philosophy and logic
10. Suggestion via tapes
11. Parents teaching children
12. Giving social status to being intelligent
13. Reducing time from response on exam to correct feedback
14. Colors, like yellow and orange rather than brown
15. Integration of current brain and behavior research

16. Handling state-of-the-art technology
17. Values in television/radio programs and advertising
18. Being inventive with others
19. Reducing time between learning and application
20. Meditation and others ways to reduce stress

In the meantime, the most effective way to improve brain functioning is to think of your brain as a technology run by your thoughts, rather than as a technology that only produces thoughts. Perceive the brain as "conscious technology." Hence, how you think you think is key. If we paid teachers for the performance of their students, then their attitude toward students would move toward one of getting their students to *think* they can improve their intelligence. According to Dr. Martha Denckla at the National Institutes of Health, this attitude change is the bottom line of all research into how the brain learns.

Schooling as a Profit Industry

American children go to school 180 days per year, whereas their Japanese counterparts go for 240 days. The tourist industry and overburdened taxpayers don't want to increase the time. But the cost factor could be ameliorated by public schools earning a living by (1) renting unused space, (2) charging for market research done by students, (3) taking contract work that fits the learning needs of students, (4) teachers developing educational software with a percentage going to the school, and (5) providing adult education and training courses.

Demographic changes have left many school facilities with underused spaces. According to the National Education Association, there will be a 25 precent drop in the high school population between 1976 and 1993. School space could be rented for elderly living, community education, and daycare centers. Not only would this cut local government costs and earn income, but it will help provide stability to children.

The presence of the elderly and the very young serves to remind students of their niche in the community. Further, the elderly are afraid to go out at night, but with apartments in unused classrooms, they could walk or wheel to the school auditorium for nightly performances, community meetings, or potting classes. Having the daycare centers near the elderly serves the children's need to receive love and the elderly's need to give love. Granted, older people do not necessarily want to have little children underfoot all the time, but they would love to give love to our future generations when they feel lonely.

Having these facilities nearby helps close the loop between the generations with love, as well as becoming a needed financial resource to the school budget.

The baby boom's children will begin to make new demands on elementary school facilities and later on high schools. But the elderly should not be moved out to make room for this growth. Instead, new modular additions to buildings should be used for the "echo boom." These modules could be taken down as the school population drops again.

Market research has become so computer dependent because labor cost is high and the computer appears to give far more precision and cross-referencing than is possible by people. However, the kind of market research necessary for local business is still largely dependent on local interviews with the public. Computer data banks are only as good as the data. Large systems make generalizations that may be off enough to be misleading for a local business. School children could fill this gap.

They have to learn about statistics, community resources, public attitudes, and they should learn about market research. Local companies could contract with the school for specific market research that could not be provided as well or as inexpensively by the larger market research companies. For example, 100 students could easily make 5 interviews in person or on the telephone in one day giving a 24-hour market research turnaround on a 500-person sample. This sample is certainly sufficient for local business needs and the speed would compete with any.

Schools could take in other kinds of contract work. The classic example is automobile repair for the industrial arts classes. Local garages will no doubt complain, but their performance over the years has earned them a low reputation that some competition would only improve.

Computer data banks are a very expensive proposition that are not turning out to be very cost-effective so far. Schools could help the situation by doing the data entry, charging far lower rates, and thus teaching computer literacy to students at the same time in the world of real work.

Teachers are developing their own curricula all the time. They could develop them while using expert system computer software. These could be sold as computer-assisted tutorials or put into international computer banks for global access via the TOK. Students with proven study-at-home performance could access such software, while reducing the demand on the physical facilities and costs of schooling. Software could also be written for the rapidly growing adult education and training market.

For those adults and programs that are not appropriate for computer-assisted instruction, the schools could open adult education and training programs at a fee.

You can think of many other examples of how schools could earn a living while improving educational performance. As the income increases, the length of the school year could also increase proportionally. As education-oriented income activities engage the sincere interest of students, they will become more inclined to want to spend more time in the new schooling environment.

Futuristic Curriculum Development

Now, it's not fair to lay all the blame for poor educational performance on the educational system. The general mood of the country is also a major factor in learning. It has been fashionable to think that we are living at the peak of human evolution. It's as if we have lost our idealism and our courage to build a global partnership for tomorrow. We need to bring idealism back into the mainstream of everyday life and to make this idealism 100 percent practical to the global population.

Without a positive vision of the future, it is unreasonable to expect people to be motivated to learn. When I was a high school teacher in New England, I discovered a strong correlation between students' views of the future and their performance in the classroom. Those who believed that the future was doomed tended to be at the bottom of the class, whereas those who saw a bright future tended to be at the top of the class. Students with negative behaviors who began to see some potential for a better future improved. This was so dramatic that I began future-orienting all my instruction and eventually created a futuristic curriculum approach that integrated futurist's forecasting techniques with teaching methods.

Essentially, the approach has four phases:

1. TRENDS—What is increasing and decreasing in the subject being studied?
2. PROJECTIONS—What *will* the subject look like at some year in the future if these trends continue?
3. IDEALS—What *would you like* the subject look like during the same year in the future?
4. POLICY—Trace the ideal conditions back to the present to see what to do now.

This futuristic curriculum approach can be superimposed on any existent curriculum in a conventional schooling environment. It simply means that during the first quarter of the course, you periodically note what is increasing and decreasing. Graphing these trends will be helpful. Then you could use the Futures Wheel explained earlier to improve your understanding of the implications of each trend.

In the second quarter, you periodically project the trends by answering how each trend will affect the others. Then the answers to these questions can be put together in the format of a scenario to see if the story makes sense and seems complete. During the third quarter you bring up the question of the ideal future conditions for the subject. You could think of this as an exercise in "correcting" the previous scenario. And last, you trace the ideal condition back to the present tense, while identifying what has to be learned or changed in the trends in the first step.

This approach nicely answers the age-old question "Why am I learning this?" People learn best, what interests them most, when they are interested in it. This is something that teachers could start doing tomorrow morning.

Futures research methods like trends and scenarios package vast amounts of information for the purpose of making decisions. One of the great challenges of the information overload problem is the efficient packaging of information. Students' lives are full of information, but not full of meaningful ways to organize that information. Students are not taught how to convert information to intelligence. This is why the most informed nation on earth is losing its competitive edge in the world marketplace. Futuristic curriculum development tends to move students' focus from information to intelligence.

There are a variety of ways to future-orient instruction. A math teacher could have students determine the statistics of one idea versus another idea in newspaper articles, TV shows, or group conversations. These trend data could be the basis for beginning the above four-step process.

This might be a natural way to introduce the elements of logic and set theory. Logic is the mathematics of ideas. Ideas are the working capital of the knowledge economy. The knowledge economy is driven by mathematical concepts. How these concepts are introduced to and retained by students will influence their financial future.

Futuristic curriculum development in mathematics would teach the techniques of mathematics so that students could apply them to present-day activities in their lives. Our mind is the interplay of the past we believe and the future we expect. By charting the past and possible futures for mathematics, we heighten our awareness of math as it is today. And we do need to heighten our awareness of mathematics today, since we are moving more toward a civilization that requires greater mathematical savvy.

In the mid-1980s, American 8th graders finished 13th out of 17 countries in math skills. U.S. elementary school classrooms' highest math scores ranked below the lowest scores in Japan.

We know that the rapid rate of change in the job market makes knowledge learned in school today less likely to be useful tomorrow. We must face that truth. If we focus on intelligence, our education will give our children the mental flexibility to integrate new skills that are useful for an expanding information economy. This is not to say that the content of basic subjects is not important, but it means that the approach to the content needs to be changed.

Our education systems must prepare us to take command of our Conscious Technology future in a global environment. Take mathematics, for example. Mystics used it to expand their insight into the nature of all existence. This attitude toward number should be taught. Numbers refer to things. Math is only abstract so that it can refer to all things. The purpose of education is to increase intelligence, share previous wisdom, and enable people to become more enlightened. The mere possession of knowledge is being automated, but our brain's ability to integrate vastly different kinds of knowledge will become increasingly important.

Spherical Education

In Chapter 2 we discussed why the belief in level theory dooms us to unending prejudice and how to apply spherical theory to begin reducing prejudice. Education can help develop the view of people in spherical terms rather than in linear terms.

Just as the sun radiates in all directions and one ray is no more or no less important than another, we can think of ourselves as radiating many abilities as rays from our being. With this metaphor we can think in terms of developing all our mental abilities. It will become less valuable to try to master one area to the exclusion of others. We need to think in terms of multidimensional or Renaissance learning based on the spherical model of the human being.

The following chart is an alternative way of looking at a student's academic profile:

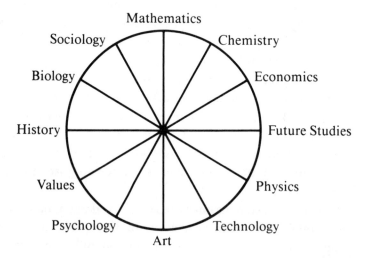

Each ray could be thought of as a measure of from 1 to 100, with 100 meaning the ultimate performance in a given area of study for that age or grade. If someone had only mastered half of the course work in mathematics, a point mid-way on the mathematics ray would be charted. If you wanted to do a quarterly picture of performance, then you would determine what the value of 100 would be for each area of study and chart the percentage of performance during that quarter.

The next chart shows the hypothetical performance of a student in all areas. This is how the student looks spherically:

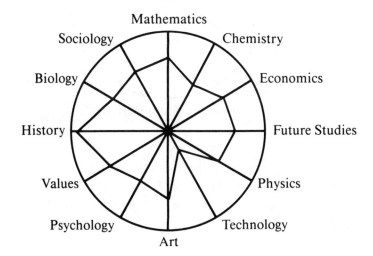

If this were done on a quarterly basis, the next quarter the teacher might have that student study the history of technology. History was a strong area, and technology was weak. Each quarter the teacher would determine what strong areas should be the focus to apply to the learning of the weaker areas. Students could also rate themselves on these charts and be asked to come up with ideas on how they would use their strengths to improve their weaknesses.

The terms on this chart are merely illustrative. You could decide what are the key indices for what you are teaching and put those terms instead. But the primary aim of the chart is to reinforce the idea of spherical learning and to give both the teacher and the student a graphic sense of the whole rather than just the parts. The following chart could be used to help develop the student as a whole person, what some refer to as humanistic education:

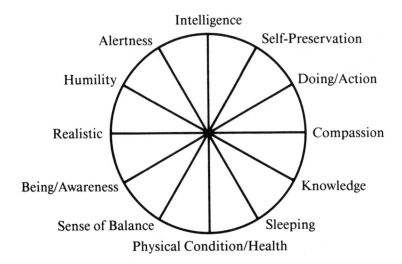

To some degree each of these can be a complementary opposite of the one at the other end of the line: Being-Doing, Knowledge-Humility, Realistic-Compassion, and so forth. Students enjoy filling out such charts and they give the teachers quite an insight into the students' self-perception.

The use of one spherical approach to evaluation was tested by Theresa Washington, Special Education teacher at Langdon School in Washington, D.C., from 1987 to 1988. She had her students rate themselves on a chart called "This is me according to me." The students wrote their names in the middle of the chart and rated themselves in terms of spelling, physical education, math, attitude, citizenship, attendance, playground conduct, art, participation, handwriting, lunch room conduct, speech, punctuality, and reading.

Washington concluded that spherical education:

> can be adapted to suit the individual classroom situation, gives the students something concrete to look at about themselves, is helpful to the teacher as far as how the students view themselves, expresses honesty as important, teaches the student what strengths to use to improve their

THIS IS ME

Spelling
Physical Education
Math
Reading
Attitude
Punctuality
Roderick Simmons
Citizenship
Speech
Lunchroom Conduct
Attendance
Handwriting
Participation
Art
Playground Conduct

ACCORDING TO ME

This is a specific evaluation chart done by an elementary school student in Washington, D.C.

weaknesses, works well to stimulate students to share with each other and get support for improvement from class mates, and tends to give almost the "whole picture" which reminds the teacher that they are to teach the whole person.

Dorothy Holmes is a third grade teacher at Bunker Hill school in Washington, D.C., who made similar comments about the spherical approach with an interesting addition. One student was doing quite well but would come in late nearly every day. Mrs. Holmes knew her family but felt uncomfortable bringing the problem to their attention. When the student filled out the spherical evaluation, "her lateness became real to her and the problem stopped," reported Mrs. Holmes. She adds that the technique gives the teacher a way to deal with a problem more effectively. Her principal, Karolyn Preston, was so impressed that she led a workshop in Florida on this approach for other principals.

Futuristic Literacy

We also need to expand our definition of literacy to include reading people and institutions and writing by action. If our action is not successful, it may be because of our inability to read people and institutions. We will have to learn the "grammar" and styles of actions in an ever more complex world with many different kinds of people than were faced by our parents. We will have to become peoplewise and institutionwise. The literacy of merely reading and writing words will not be sufficient for the intensity of human interaction in the future.

Globalization of Education

People learn best what interests them most, especially when they can get immediate application and feedback. This utopian view of education was not possible to implement in the past, but it will be in the future. With the increasing integration of computers and communications, students will access education worldwide.

Dr. Coleman, a leading American educational researcher, has pointed out that the school 100 years ago was information-rich relative to the information-poor community and that a child's primary function was to help the family business. Schooling was secondary. Today, the school is information-poor relative to the community and a child's only role is being a student. Hence, young people feel less necessary and know that "the action" is not in the classroom.

Increasingly, education will fall into three categories. First is computer-assisted instruction—whatever can be automated should be automated by the best minds we can get. Second is the apprentice experience—we need to engage our youth in the world of work and have them see for themselves how knowledge is used in the workplace. And third is humanistic education—to develop the whole person and the integration of computer-assisted instruction and apprentice experiences, as well as to monitor intellectual development. The school will still be the central focus to monitor, plan, and evaluate the proper balance of education through these three means.

One of the key values in our attempts to make computer-assisted instruction more intelligent will be the testing of all of our assumptions about how the mind learns. We will also be more objective about how a

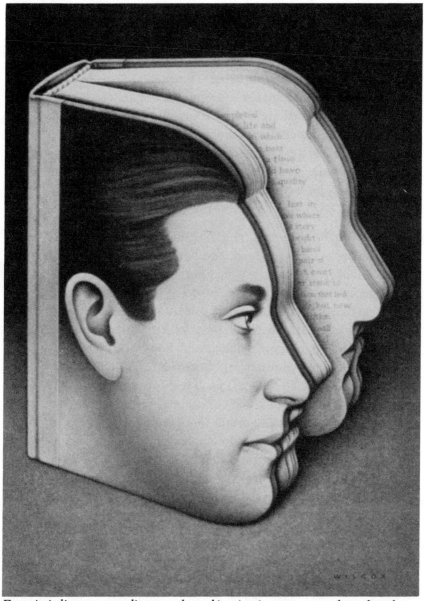

Futuristic literacy: reading people and institutions as we read words today.
Drawing courtesy of Champion

machine increases human performance as compared with how a human teacher does.

According to Education TURNKEY Systems Inc., $1.25/student-hour is spent for classroom education, whereas $1.10/student-hour is spent for computer-based instruction. This gap should widen. New Jersey Institute of Technology studies indicate that computer-assisted instruction produces better retention than classroom instruction. Sesame Street costs $0.01/viewer-hour. One compact disk for data storage can hold 20 encyclopedias or all the texts necessary for a college education.

The American educational futurists Chris Dede and H. Jerome Freiberg identify five functions for such educational technology in the Fall 1986 issue of *The Educational Forum:*

> 1) "Intelligent" tutors, which use the Socratic method and understand what, whom, and how they are teaching; 2) "Intelligent" coaches, which provide a model of expert performance in a learning-by-doing situation, intervening based on a pedagogical strategy of hints and "frontier" knowledge; 3) "Idea processors," which facilitate building and manipulating a sophisticated, non-linear web of interconnected concepts; 4) "Microworlds," which create limited alternative variations of reality (e.g., a universe in which the force of gravity alters in different ways at the learner's option) as a means for developing a qualitative causal understanding of complex phenomena; and 5) "Empowering environments," e.g., "intelligent" word processors, databases, spreadsheets, graphics tools, music construction sets.

The ideal of equal access to education is only possible electronically. The best interactive computer programs for specific subjects along with all the knowledge in the Library of Congress will be available worldwide via satellite, as explained in Chapter 6. Also described in that chapter was the Tree of Knowledge (TOK), which integrates computer, audio, and video capabilities into an attache case for communications and retrieval via high-powered satellites. Initially, the teacher, but later the student, could meander through many inquiry paths available on the TOK to find countless challenges to the mind. This makes the old ideal of student-centered, self-paced, and learning from primary sources possible. Idealistic? Yes, but increasingly practical today.

For example, interactive compact disks can store a quarter of a million pages of text. These could be programmed with motion pictures, print, and voice to make education more exciting and complete. With a built-in testing program, a student's responses can elicit the next set of materials for the appropriate complexity and instruction. It is now possible to get all of the educational materials stored in the Educational Resources Information Center (ERIC) database for every school. This vast collection of educational materials is now stored on compact disks (CDROM) and can be purchased for $1,200.

It has already been proven that remote education via computer communications results in the same or better learning than classroom instruction. According to Dr. Starr Roxanne Hiltz in "The Virtual Classroom on EIES: Final Evaluation Report,"

> You can say that there is no difference in test scores, though in computer-related courses in particular, we are getting better grades [than from those who take the same course, with the same teacher, and the same text, but in a classroom situation].
>
> On the other hand, for students with adequate access and microcomputer skills AND COMMAND OF WRITTEN ENGLISH—they consistently SAY that it gives them better contact with professor and other students than do traditional courses. You have to emphasize that the virtual classroom [via remote computer access] has consciously been implemented with a group or cooperative learning strategy—the students work together on many assignments. They DO get to know each other informally.

The following chart compares the results of the same test taken by students who received their instruction via remote access on the computer (ONLINE) with those who had face-to-face (FTF) classroom instruction and those with both (BOTH) methods of instruction:

DIFFERENCES IN GRADES BY MODE AND COURSE
QUASI-EXPERIMENTAL DESIGN

MEAN MIDTERM EXAM GRADE

COURSE	ONLINE	FTF	BOTH
CIS 213	90.7	80.1	85.4
INTRO SOCIOLOGY	75.2	75.9	75.5
STATISTICS	68.8	69.5	69.6
ALL	78.5	75.2	

MEAN GRADE ON FINAL EXAM

COURSE	ONLINE	FTF	BOTH
CIS 213	79.3	78.8	79.1
MATH 305	79.0	81.6	80.3
INTRO SOCIOLOGY	68.4	68.7	68.5
STATISTICS	53.6	56.4	55.0
ALL	70.1	71.4	

I have taught two graduate courses and one adult education class via computer communications. I agree that the students get better access to me via computer than they would if we were in a classroom situation. It is a good deal for the student, but it is a lot of work for the instructor, since you have to respond to each student uniquely. In a classroom you ask a question, get an answer, correct it if wrong, and then go on. Not so in the "virtual classroom." Each student gives an answer to the question, and there will be differences in these responses, requiring unique responses. This means that each student is getting a private tutorial that the other students can observe. Hence the primary problem with this approach is the overworked teacher. The hours of instruction and preparation the telelecturer puts in per course far exceed that of a conventional classroom teacher.

One of the more successful computer network college programs is managed by Connected Education, Inc. College credit is awarded by the New School for Social Research in New York. In the past two years 60 graduate and undergraduate courses have been offered entirely via computer conferencing to more than 300 students across 24 states in the

United States and overseas in such countries as Japan, Singapore, the Middle East, Norway, Denmark, England, Iceland, South and Central America, and Canada.

Most participants are professionals in the business, public sector, and educational communities, and all took full-credit courses without interrupting their daily activities, in the privacy and convenience of their homes or offices. Students who traveled extensively in their jobs were able to take courses simply by "logging on" from the nearest telephone.

Along with the obvious advantages of making the best instruction available to all students, the TOK could also serve as as a clearinghouse and medium for apprentice experiences. In the past an apprentice had to be at the same location as the master craftsman. Going to school and being an apprentice at the same time was not possible. It will be possible via the TOK. A student studying carpentry assisted by a computer programmed unit on ornate finishes, for example, could switch to the video option on TOK to show his or her master in China what his or her work looks like. The master in China would evaluate the apprentice's piece as seen on the video screen of the master's TOK in China and send back comments for further improvement. The Chinese comments would be computer translated into English via an intermediary host computer for language translation mutually accessible via both parties' TOKs.

Why would the master craftsman in China do it? First of all, it doesn't require much time and people get a kick out of working with people at great distances, especially young people. Second, masters might be interested in forming relations with people to begin to explore foreign markets for their crafts.

INTELSAT, the 113-nation satellite cooperative, might open a subdivision called INEDSAT in cooperation with the U.N. that would give economic credits for international apprentice assistance. These are just some examples of how we can have our students be apprentices to master teachers anywhere via TOK.

The education system could take the lead in this new direction by (1) writing, finding, and editing computer-assisted learning programs; (2) compiling community resources for computer storage; (3) helping students make the shift from the classroom to the world at large for learning access; (4) beginning to integrate the general population into computer networks for lifelong learning; (5) guiding the students' development; (6) constantly evaluating and improving computer-assisted programs and apprentice/master relations; and (7) developing the management position in the looming INEDSAT or TOK on behalf of students.

The third category of education after computer-assisted instruction and apprentice experiences is humanistic education. The human personality needs to grow in the medium of human interaction that will not be satisfied by working on a computer terminal or as an apprentice. Here it is difficult to imagine replacing the classroom and teacher. There is already a large literature on games, simulations, theater games, and group experiences to stimulate personal growth and inquiry into values. So that need not be discussed here other than to say that the teacher will have to take the lead in humanistic education and make a balance among the three categories to ensure the development of the whole person.

Private business will continue to take over public education and interlink with public education. We have seen speed reading, language training, and computer camps conducted by business that resulted in better educational performance than from counterparts in the public educational systems. And after all, a school district should be able to contract with whoever produces the best intellectual growth among its youth. We've got the money to buy whatever we want in education. And for my money, I want to buy intelligence. Let the public and private sector compete to make us all more intelligent.

Chapter Thirteen

Three Future Scenarios
For Conscious Technology

History teaches us that any good idea can be developed negatively. Christianity had its Inquisition and computers have had their viruses. Conscious Technology is no different. The first two scenarios we shall consider are intended to illustrate some of the leading indicators and consequences of more negative futures for Conscious Technology. The content of these scenarios should not be taken too seriously. They merely illustrate some of the possible misapplications of the ideas in this book.

The first scenario portrays an advanced technological society that has rejected the mystical aspects of human nature. Although the Soviet Union is not yet an advanced technological society, it is nevertheless beginning to wrestle with this issue today. *Clockwork Orange* by Anthony Burgess and the television series *Max Headroom* are good examples of the long-range consequences of separating the mystical from the technological.

In the second scenario, people become so insecure about technological growth that they embrace old metaphysical views cloaked in religious and occult authority. Such authorities disdain technocratic competency. This is a contemporary reality that is drowning Iran.

The third scenario is not quite as negative. It describes a future in which mystics and technocrats tolerate each other but have not yet integrated their views. To some degree this is much like Japan today, where there is mutual respect for the mystical and the technological.

I have not included a separate positive scenario in this chapter because that would be repetitious of the key elements in the first 12 chapters.

Scenario 1: High Tech–Low Mystic

Because so many New Age and occult groups insisted on the truth of their metaphysics—rather than the value of their attitudes—the general public grew wary of anything having to do with the mystical dimensions of life and embraced everything technological. It was reasoned that since people continued to abuse the mystical (as discussed in Chapter 3), there was something inherent in the phenomenon that could not be trusted. Because the mystically oriented could not be trusted, society turned to the technocrat.

Instead of being "future shocked" by technological change, most people simply habituated to it and senselessly accepted technological dominance of their lives. Technology became their religion. During the 1990s the great corporate mergers and acquisitions created superinternational corporations that employed millions of people and controlled enough mobile assets to act independently of governments. These robotized humans with feelings dulled found outlets in chemical and electronic forms of hedonism.

Divorcing mystic attitudes from technocratic management stifled the human spirit. Too many managers could not distinguish between "loose cannons" and "lead cannons" or crazy ideas from genuinely innovative approaches. So they tended to discourage both. This is especially dangerous in a Conscious Technology civilization since the time from thought to action is dramatically reduced. Apathy, superficial thought, and mediocre action spread rapidly. Wisdom was not important. Just getting through each day without a hassle became the goal of life.

The push to increase intelligence 10 points in 10 years focused solely on content scores rather than tests that measured brain functioning, reasoning, or intelligence. Education stressed techniques of knowledge retention rather than *being* knowledgeable or *being* intelligent. People learned techniques to appear more enlightened, rather than having experiences to be more enlightened. As the "right" technique for the situation had to be remembered, human spontaneity atrophied. Nevertheless, the TOK was well used to assist in data bank access and acted as an international score-keeper for the 10–10 program.

In this more negative scenario, tools of consciousness increased the power to enslave. The TOK was used too often in a one-way mode for watching vast amounts of global television and holography. Individual freedom meant the freedom to consume the media of your choice. The result was many people whose consciousness became more receptive than productive. As technocratic complexity increased, some stayed on top of change; many more gave up and became docile, as illustrated in *Brave New World* by Aldous Huxley.

Technocratic management did have the advantage of stalling the greenhouse effect by swapping Third World debt in exchange for local projects that saved tropical rain forests, developed national youth corps to plant trees, and converted much of the electric supply to INSOLSAT to lower carbon emissions. The protective ozone layer in the atmosphere was periodically built up by ground and satellite laser beams striking the depleted areas.

Without taking the subjective into account, the reliability of technocratic forecasting was too poor for labor unions to take seriously. Since few labor unions used job forecasting and retraining in cooperation with business and government, the skills of the labor force deteriorated relative to the demands of the technocratic society. Fortunately, the unemployment rate did not go up because the global economy grew sufficiently to keep the poorly skilled employed and accommodate the new entrants into the labor force. Their incomes were supplemented by an average 20 percent return on investment through the global market investment options on their TOK.

The qualitivity increases that kept the global economy growing at 4 percent annually were due to dramatic advances in bioengineering, telecommunications, and software design for robots and other forms of automation, not because of increasing skills, knowledge, and wisdom in the labor force. With the end of the Iran-Iraq war, Mexico's jump in production, and China's and Africa's new finds entering production, the oil price stayed low enough to prevent global inflation.

Sensing that humans were less in command of their lives, political opportunists joined forces with several key mass media programmers to gain power. These strange bedfellows added subliminal messages to television programming communicating that anything mystical was ignorance and technology was the only way to enlightenment. The messages were part of world media coverage of such events as the human exploration of Mars, the world soccer cups, the completion of the mapping of the human genome, the birth of the first space-adapted cyborg, the destruction of a comet headed for earth, and other such events that attracted the species as a whole.

The puny vision of these new politicians was well illustrated in the television series called *Max Headroom*. It brilliantly portrayed an alienated society of powerless, purposeless, unethical people without a sense of community, manipulated by technocrats as technology replaced human relationships.

Because the romantic has little reinforcement in such a society, the divorce rates continued to rise producing a more psychologically insecure generation. The growth in general apathy was matched by the rise in numbers of violent criminals preying on the technologically cowed public. The government responded with chemical and electronic behavior control rather than education and appealing to community values.

Pea-sized spies developed by government police, corporate intelligence, and jealous lovers were everywhere eliminating privacy. Even rural populations that fled the "solid state cities" and electronic highway robbers for greener pastures were not safe from these electronic bumble bees. Beyond the electronic burglaries of the late 20th century, criminals during the early 21st century electronically masked their identity, remotely influenced the minds of others while leaving a trail that pointed to innocent people. Average individuals using their TOKs were never really sure who they were dealing with or even if they were dealing with a person at all. This insecurity coupled with staggering technological power resulted in many seeing themselves in the center of a world that was unreal or could not be trusted.

Compounding this was the failure of parastroyka and glasnost. The USSR was not able to reconcile communism and spiritual freedom. As Eastern Europe and the Soviet autonomous regions began moving away from Moscow's grip, the progressive elements lost control to the more Stalinesk leadership. Computers and communications were used with devastating effectiveness to identify and destroy opposition making it easier to bring back the police state. Internationally, the Soviet agents had so infiltrated the Electronic Peace Corps that American field volunteers could no longer trust their electronic mail from previously reliable information sources in the richer countries.

Simultaneously, the Soviet Union increased the intensity of its information warfare directly with NATO countries to keep the West too busy to exploit the crisis in communism or complete the deployment of space-based defenses of SDI. Beginning with the announcement of conventional force reductions in Europe, the Soviets made peace initiatives every several months. This mobilized public opinion that forced Western politicians to keep cutting their military budgets and both sides to keep negotiating. The Intermediate Nuclear Forces Treaty in 1987, Chemical Protocols in 1990, Convention Force Reductions in 1991, International Biological Weapons Accords in 1993, and the Strategic Arms Reduction Treaty of 1995 eventually became known collectively as SALT III. The success of these five agreements gave the false impression that the world was at peace during the height of the undeclared information war of the 1990s.

After significant pressure from both China and India, a truce was finally achieved in the early 21st century. The informal merger of western political and media leaders struck a deal with Moscow, Beijing, and New Delhi to form a New World Court of the United Nations. This New World Court cemented the alliance of business, government, and the media, which left the nongovernmental organizations and general public powerless to bring about any significant change. Although they were fully involved in a global participatory system via the TOK, which fed issues to the New World Court, they had no say in the outcome. The illusion of participation kept the public pacified.

If it turns out that intelligent life is a pattern of matter and energy, then the extreme end of this scenario is the replacement of cytoplasm by technology as artificial intelligence migrates to the stars . . . making new patterns as other sentient forms are encountered, until life's patterns permeate the universe and force the end of cyclic Big Bangs and the beginning of universal being.

Now, take a deep breath, let it out slowly, and get ready for a different view of the future.

Scenario 2: Mystical Abuse–Technological Introversion

At the turn of the millennium, miniaturized hardware and seemingly intelligent software proliferated so rapidly that people were constantly trying to figure out how to apply these wonders. The quality and availability of documentation for these innovations did not keep pace. Consumers suffered from overchoice and lost confidence that anything could be modified to fit their circumstances. Angry users junked devices of vast capability. Cities became littered with high tech corpses. At the other extreme, gigantic construction projects were fraught with delays and budget overruns.

As the 21st century civilization became increasingly complex and increasing numbers of people rejected new technology, the public sought solace in the mystical. Both New Age socialism and religious fundamentalism grew dramatically. Even communist leadership was forced to work through established religions to keep power. This spiritual renaissance renewed peoples' faith that an enlightened civilization was possible. Massive spiritual gatherings in India, Pakistan, and China reminded the more technocratically inclined to keep a low profile.

New Age optimism became mainstream in the industrial world and people with the "right stuff" became "psychonauts" pushing the limits of their minds. Unfortunately, feelysis was used to reject analysis; empiricism was ridiculed in a similar fashion as the Red Guard did during the Chinese Cultural Revolution in the 1960s; and the best minds turned in upon themselves. Just as people pretended to be wealthy or in high social status, many now pretended to be spiritually advanced. Research that demonstrated the power of thought in healing opened the doors to many exaggerated claims by religious healers. Enough turned from high-tech hospitals to cause their financial failure. Bionics and genetic engineering became esoteric fields of study with a very small market.

Because the next generation turned to the study of the humanities far more than science and engineering, the global economy eventually slowed to a halt throwing much of Africa into Ethiopian-like depressions. This gave strength to fundamental movements like the Islamic Brotherhood that seized power across the Moslem world including parts of Soviet central Asia. Intolerance of new thought blocked innovation so necessary for the success of the Third World. Intermediate technology and intentional rural communities such as Findhorn in Scotland and Auroville in India were glorified as the responsible road to enlightenment.

Ballots and bullets gave way to large-scale C-T exercises to persuade the masses of the new leadership's divine right to rule. Like Khomeni using the audio cassette for his messages from his exile in France as the technology to take over the consciousness of Iran, so too others who abuse the mystical used global television and TOK programming to expand their power. Subliminal anti-science messages and emotional appeals for a "New Age Order" rallied the public to support these new politicians.

Although it was demonstrated that humans could be programmed to become geniuses, the fundamentalist backlash against tampering with nature prevented the commercialization of these methods. Nevertheless, some centers were established underground for increasing human intelligence. These intelligence centers rapidly developed businesses that provided a reliable supply of advanced technology for the dominant economy. The centers also served to keep the knowledge of advanced technology alive, much like the monasteries of the Catholic Church that preserved knowledge during the Dark Ages. The irony of this was not lost on the underground technocrats, who called their centers "Benedictine IIs" after those 12th-century monasteries that developed music and architecture and invented the water wheel.

The extreme end of this scenario is the slow and undramatic extinction of the human species unless interrupted by extraterrestrial intelligence, new religious leadership, or the successful revolution by the Benedictine IIs.

Now, take one more deep breath, let it out, and off we go to the last scenario.

Scenario 3: Oil and Water Truce

Oil and water can exist next to each other without altering the others' composition. However, the temperature or growth of one can change the temperature or shape of the other. This characterizes the relationship of the mystical to the technological in the third scenario.

The public's reaction to the integration of technology with their minds was equally divided among those who habituated, rejected, or participated with these changes. Those who habituated, acquiesced to technocratic control and will be referred to as Group 1. They tended not to believe in life after death and welcomed genetic engineering and bionics to prolong life. Those who rejected these changes sought religious or occult leadership and will be referred to as Group 2. They preferred to use meditation, prayer, yoga, and T'ai Chi to keep their health, while some of Group 2 believed that life after death made much of all this irrelevant. Those who consciously participated in rapid technological changes designed their own lives becoming their own leaders and will be referred to as Group 3. They were embarrassed by Group 1's and Group 2's approaches to health seeing their future as being both cyborgs and yoga masters. Group 1 and 2 used technology to control belief and behavior. Group 3 designed tools to enlighten and empower.

The key characteristic of this scenario is the mutual but superficial public tolerance among the groups. Since prosecution from external sources helps keep a group's internal loyalty strong, the bonding of these groups slowly deteriorated.

Meanwhile, corporate power grew faster than government's ability to control. Even individual power became a factor in human affairs. With laser-launched personal microsatellites, people had global access via their TOKs without government involvement. Anticipated by Alvin Toffler's "ad hocracies" in *Future Shock,* individuals could make temporary and ad hoc arrangements that were faster and more flexible than either corporate or government actions. Small and quick can beat large and slow. As a result, the individual's role in such global management systems as INSPACECO became surprisingly dominant. Individual launchers, living quarters, and communications systems were developed at an extraordinary rate, speeding the individual access to space migration.

The momentum initiated by the economic integration of Europe as well as that of American with Canada and the South American merger of Brazil and Argentina led to global acceptance of a world market. With telepresent manufacturing, production control was in one country and manufacture was simultaneously carried out in many other countries. Minute modifications and customizations were made via the customer's TOK in still another country.

Group 1 eventually acknowledged the spiritual bankruptcy of its technocratic culture, as conditions of Scenario 1 began appearing in areas under its control. New leadership was sought among Group 2 and Group 3. Likewise, Group 2 finally admitted that technological augmentation of human capability did not have to reduce spiritual development and that technocratic management did help society run better, as conditions of Scenario 2 appeared in areas under its control. As Group 2 became aware that humans are a technology of life, its members became willing to listen to Group 1 and Group 3.

Because Groups 2 made enlightenment a fad and argued over the best ways to eliminate greed and prejudice, Group 3 members used their norms to get them to be open to Group 1. Because Group 1 worshiped technique, Group 3 focused on helping them practice prayer, meditation, biofeedback, and yoga with Group 2. Early meetings of the groups were held at free association night clubs for intellectual jazz and stream of consciousness conversations.

Because spherical theory rather than level theory structured Group 3's view of reality, its members did not set themselves up as leaders for Group 1 and Group 2, but as a conduit between them. In the same way that we use the transition from the Industrial Age to the Information Age as a framework to make sense of change today, so too, Group 3 used Conscious Technology as a framework to help Groups 1 and 2 understand changes and reduce their mutual prejudice. C-T exercises were created on the TOK as games for Group 1 and Group 2 to play at their leisure. These games led to joint designs of entertainment, trade, technology, and new electronic communities. The first 12 chapters of this book detailed many of the ideas and policies that eventually brought these groups closer together giving birth to the first world renaissance.

Even though nuclear weapons could be dismantled, the knowledge of how to build them could not be erased. Hence, it was still possible that one day an intelligent but deranged mind could endanger terrestrial civilization. When those who previously abhorred leaving the earth acknowledged that space migration was an insurance policy for life's survival, INSPACECO plans for the serious development of space finally got underway.

This created sufficient interest in interspecies communications research to generate a series of breakthroughs that would help us communicate one day with extraterrestrials. The United Nations University created its own "aliens" via genetic engineering, bionics, and artificial intelligence in order to experiment with extraterrestrial communication. The UNU eventually developed an intermediary language or set of procedures that worked well enough to give the researchers the eerie feeling that they were indeed communicating through a time machine to their own future. Nevertheless, it did give our "Spacekind" the confidence to venture forth from the solar system in search of new life.

One vignette of the long-range view of Conscious Technology in this scenario was well envisioned by Freemand Dyson in *Infinity in All Directions*:

> The last of my projects is the "space butterfly." That is a way of exploiting for the purposes of space science the biological technology . . . which allows a humble caterpillar to wrap itself up in a chrysalis and emerge three weeks later transformed into a shimmering beauty of legs and antennae and wings. Sooner or later, probably fairly soon, we will understand how that is done. Somehow it is programmed into the DNA and we should soon learn how to do it. It is likely that, within the next twenty-five years, this technology will be fully understood and available for us to copy. So it is reasonable to think of the microspacecraft of the year 2010, not as a structure of metal and glass and silicon, but as a living creature, fed on Earth like a caterpillar, launched into space like a chrysalis, riding a laser beam into orbit, and metamorphosing itself in space like a butterfly. Once it is out there in space, it will sprout wings in the shape of solar sails, thus neatly solving the sail deployment problem. It will grow telescopic eyes to see where it is going, gossamer-fine antennae for receiving and transmitting radio signals, long springy legs for landing and walking on smaller asteroids, chemical sensors for tasting the asteroidal minerals and the solar wind, electric-current-generating organs for orienting its wings in the interplanetary magnetic field, and a high-quality

brain enabling it to coordinate its activities, navigate to its destination, and report its observations back to Earth.

The "Space Butterfly" will be one of an unending progression of our future species. As we migrated through the solar system to the galaxies, we became a new species—the result of mixing genetic engineering, bionics, and artificial intelligence. We became Conscious Technology whose purpose it was to mate with other sentient beings and permeate the universe to prevent the collapse or entropy of the universe.

*   *   *   *

Until we change our view of what is possible, more of the same is inevitable.

Again, the content of these three scenarios should not be taken too seriously. They are not predictions. But they do serve to remind us that there is no inevitability to tomorrow, that good ideas can get twisted, and to question whether we will habituate, reject, or participate in the intensity and complexity of the 21st century.

Toward the end of the first chapter, Conscious Technology was given the formal definition that it was the network created by the interaction of six elements. There are many ways that each element will develop over the years and even more ways that they will interrelate to make the real Conscious Technology Age.

Today it may seem impossible to perceive the six elements as one interrelated future, but not to our future mind. Because each reader of this book will stress different elements of the network definition, the conversation among readers will come closer to charting the character of our future mind.

Index